DIGITAL MARKETING
QuickStart Guide®

DIGITAL MARKETING

QuickStart Guide®

The Simplified Beginner's Guide to
Developing a Scalable Online Strategy,
Finding Your Customers, and
Profitably Growing Your Business

Benjamin Sweeney

Editors: Bryan Basamanowicz, Marilyn Burkley
Cover Illustration and Design: Katie Donnachie, Copyright © 2022 by ClydeBank Media LLC
Interior Design & Illustrations: Katie Donnachie & Brittney Duquette, Copyright © 2022 by ClydeBank Media LLC

First Edition - Last Updated: August 24, 2022

ISBN: 9781945051098 (paperback) | 9781945051128 (hardcover) | 9781945051463 (ebook) | 9781945051913 (audiobook) | 9781636100272 (spiral bound)

Publisher's Cataloging-In-Publication Data
(Prepared by The Donohue Group, Inc.)

Names: Sweeney, Benjamin, author.
Title: Digital marketing QuickStart Guide : the simplified beginner's guide to developing a scalable online strategy, finding your customers & profitably growing your business / Benjamin Sweeney.
Other Titles: Digital marketing Quick Start Guide
Description: [Albany, New York] : ClydeBank Business, [2021] | Series: QuickStart Guide | Includes bibliographical references and index.
Identifiers: ISBN 9781945051098 (paperback) | ISBN 9781945051128 (hardcover) | ISBN 9781945051463 (ebook)
Subjects: LCSH: Internet marketing. | Success in business.
Classification: LCC HF5415.1265 .D66 2021 (print) | LCC HF5415.1265 (ebook) | DDC 658.872--dc23

Library of Congress Control Number: 2021934425

Author ISNI: 0000 0004 9416 4830

For bulk sales inquiries, please visit www.clydebankmedia.com/orders, email us at orders@clydebankmedia.com, or call 888-208-6826. Special discounts are available on quantity purchases by corporations, associations, and others.

PRAISE FOR

QuickStart Guides.

Really well written with lots of practical information. These books have a very concise way of presenting each topic and everything inside is very actionable!

– ALAN F.

My new book is so helpful, it's so easy to understand and I can recommend it to any client no matter what level of expertise they have (or don't have).

– AMANDA K.

Everything is written in a beautiful font which is great for people who get bored with reading.

– ANGEL L.

The book was a great resource, every page is packed with information, but [the book] never felt overly-wordy or repetitive. Every chapter was filled with very useful information.

– CUTRIS W.

I appreciated how accessible and how insightful the material was and look forward to sharing the knowledge that I've learned [from this book].

– SCOTT B.

My new QuickStart Guide is very easy to follow, it's really well written and it breaks everything down, especially the essentials.

– ARIZE O.

After reading this book, I must say that it has been one of the best decisions of my life!

– ROHIT R.

This book is one-thousand percent worth every single dollar!

– HUGO C.

The read itself was worth the cost of the book, but the additional tools and materials make this purchase a better value than most books.

– JAMES D.

This is a "go-to" book for not only beginners but also as a refresher for experienced practitioners.

– CHARLES C.

I finally understand this topic ... this book has really opened doors for me!

– MISTY A.

Contents

INTRODUCTION 1
Why Digital Marketing? 2
Why I Wrote This Book 3
Who This Book Is For 4
How This Book Is Organized 6

PART I – DIGITAL MARKETING 101

| 1 | A CRASH COURSE IN MARKETING CONCEPTS 13
What Is Marketing? 14
Why Is Marketing Important? 16
Different Marketing Perspectives 20
The Marketing Mix 26
Alternative Interpretations of the Marketing Mix 29
Brand Positioning 30
Tying It All Together 31
Traditional Marketing vs. Digital Marketing 33

| 2 | CORE DIGITAL MARKETING CONCEPTS 37
Customer Lifetime Value (CLV) 37
Calculating CLV 38
CLV and Average Order Value 40
Key Digital Marketing Concepts 41
A Review of the Media Mix 43
Using the Media Mix to Best Effect 49

| 3 | WHO ARE YOU SELLING TO? 53
Your Market 53
The Customer Avatar 56
Narrowing Your Market through Segmentation 63
The Customer Journey 71

| 4 | WHAT ARE YOU SELLING? 75
The Value Ladder 75
Crafting an Offer 79
Crafting a Hyper-Compelling Offer 83

| 5 | WHAT ARE YOUR OBJECTIVES? 89

What Do You Want to Achieve? 89

SMART Goals 91

Digital Marketing SERVEs 92

SERVE and Effective Goal Setting in Action............................... 95

Potential Obstacles 97

On Budgeting 99

PART II – TOOLS OF THE TRADE

| 6 | COMING IN FOR A LANDING 105

Thinking about Your Website as a Tool 105

Exploring the Role of Landing Pages..................................... 108

Opt-In Pages... 110

Sales Pages 111

Webinar Registration Landing Pages..................................... 117

Best Practices 117

Metrics to Measure... 125

Compliance 127

| 7 | CAPTURING TRAFFIC 131

Attracting Traffic through Earned Media 131

Search Engine Optimization (SEO).. 134

SEO for Two Sets of Readers 137

Optimizing for Human Readers.. 148

Keywords 149

Content Is King 150

What Is Content?.. 151

The Strategic Role of Content.. 153

Content and Audience Temperature 154

Social Content 156

Associated Metrics 161

| 8 | DIRECTING TRAFFIC..................................... 165

Paid Search 168

Display Advertising 171

Video.. 174

Shopping... 175

Selecting Keywords 176

Associated Metrics 181

| 9 | SOCIAL 189

    The Evolving Nature of Social Media 189

    Social Media Marketing and Campaigns 191

    Advertising on Social Media 196

    Chat and Messenger 202

    Damage Control at the Speed of Social 203

    Associated Metrics 204

| 10 | FOLLOWING UP WITH EMAIL 209

    The Money Is in the List 209

    Getting Subscribers 210

    The Anatomy of an Email 212

    Converting Subscribers 217

    Intimacy Equals Extreme Personalization 219

    An Email Sequence Crash Course 222

    Associated Metrics 223

PART III – EXECUTION

| 11 | BUILDING A SOUND MARKETING STRATEGY 231

    The Digital Marketing Funnel 231

    Tying It All Together – Lifecycle Marketing 239

    Building a Funnel 245

    A Final Thought on Digital Marketing Funnels 254

| 12 | DIGITAL MARKETING EFFICIENCY 257

    Behavior-Based Automation 257

    Optimizing Campaigns 263

    Troubleshooting Poor Performance 265

    The Larger Role of Digital Marketing 270

CONCLUSION 277

APPENDIX 281

ABOUT THE AUTHOR 285

ABOUT CLYDEBANK MEDIA 287

GLOSSARY 289

REFERENCES 299

INDEX 301

BEFORE YOU START READING,
DOWNLOAD YOUR FREE DIGITAL ASSETS!

 Strategic Planning Worksheet

 SEO Fundamentals Checklist

 Digital Marketing Toolkit

 Customer Avatar Worksheet

TWO WAYS TO ACCESS YOUR FREE DIGITAL ASSETS

Use the **camera app on your mobile phone** to scan the QR code
or visit the link below and instantly access your Digital Assets.

or

www.clydebankmedia.com/digitalmarketing-assets

SCAN ME   VISIT URL

Introduction

Business has only two functions—marketing and innovation.
— PETER DRUCKER

The lights are on, the door is unlocked, and you're open for business. Or you've paid your hosting fees and your inventory is listed on your e-commerce site. Your gym, bar, flower shop, or dog walking service is ready to do what it does best. You just need one more thing: no matter the shape, size, or flavor of your business, you have one burning need above all others—customers. A business's need for customers is a tale as old as time. The specific methods by which those customers are found, enticed into parting with their money, and convinced to come back for more have varied throughout history, but one element remains constant: the human element. Digital marketing tactics are the latest in a long line of commerce and exchange techniques that stretch back to trade caravans and the earliest of human settlements.

This is a book about people. In it we will discuss reaching people, understanding their needs, communicating with them, and providing them with value. Maybe you're a new entrepreneur who needs to stand apart from the competition, but you only have a small team and modest resources. Or maybe you've been in business for years and are afraid that the opportunities provided by digital marketing are passing you by. People who know nothing about marketing or digital tools will find tremendous value in this book— as will marketing students, veteran marketers, freelancers, entrepreneurs, managers, decision makers, and influencers.

The truth is that digital marketing has, well, a marketing problem.

For too many people, digital marketing is perceived as complex, expensive, and bewilderingly technical. The idea that digital marketing is a black box is reinforced by marketing agencies that need their clients to outsource marketing, by legacy media outlets clinging to advertising dollars, and by marketing coaches who have high-ticket courses and seminars for sale (to name just a few). In reality, modern digital marketing methods are intuitive, user-friendly, cost-effective, and more accessible to businesses of all sizes than ever before. Put bluntly, there is no better way to put your message—or product, or service—in front of more people for a lower price.

Why Digital Marketing?

What sets digital marketing apart from other marketing avenues, above all else, is scale. Imagine it's 1940 and you've hired an army of copywriters, printers, and illustrators to push out print ads, radio ads, and mass mailings, only to see the first television ad beamed directly into consumers' living rooms in 1941. Incidentally, that first commercial cost $9, upwards of $165 in today's dollars, and was a spot for the watchmaker Bulova.

Fast forward to 1955, and total TV ad spending surpasses the $1 billion threshold. For savvy marketers, television was a revelation. Everyone wanted a TV in their home, and in short order the same people that marketers across the country wanted to reach were spending more and more time looking at their TVs. Reaching people at scale was never easier.

Today, Google's search engine processes more than 40,000 search queries every second of every day, on average. Facebook has 2.89 billion monthly active users—over a third of all humans alive right now—and more than two billion emails find their way to inboxes around the globe daily. The sheer number of smartphones, computers, and "always online" devices presents marketers with that same revelation of TV in 1941 but at a scale that's so large it's hard to wrap your head around. In fact, in much the same way that cell phones are just called "phones" now, digital marking is so ubiquitous in our lives and so integral to the ways that businesses reach customers that it may as well just be called "marketing."

So why *digital* marketing? Digital marketers have the ability to reach truly massive audiences in the blink of an eye at a cost that is much lower than that of traditional marketing methods. Digital marketing tools have enabled small businesses that would otherwise have languished in local markets to go global and deliver value to customers who may never have heard of them otherwise. Artists and craftspeople with even a minimal understanding of, and investment in, digital marketing tools can find, connect with, and sell their work to patrons who otherwise would never have realized they existed. However, digital marketing need not be global to be effective. Local businesses that use the same digital marketing principles outlined in this book can stay relevant in the minds of dedicated customers and deepen their connections to the community around them.

One of the other aspects of digital marketing that makes it so attractive is how measurable the results are. Sure, a billboard by a busy stretch of highway may be seen by thousands of people, but how many of them act as a result? No one knows. There are imperfect ways to measure the effectiveness of traditional advertising, but they pale in comparison to the precision of digital marketing with its ability to account for each dollar spent. Armed with the unique insight offered by digital marketing, marketers can see what works, what doesn't, and how they can tweak their efforts to reduce marketing costs even further.

Digital marketers reach prospective customers where they are spending their time—on their phones, on their computers, on social media, in their inboxes, and with the content they consume. Additionally, given the wealth of information and metadata that we generate in our travels around the internet, digital marketers can learn more about their target customers, uncover new prospective customers, and track the responses to marketing efforts in near real time. Marketing in digital spaces also opens up the conversation in ways that are new and exciting for businesses. Marketing in the twenty-first century truly is a two-way conversation. Not only are companies learning more about their customers, but their customers are learning about the businesses they patronize. This two-way exchange increases brand loyalty and personalizes brands in ways that eluded marketers in the past. Plus, there is no better insight into customer preferences and needs than a conversation directly with the source!

Why I Wrote This Book

ClydeBank Media was founded in 2013 as a digital-first publisher. We're a book publisher, of course, but from a business model and marketing perspective we're also an e-commerce brand. ClydeBank Media doesn't have a physical storefront. We don't have retail shelf displays or window dressing. Online-only stores are long past the point of being novel, but we mention the fact that ClydeBank Media is online-only because that has been tremendously influential in the ways that we think about our customers, how to reach them, and the future of our business. As a result, our team was engaging with the world of digital marketing from day one.

All the concepts covered in this book reflect my hands-on experience working in the world of digital marketing. As a startup with a focus on growth, we've tried everything at least once. The digital-first nature of our business means that if we're not making money with digital marketing, we're probably not making very much money at all. Whether you are a digital-first business like we are, or you have a brick-and-mortar business, or some combination of both, you are likely aware that there is no escaping the digital revolution. Today's customers always have at least one foot in the digital world, and they have evolved into savvy digital shoppers.

I wrote this book for a few reasons. It's easy to look back over the years and draw a straight line to our current success—the reality is that things are a little more complicated than that. We've had false starts, made decisions that later made us scratch our heads, and made outright mistakes that have cost us money. That's why I feel that my experience and what I've learned uniquely positions me to present an unvarnished view of the world of digital marketing. Where to start, what to do, how to succeed, and—critically—what to avoid has been the story of our business for the last several years.

I also wrote this book because I don't want anyone to be left behind. The business environment is a competitive one. So is the job market. When businesses thrive, so do the communities they serve. When job seekers have more marketable skills, their work is more rewarding, and they can live more comfortable and fulfilling lives. The rise and ubiquity of digital marketing hasn't just given professionals another line item on their resumes but has also created entirely new career paths and job opportunities that didn't exist even a decade ago. In short, there is a wealth of opportunity available in digital spaces. Armed with the information in this book, you will be equipped to take full advantage of those opportunities.

Who This Book Is For

While anyone interested in marketing can benefit from this book, there are some people who will find it particularly useful.

Entrepreneurs, Artists, and Influencers

From "wantrepreneurs" to "solopreneurs" and every kind of business owner or decision maker in between, starting and growing your business without an understanding of marketing principles and how to put them into practice in digital spaces will be a huge challenge. If you're an entrepreneur who is hands-on with your digital marketing efforts, this book provides a solid grasp of the fundamentals you will need to know to reach customers, grow your business, and make more money. Not just by running ads, but by creating holistic digital marketing campaigns, interpreting the results and feedback from those campaigns, and building on successes to keep costs low and thrill your customers. Plus, as a primer on digital marketing automation, this book will also teach you to improve the effectiveness of your marketing activities while keeping time and effort to a minimum. As any entrepreneur who is trying to do it all knows, the most valuable resource at your disposal is your time and attention. Automating your lead-generation efforts, digital advertising, email follow-up, and more frees up time to work on improving and growing your business in other areas while saving time and money.

Planning to outsource your digital marketing efforts? Don't put this book down! Understanding digital marketing fundamentals means you are better equipped to work with agencies, freelancers, and other digital marketing outsourcing partners. Not only will you be able to better communicate your needs, but you will be better able to interpret the results and provide feedback for your collaborators.

Today's entrepreneurs aren't just business owners. Creators and makers are finding that a mastery of digital marketing can make a world of difference when it comes to getting ears for their musical projects, eyeballs on their design work or art, and more ways to monetize their hobbies.

Professionals and Freelancers Looking for a Saleable Skill

Digital marketers are in demand. The Bureau of Labor Statistics projects that demand for professionals with marketing experience will grow faster than demand for most other occupations. While there are still jobs in traditional marketing, today's marketing positions necessitate experience in digital spaces. The gig economy is also fertile ground for experienced digital marketers to succeed. Freelancers who find their niche in email marketing, social media management, search engine marketing, or pay-per-click management can develop a healthy business solving digital marketing problems for their clients. If you are looking to learn digital marketing to gain employment—either as a freelancer or with an agency on a more permanent basis—this book will give you an advantage in the marketplace.

Students and Marketers Looking to Expand Their Skill Sets

Marketing students and business students owe it to themselves to build a strong digital marketing foundation. Likewise, marketing professionals who have limited experience with digital marketing concepts should start here to bring themselves up to speed and stay current in their field. If you are already a member of the marketing industry, don't worry, the digital ship hasn't sailed. If anything, digital marketing is easier than ever to break into and put into practice.

How This Book Is Organized

Digital Marketing QuickStart Guide is organized into three parts: "Digital Marketing 101," "Tools of the Trade," and "Execution."

Part I, "Digital Marketing 101," provides a catch-up opportunity for readers who are not overly familiar with basic marketing concepts. These concepts are fundamental to marketing activities no matter the environment, whether a billboard or a Facebook ad. This part of *Digital Marketing QuickStart Guide* serves as a detailed walk-through of the basics of understanding what you're selling, who you're selling to, how to segment your market, and how best to set and achieve your marketing goals.

Part II, "Tools of the Trade," gets down to business with the information you need about the tools that will fill your digital toolbox. We discuss at length websites, search engine optimization (SEO), keyword selection, paid search placement and pay-per-click (PPC) advertising, social media, and email campaigns. These are the nuts and bolts that will power your campaigns and the relationships you have with your customers. By the end of part II, you will have a solid understanding of how different digital marketing tools fit together, which ones are the best fit for your marketing goals, and how savvy digital marketers use these tools in unison to power successful digital marketing campaigns.

In part III, "Execution," you'll learn how to take the tools covered in part II and put them to work in a cohesive way. Use digital marketing tools to create sound marketing strategies, build your digital marketing funnel, assess and optimize campaigns, troubleshoot underperforming ads, and more.

The content of the book moves logically from beginning marketing concepts to the fine-tuning of a campaign, but you can read and use it in any order that is most advantageous to you (though we don't recommend skipping anything!)

Chapter by Chapter

» Part I – Digital Marketing 101

» Chapter 1: Digital marketing gets a lot of attention and is the focus of this book, but it's important to understand that digital marketing uses timeless marketing fundamentals that have been honed over decades. "A Crash Course in Marketing Concepts" explores the overall field of marketing, detailing the basic concepts and elements that guide all marketing efforts, regardless of where the message appears. This chapter will be particularly valuable for readers who haven't studied marketing or are not overly familiar with the basics of the topic.

» Chapter 2: "Core Digital Marketing Concepts" outlines concepts that apply specifically to digital marketing as well as other business concepts, such as product design, process design, and strategic pricing. Chapter 2 dives into the importance of customer lifetime value and the differences between—and different uses of—earned, paid, and owned media. It also defines some of the marketing concepts that are used throughout the rest of the book.

» Chapter 3: Before you make the first keystroke of your first campaign, there are quite a few things to get squared away. In "Who Are You Selling To?" you'll learn about market scope and identifying your target audience. We walk through the process of creating a customer avatar, understanding the customer journey, and how these concepts impact the decisions you'll make when planning and executing campaigns.

» Chapter 4: "What Are You Selling?" introduces the all-important value ladder, a tool that helps you organize related products or services into a sequence and keep customers advancing—or ascending—through your product offerings to spend more and more. We explore how to use upselling and downselling tactics and how to craft an offer your customers will find difficult to refuse.

» Chapter 5: Like any business activity, digital marketing should be undertaken with concrete goals in mind. "What Are Your Objectives?" will help you clarify what you're working to achieve, whether it's increased sales and profits, improved generation of leads, or the launch of a new product or service. Once you've identified your objectives, you'll rely on SMART goals to reach them—that is, goals that are Specific, Measurable, Actionable, Relevant, and Time-Bound. With a clear set of goals in mind, you are ready to move on to evaluating the tools at your disposal.

» **Part II – Tools of the Trade**

» Chapter 6: "Coming In for a Landing" explains the importance of building a website that serves as a point of contact and enables you to stay in touch with visitors, and how to use specific pages, such as a landing page or a squeeze page, to convince visitors to take action. You'll learn more about the power of compelling headlines and copy and how to use various types of social proof to convert traffic into paying customers.

» Chapter 7: "Capturing Traffic" discusses how to use earned media to attract traffic to your landing pages. We also take an in-depth look at how to use search engine optimization to capture organic web traffic from search engines like Google, along with how to create and deploy content strategically.

» Chapter 8: In "Directing Traffic" you'll learn the ins and outs of selecting keywords to drive customers to your site, as well as how to track and analyze the success of keyword-driven advertising campaigns. Learn how pay-per-click advertising is used to drive traffic from everyday internet searches while keeping budgets in check.

» Chapter 9: In "Social," we dive into the world of marketing and using social media and social advertising while smashing misconceptions about what it means to be a social brand. We also explore marketing via chat, ways to stand out in the competitive social media spaces, and driving revenue from social media.

» Chapter 10: The money is in the list. In "Following Up with Email" you'll learn why email marketing is still one of the most powerful tools in a digital marketer's toolbox. We break down how to build and get the most value out of a robust email list.

» **Part III – Execution**

» Chapter 11: Now that you have a firm understanding of the tools available to you, it's time to put them to work. "Building a Sound Marketing Strategy" explains the importance of building a scalable digital marketing funnel. We also discuss how to use lifecycle marketing methods to advance traffic through the digital marketing funnel and turn traffic that has never heard of your brand into raving fans.

» Chapter 12: "Digital Marketing Efficiency" discusses the ways in which new and veteran marketers can get the most out of the tools and tactics covered in this book. The chapter also takes a look at the ways you can troubleshoot poor performance and use marketing automation to scale your marketing efforts with ease.

PART I

DIGITAL MARKETING 101

1

A Crash Course in Marketing Concepts

Chapter Overview
» Marketing, defined
» A review of basic marketing concepts
» The marketing formula explained
» The marketing mix and the brand positioning matrix

Marketing is everything you do to attract customers willing to buy your products or services. Some marketing tactics are designed to make potential customers aware of your offerings in hopes of persuading them to buy from you. Others work by attracting your target market to your company so that you can sell them something.

Marketing is different from sales in that marketing consists of the promotional strategies and tactics you use to convert someone from a prospect into a paying customer. That last step—where you negotiate when, where, and how the customer is going to hand over their credit card or cash—is where sales gets involved. They are two different steps in the process you'll use to make money in your business.

Before we dive into the specific tools and tactics that digital marketers use to grow their businesses, it will be useful to revisit the basic concepts of marketing in general. You might wonder whether these more traditional forms of marketing and their principles have been rendered obsolete by digital marketing.

In a word, no.

"Traditional marketing" is, in fact, more alive and well than ever before. While the methods of communication, tools of persuasion, and reach of marketing efforts are subject to the same breakneck pace as the development of technology—meaning they evolve and adapt, too—the one constant is the human element. Marketers want to reach people. This is true whether they are going door-to-door or sending a mass email. The distinctly personal aspect of marketing—whether face-to-face or through a computer screen—has largely remained the same over the years. So it's helpful to have that background knowledge before we get to the digital-specific stuff.

In this chapter we will review some of those foundational marketing elements and discuss their strategic role for marketing decision makers.

QUESTION

?

You may be asking yourself, "Can I just skip this section?"

This book is designed to be a helpful reference guide, so you can jump around if you so choose, but it is also laid out very purposefully. These concepts aren't strictly related to practical digital marketing, but they are critical to building a cohesive and successful digital marketing strategy—or any marketing strategy, for that matter. You will use them in your first campaign, your tenth campaign, and your thousandth. They are worth reviewing and keeping in the back of your head as you build your strategy from the ground up.

What Is Marketing?

The American Marketing Association (AMA) defines *marketing* as "the activity, set of institutions, and processes for creating, communicating, delivering, and exchanging offerings that have value for customers, clients, partners, and society at large."

A more common way to think of marketing is as the collection of activities that businesses use to make it known that they exist, and to convince consumers that the business is likeable and trustworthy enough to buy from, or at least to consider buying from. But marketing isn't just one activity. In practice, it is the management, coordination, and execution of a wide range of promotional activities and processes. These processes commonly include advertising, sales promotions, market research, brand management, distribution, and public relations—each of which is a specialized discipline in its own right.

DIGITAL ASSETS

To help you pull together all the pieces of your marketing plan from the outset, please download and fill out the Digital Marketing Strategic Planning worksheet we've designed that walks you through developing your brand, outlining your offer, and choosing the marketing methods that will work best for your company as you read each chapter. You can find the worksheet with your Digital Assets at www.clydebankmedia.com/digitalmarketing-assets.

Because of their impact on revenue, or sales, the activities that the sales and marketing department of a company undertake are absolutely critical; in many cases, the sales and marketing departments are an organization's primary point of contact with customers. Because of this, when a marketable entity communicates with a customer, and vice versa, the outcome of this conversation is entirely shaped by the skill and sophistication of that entity's marketing department. Here a marketable entity is any "thing" that can benefit from identifying, anticipating, and satisfying the requirements of customers. A *marketable entity* is commonly a company, brand, or organization, but just about anything or anyone can implement marketing techniques and practices. For example, self-marketing (now more commonly referred to as personal branding) is the practice of promoting a person or personality as one would a company or product. Similarly, political campaigns use marketing techniques and tactics to "pitch" candidates.

There are numerous examples of marketable entities that are not companies or products. Despite being on the cusp of his seventies, Sir Richard Branson is a veritable poster boy for personal branding. He is the founder of the Virgin Group, a multinational conglomerate owning a portfolio of more than four hundred companies, including Virgin Atlantic airline and Virgin Mobile services. Branson himself does not shy away from the camera or social media. In his numerous media appearances, he is always cheery and smiling, projecting the image of someone who is open and relatable, despite being a man of considerable wealth. This perceived authenticity has been a distinct asset for Branson as an entrepreneur and businessman and has been a key factor in why the numerous commercial brands his own personal brand is associated with have grown steadily through the years.

For much of modern history, the conversation between marketers and customers was largely a one-way exchange. Billboards, catalog sales, circulars, coupons, TV and radio, etc., allow the opportunity for a marketable entity, such as a company, to present a message to an audience about its products or services. But that same audience (the customer) doesn't have a clear channel of communication through which to respond when presented with those messages.

As you are already well aware, the advent of the World Wide Web has completely changed that dynamic, and now the conversation between marketable entities and their audiences is much more of a two-way exchange. Through social media, email, live chat, and phone, prospects and customers can reach out to brands or organizations directly. This shift has empowered consumers in ways that marketers never could have predicted but have now come to embrace. In addition to providing simple feedback, audiences can amplify a message by sharing it with their followers, or they can rally others to a cause by adding their own commentary and stories—all at no cost to the marketer. There is a downside to this two-way messaging, of course. As audiences have become more empowered, they have also become more critical of companies and their marketing efforts and rarely hesitate to severely punish missteps.

Why Is Marketing Important?

No matter how sexy, exciting, new, or tech-enabled your product or service is, it simply will not sell itself. This is especially true if your potential customers don't understand how your product solves a problem they have or fulfills a burning need. Most important, even if your product was so compelling that every consumer snapped it up without a second thought, people's attitudes and preferences change over time. Marketing—digital or otherwise—is the way your company puts your product or service in front of customers, helps them understand why your offering is the best fit for their needs, and keeps your company abreast of changing customer preferences.

MY TAKE

It can be easy for entrepreneurs to develop tunnel vision when focusing on their products—after all, working so hard on getting one thing exactly right takes focus and dedication—but this becomes a real risk when it's time to look at the big picture. A "build it and they will come" mentality is not only misguided, but it can have a serious impact on the success of an emerging company. The development of marketing strategy at the expense of product design, and vice versa, can result in wasted marketing dollars, last-minute product changes, and product launches without validation of true demand. In both product design and marketing strategy, focus on the needs of your target market and don't undertake one action without committing to the other as well. That is, don't develop a product and then try to find a target market for it. Let your market drive product development.

We humans like to think our decisions are based on reason and logic and, by extension, so are our buying habits and preferences. But the reality is that purchasing decisions are more often driven by emotion, and it is through marketing that savvy professionals aim to influence those emotional connections that lead to purchases.

Although the end goal of marketing is a sale, there are numerous objectives that marketing can help achieve:

Marketing Reaches Customers

The most straightforward use of marketing activities is to reach—meaning communicate with—potential customers and share your message with them. That message could be about a new product, a sale, anything you feel is important to share and helps you achieve your business goals. Reaching new customers, maintaining relationships with existing customers, and attempting to win back customers who have defected to competitors is the lifeblood of any business.

Marketing Provides Customer Clarity

Reaching customers is essential but is only half of the equation. Knowing what to say to those individuals when you have won their attention is just as important. Today's two-way conversation between marketers and their audiences means that you can often identify exactly who is interested in your products and services. The more you understand the wants, needs, fears, and concerns of the people your business interacts with, the more effective you will be when communicating with them.

NOTE

Understanding who you're talking to and crafting messaging that resonates is classic marketing in a nutshell. Dedicated and diligent market research uncovers key aspects of the people who will become your target market (the people most likely to buy your product or service) but it also uncovers another group of people: those who *aren't* interested in buying what you're selling. There are many reasons we don't buy things. We may not understand how a product or service improves our lives or solves our problems. The price may be too high. The product may not be available where we shop, or it might not be as good a fit as another product we already use; the list goes on. Identifying the type of people who don't have a need for what you are selling is important, because your marketing efforts will be much less effective when speaking to this group.

Marketing Explains Benefits

Though they are sometimes used interchangeably in casual conversation, the terms "feature" and "benefit" have very different definitions in the world of sales and marketing. A *feature* is a particular aspect of a product or service that provides value and differentiates it from others. A *benefit* is the value that a feature provides to the customer. For example, a tech-enabled feature on many new cars is the ability to make phone calls through a synced phone using voice commands. The technology that makes this possible is the feature—it provides value and differentiation. The ability to make calls safely (and, in many states, legally) without looking away from the road is the *benefit* to customers.

FEATURE	BENEFIT
A golf ball is made from a new type of shell and has a unique dimple pattern on the surface.	*What this means for you* is that your shots will go farther and fly straighter.
A new running shoe has a unique foam core in the sole.	*What this means for you* is less shock to your ankles and knees when running on hard surfaces.

People buy benefits, not features.

The most important thing to remember about features and benefits is that **people buy benefits, not features.** Features are necessary to produce the value—benefit—that people will buy, but no one will buy a product based on features alone. A feature-packed product may be a true marvel, but if customers don't understand how those features translate into benefits in their own lives, they won't be interested. Marketing is the key to bridging this gap. As the saying goes, don't sell the steak—sell the sizzle.

A good way to think about the difference between features and benefits is to translate a feature into a "what this means for you" statement. For example, a car salesperson may say, "The newest model of this sedan includes wireless connectivity to your phone and recognizes your voice to enable hands-free calls through the car's speakers. *What this means for you* is that you can keep your eyes on the road and make calls safely and confidently."

Marketing Defines Your Brand

A *brand* is the sum of feelings, associations, and perceptions that people have regarding a company and its products. The concept of "brand" can be tough to nail down. Even the definition of what exactly a brand is can be a point of contention.

A logo, for example, is part of a brand's image, but a brand is much more than a logo. Packaging and color palettes are part of a brand, but a brand is about more than just the way products are dressed. And it's more than just a mission statement. If a company is a person, then that company's brand would include their personality. Are they fun and enthusiastic or serious and professional? Do they wear bright, sporty clothes or do they dress more conservatively? Are they a person you think of when you want to relax, or are they a person you would rely on for advice or help? These intangible elements that surround a product or a company coalesce into that company's brand.

Branding, or the activities associated with refining and spreading brand elements, is a marketing function. A brand's perception helps customers connect with it and acts as shorthand for the experience those customers can expect. A well-defined brand can be a differentiating aspect between two otherwise similar products, or it can justify higher prices for products that are perceived as premium or luxury. Remember, a brand is the *sum* of feelings, associations, and perceptions; any of these individual brand elements can have negative connotations as well. A brand that is seen as cheap, socially irresponsible, of poor quality or value, or otherwise objectionable will face an uphill battle when it comes to winning new customers and retaining existing customers.

Marketing Moves the Conversation to the Emotional Space

A message that is tailored to speak to the exact wants, needs, fears, and concerns of customers is much more likely to hit the emotional points that trigger a sale. Earlier in this chapter, we touched on the idea that for most purchases, the decision to buy is an emotional one. Reaching customers, learning about them, educating them, and explaining what features mean to them—presenting a well-defined brand—culminates in the transition from rational decision making to a more emotional commitment. The point at which logic gives way to emotion is known as *affective override*, and that point is when marketing is most effective.

Different Marketing Perspectives

Now that we have established exactly what marketing is and why it is necessary, let's look at some of the traditional marketing elements and how they work in digital environments. Crafting an effective marketing strategy can be a daunting task. Fortunately, there are a few basic principles that hold true regardless of whether you're working in a traditional or a digital space. Together, these principles form what is generally referred to as the *marketing formula*:

Market

The market is the group of individuals you are targeting. For example, men and women between the ages of eighteen and thirty-three in Los Angeles, or all the brick-and-mortar clothing retailers in the United States under nine thousand square feet in size per location. Subsets of those groups are called *market segments*.

Media

Media, or the medium, is the channel through which you will be sharing your message with your market. This can include mass media, such as major broadcast television, or much more personal methods of communication, such as email, SMS texting, and in-person conversations.

Message

The message is the content of what you want to share with your market. When marketers craft a message, it is always done with a goal in mind. What is the desired action that the market—your target audience—should take after reading the message? Do you want prospects to visit your new website? Stop by your new storefront? Are you reminding your market that you are open for business? What's the point of your communication and what do you want your market to do?

When the three aspects of market, media, and message work together in harmony, marketers find success. When one of the sides of the triangle is not a good fit with the others, marketing efforts begin to underperform and don't deliver satisfactory results. Synchronicity between market, media, and message is essential (figure 2).

GRAPHIC

fig. 2

MEDIA

As a marketer—or someone who has become a de facto marketer by virtue of being a small business owner or entrepreneur—how do you determine the best way to deploy your market, media, and message? The answer is strategy. All businesses have the overarching goal of profitability, but there are often objectives and steps along the way that can help ensure that the marketing tactics you use will yield optimal success for your business.

Small businesses often focus more on growing their customer base and increasing the amount that each customer spends. Larger corporations often pay more attention to market share increase and maximizing the value of their product lines. Whatever the size of your venture, these strategic, long-term goals can be accomplished through careful implementation of the marketing formula.

Let's look at some distinct categories of marketing that use different versions of the market/media/message mix. As we do, think about campaigns you have seen or have executed yourself. How do these marketing perspectives relate to different products or services? How do they relate to different markets or groups of people? Most marketing efforts can be divided into two overarching categories: outbound and inbound.

Outbound Marketing

Outbound marketing is the catch-all term for marketing that is disseminated or issued by a company or marketable entity. It's when the entity initiates the conversation with its target audience.

This form of marketing is generally known as ***push marketing*** because it "pushes" the message out to the target audience, whether they are actively interested in hearing it or not. Traditional forms of advertising, such as print, radio, and TV, are perfect examples of push or outbound marketing. Digital versions include online pop-up ads, Facebook ads in one's news feed, and promotional emails.

Inbound Marketing

Inbound marketing is, as you would expect, the opposite of outbound marketing. It is marketing that happens in response to consumers who are actively seeking out a product or service. Inbound marketing is synonymous with the term ***pull marketing*** because inbound tactics "pull" customers along a chosen path toward a purchase, instead of reaching out to them.

Giving away a free resource that solves a problem for a customer or writing an informative article that appears in search results are both inbound marketing tactics. In these instances, potential customers seek out a solution to a problem they are already experiencing, meaning they are primed to receive value from a brand that can put information in front of them.

fig. 3

INBOUND MARKETING TACTICS	OUTBOUND MARKETING TACTICS
PODCASTS	PRINT & BROADCAST ADVERTISING
WEBINARS	BILLBOARDS
FREE EBOOKS	PPC ADVERTISING
VIDEOS	DIRECT MAIL
FREE COURSES	TRADE SHOWS
SEO	NEWSLETTERS

Examples of common inbound and outbound marketing tactics

The advent of search engines, high-speed internet, mobile connectivity, and social media have radically changed the ways in which marketers think about and deploy inbound strategies. Once upon a time, inbound marketing was the sole realm of massive corporations—marketable entities that had deep enough pockets to collect sufficient amounts of data about their customers and leverage their existing customer awareness. Moreover, to further boost awareness, they could deploy aggressive outbound campaigns as needed, which in turn set the stage for the generally more cost-effective inbound marketing efforts. Today, the ubiquitous, accessible, and cost-effective marketing tools that are available to businesses of all sizes are driving an inbound revolution in the digital marketing space. Still, no marketing strategy is complete without a plan to both push messages to customers and pull them to your business. You need to do both.

Direct Response Marketing

Direct response marketing is a specific type of outbound marketing designed to elicit an immediate response or action from your target. This type of marketing is generally used with buyers who are aware of the problem a product or service solves and are much closer to making a purchase. A sales page, a promotional email or text, or a chat message that encourages the recipient to take action *now* are all examples of direct response marketing in action.

There is no limit to the kinds of media that can be used for direct response marketing, but personalized, targeted media often generates the best results. As with all other marketing messages, direct response efforts use messages that are crafted with a purpose. In this case, the purpose is almost always made clear in the *call to action* (CTA). A CTA is a request that your audience take a particular action, which is a step toward making a purchase.

An email that is advertising a sale may end with the CTA "Shop Now!" with a link to the relevant product selection. Or a CTA may encourage website visitors to start a free trial, make a donation, join an email list, or leave a review. As with any other strategic marketing elements, direct response calls to action should work in unison with the overall message and target market and should be appropriate for the delivery media.

A classic staple of the direct response approach to marketing is the sales letter. These long form letters were traditionally written using persuasive language that was tailored to a very specific audience. Today's digital iteration takes the form of sales pages, persuasive emails, landing pages, and sales funnels, all of which will be covered in detail later in this text. Direct response principles work in conjunction with these and other inbound methods to deliver a one-two punch that thrives in digital environments—inbound techniques bring in customers who know they have a problem that needs a solution, and direct response tactics are used to close the sale.

Awareness Marketing

Awareness marketing is the general term for marketing efforts that aim to increase brand recognition and awareness in target markets. It is a form of outbound marketing—its goal is to encourage potential customers who may not be aware of your product or service to seek you out based on the solution you provide. Awareness marketing works well in conjunction with other outbound marketing tactics, but when used alone it generally doesn't produce the results marketers are looking for.

Frequently used in traditional, nondigital marketing, there are many examples of awareness marketing—the entire industry of out-of-home advertising is ideal for delivering awareness-based messages. *Out-of-home advertising* consists of billboards, banners, benches, city buses, and anything else that is visible when people are out and about.

In the digital realm, awareness marketing takes those out-of-home principles a step further. Not only is a digital awareness-based message spread via digital ads, content placement, and influencer mentions (to name a few), but it is also targeted and relevant.

NOTE

The most notable examples of hyper-successful brand awareness efforts include those for consumer products such as Kleenex and Q-Tips. The brand awareness surrounding these products is so prevalent that we often use their brand names interchangeably with the generic product names–facial tissue and cotton swabs. Branding experts often point to this development as a marketing misfire, rather than the resounding success that it appears to be. After all, if I go to the store to "buy some Kleenex" and purchase a box of facial tissue from a competitor without batting an eyelash, what has

Kleenex really achieved? Nothing, in that instance, since awareness does not seem to lead to a preference for the Kleenex brand.

Content Marketing

Perhaps the most effective inbound marketing concept of all time, **content marketing** is the practice of creating, publishing, and distributing content of potential interest to targeted audiences. This content is rarely overly promotional. Instead, it is focused on providing value to audiences and stimulating interest in the relevant brand. Combined with search intent and search engine optimization principles, content marketing is one of the most effective tools in a digital marketer's toolbox.

Today, content marketing is most closely associated with blogs, social media, and video content campaigns, but the concept emerged a long time ago with entrepreneur Benjamin Franklin. Franklin was a trailblazer in many disciplines—he was an inventor, a statesman, a writer, a scientist, and a civil activist. He was also a successful printer and publisher. First published in 1732, his *Poor Richard's Almanack* was a serial lifestyle booklet that included puzzles, stories, engaging wordplay, and other entertainment. It was a successful publication in its own right; however, it was also a valuable way for Franklin to showcase his skills as a printer and to drum up new business. This is perhaps one of the earliest examples of successful content marketing.

Conversion-Based Marketing

Unique to the digital space, **conversion-based marketing** is a broad term for all the marketing efforts that go into converting internet traffic into paying customers. A dive into the numbers truly boggles the mind. Google receives more than 63,000 searches *per second*. That translates into roughly 5.5 billion searches per day—more than two trillion a year. And that's just Google. Combine social media, news sites, your favorite blogs … the list goes on. Capturing even just a tiny slice of that traffic and converting it into paying customers is the broad goal of digital marking efforts. Digital marketers start by identifying the people who are making searches on popular search engines, then they create content and offers that speak to solving the problems those people have—using tactics and techniques that are covered in later chapters of this book.

Conversion-based marketing is laser-focused on that all-important conversion event: the point when a person on their computer, phone, or tablet (and now potentially their fridge, microwave, or washing machine) stops being merely "traffic" and becomes a customer. This could be the moment when the customer actually pulls out their credit card, or it could be any one of the equally important steps along the way. Due to the wealth of data available to digital marketers, conversion-based marketing efforts have the opportunity for endless tweaking, sophistication, and refinement. Conversion-based principles can be applied to digital campaigns that are based on both inbound and outbound objectives and tactics. And they are particularly well suited to the revenue-based objectives of businesses of all sizes. In short, conversion-based marketing is the primary language of budget-minded digital marketers, meaning it is the single most utilized strategic marketing concept in the digital space right now.

Though they are presented separately, the aforementioned strategic approaches are, collectively, the gold standard. Using a *combination* of digital marketing strategies will yield the best results, rather than picking and choosing single tactics. Therefore, this book focuses primarily on using a blend of these marketing perspectives.

The Marketing Mix

Most marketing efforts are essentially defined by the market, the media, and the message—the "marketing formula."

The exact way in which these elements are deployed is based on the strategic goals that marketers want to achieve. We know that marketing strategies are informed by strategic goals, but what informs those goals? Not to be confused with the marketing formula, the **marketing mix** is a combination of characteristics that describe exactly what it is you are selling. These characteristics help determine what shape your marketing formula should take and therefore what strategies make the most sense when it comes to executing marketing campaigns.

The marketing mix is by no means a recent concept. The term was first used by Harvard professor Neil Borden in 1953 during an address directed to the American Marketing Association. Borden said that the four components of the marketing mix—product, price, place, and promotion—impact every marketing campaign. Nearly seventy years later, it turns out that Borden is still right.[1]

The marketing mix is also commonly referred to as the *4 P's of marketing*. The four Ps are product, price, place, and promotion. They represent specific aspects that vary from product to product and are the basis for constructing and executing campaigns.

Product

Your product is, literally, what you are selling. It could be a tangible product or an intangible service, but in either case the associated product lifecycle informs marketing strategy. The *product lifecycle* of a product (or service lifecycle for a service) generally consists of a series of stages that begins with introduction, progresses to growth, achieves maturity, and then moves into decline (figure 4). Although decline is a natural lifecycle state, it can be headed off, extended, or otherwise precluded, perhaps by reigniting the lifecycle all over again, beginning (again) with introduction.

STAGES OF THE PRODUCT LIFE CYCLE

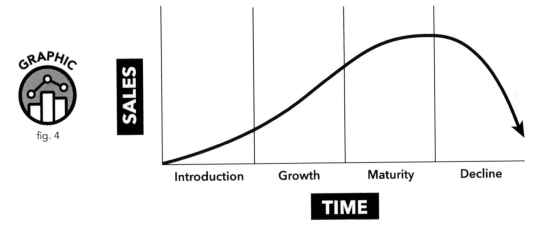

GRAPHIC

fig. 4

Take, for example, the launch of new iPhone models. In the space of a few years, the latest model is introduced, sales skyrocket as millions of consumers decide to upgrade their phones, at a certain point sales level off, and then the cycle shifts into decline as consumer interest wanes in anticipation of the next model. When the next model is announced, excitement builds again for the new introduction, and the process starts over.

In the world of automobiles, each new model has a very compressed introduction and growth phase. Both start and come to conclusion within a brief period, several months before their nominal year begins. A 2021 vehicle, for example, is introduced in 2020. It hits the maturity phase during 2021 and is in decline at the point when the 2022 model is released. Trendy summer shorts or tank tops will have an even shorter product lifecycle, experiencing all the lifecycle stages in just a matter of weeks, quickly replaced by fall sweaters and coats. A pharmaceutical product, on the other hand, could have a lifecycle that lasts a decade or more. A new drug introduced into the market enters the growth stage after a year or so, once physicians understand its benefits for their patients. It is then prescribed until demand and production level out (maturity). As other products are released and generics start grabbing market share, the drug may start to enter decline.

Marketing objectives are different at each stage of the product lifecycle. In the early stages of introduction and growth, it is essential to attract new customers. As the product reaches maturity, the market may not change significantly and the media may stay the same, although the message may change and adapt. Other product-related concerns that marketers should be aware of include features and benefits (and how to effectively present benefits), target market (the people who have the problem this product solves), and competitive products and substitutes. Each of these aspects inform the specific tweaks marketers will make to their own market, media, and message mix over the product lifecycle.

Price

Pricing is both a strategic decision and a very important aspect of your product's marketing plan. Determining the best price for your product is equal parts art and science. Are you a new entrant to an industry? If so, it might make sense to use a ***penetration pricing*** strategy, pricing your products lower than the market price to aggressively capture market share and "penetrate" a market. Once the target market share has been achieved, you may adjust your prices closer to market value. Lower pricing or discount pricing can also be used defensively to dissuade new entrants from capturing market share in an industry where you are heavily entrenched. A ***value pricing*** strategy assigns price based on customer-perceived value. Marketing efforts are critical in determining what that perceived value should be.

Pricing can be complicated, though. Marketing efforts must take price into account to provide the highest level of success (and profit). Ignoring price when crafting a marketing strategy is a recipe for disaster.

Place

Place describes the distribution channels used to physically deliver the product to customers. If your business has product placement in North America, a marketing campaign in Europe doesn't make much sense. Likewise, if your product is perceived as being premium or luxury, a market/media/message mix that excludes potential customers with high levels of disposable income is a poor strategy. Right now, an emerging trend is increased popularity of *direct-to-consumer* (DTC) brands, or those that distribute directly to their customers.

Promotion

Promotion reflects the *promotional mix*, which consists of advertising, public relations, personal selling, and sales promotion. Different promotional mixes are appropriate for different products. No one would purchase a house or a car sight unseen—those high-cost products require a certain amount of personal selling in their promotional mix. The opposite could be said for lower-priced fast food or packaged food products; they usually rely on relatively little personal selling and much more on advertising and sales promotion.

Alternative Interpretations of the Marketing Mix

The 4 P's of marketing aren't the only game in town. An alternative interpretation called the *5 P's of marketing* includes "people" in addition to the traditional 4 P's. Using this interpretation of the marketing mix, "people" refers to sales staff involved in the selling process. In some cases, there are digital equivalents to personal selling. Some Instagram influencers, for example, have been tremendously successful using a personal selling model adapted to the social space.

Other interpretations of the marketing mix include the customer-centric *4 C's of marketing* and the *service marketing mix* for businesses, both of which are built around delivering a core service. The 4 C's consist of customer wants and needs, cost, convenience, and communication. The service marketing mix includes the 4 P's plus "people," "process," and "physical evidence."

MY TAKE

How should an entrepreneur or business decision maker cut through the alphabet soup? Between the C's and the P's, it can seem like no matter which strategic core you choose, there is an alternate model that might be a better fit–the grass is always greener. The most important thing you can do is stick to the model you select. Be flexible and think holistically about what you want to achieve, the value your product or service provides, and who your target market is.

Brand Positioning

Brand positioning refers to how your brand is perceived by customers and your target market. Are you a premium luxury brand? Do customers think of your brand as fun and cool, or are you outdated? The key word here is "perception." You yourself may have a distinct impression of your own brand, but for your customers, perception is reality. Successful brands use three primary criteria when considering their brand positioning strategy:

» **Customer Relevancy:** How good is the brand's *perceived* fit for the target market? A standout product or service that is wrapped in an irrelevant or uninteresting brand will face a tough time in the market—even when pitted against inferior products.

» **Differentiation:** A unique positioning is critical for brands that want to stand out in a crowded marketplace and want to be able to charge top dollar for their products or services.

» **Credibility:** A brand must be able to deliver on its promises. Customer relevancy is meaningless if your customers are disappointed or feel as though they were duped after buying your product.

Marketing efforts and brand positioning must be a match for a product's target market. You are going to hear that more than once here. What you need to remember is that your target market consists of the people who are most likely to purchase your product or service (and therefore will be most receptive to your marketing efforts).

The Brand Positioning Matrix

The *brand positioning matrix* is a visual representation of the various brand positions within an industry. They are helpful for evaluating the generally competitive nature of an industry and assessing where your brand fits. The matrix is constructed with x and y axes that divide the chart into quadrants. Each axis represents a scale of two different criteria, and brands are placed in the appropriate quadrant. The criteria used for evaluation are whatever make the most sense for the given industry. For example, automotive brands are often plotted with luxury versus sporty on one axis and inexpensive versus expensive on the other. Toyota is sporty and inexpensive; Mercedes is luxury and expensive. Brands are plotted on the matrix until all relevant industry players are represented. Remember, this isn't about each individual product line offered by each brand. Both Toyota and Mercedes make a wide range of vehicles in a range of price points. The idea is to attempt to capture the overall customer perception of a given brand and plot it accordingly.

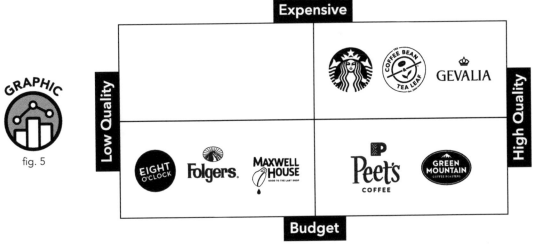

GRAPHIC

fig. 5

A brand positioning matrix showing various pre-ground coffee brands.

Figure 5 is an example of a brand positioning matrix that plots leading pre-ground coffee brands for home brewing. There's no accounting for taste—your opinion may differ from the plots here. The point of the matrix is to represent how the brands have tried to position *themselves*. Starbucks and Gevalia brands are positioned to be perceived as expensive and of high quality, making them premium brands. Notice that there are no brands that fall into the expensive/budget quality quadrant. After all, who would want to pay an arm and a leg for low quality coffee?

Tying It All Together

All the marketing aspects we have just discussed work in concert with one another. Each needs to be considered, regardless of the industry in which you operate or whether you're employing traditional methods, exploring digital methods, or using a combination of both. Building your marketing strategy the right way is crucial and will produce more consistent results down the road.

What you are selling determines your brand positioning elements, which in turn inform your marketing formula.

Figure 6 is a visual representation of how these key elements fit together. Marketing at the campaign level is composed of different configurations of the market/media/message mix. These are determined by brand positioning criteria—how you want customers to perceive your brand—which in turn are a function of the product you sell, your pricing strategy, the promotions you will use to push sales of that product, and the distribution channels that will be used to deliver the product. Let's look at an example.

Today is the first day of business for my new water bottle company. My water bottles have a proprietary design with a lid that seals closed to prevent leaks, but which can also be opened with ease for convenient drinking. My marketing mix consists of the following:

>> **Product**: A premium water bottle that keeps water chilled, does not leak or spill, and is easy to open and use. The bottle comes printed in a variety of trendy patterns and colors and is on the more expensive end of commonly available water bottles. I want my bottle to be perceived as luxury, ecofriendly, fun, and high quality.

>> **Price**: I am implementing a premium pricing strategy. My bottles are priced higher than others and are made from higher quality materials, and my goal through marketing and branding is to position my bottle as a status symbol accessory. This is relevant to my target customers, who have high-powered jobs and disposable

income. These people want every accessory they own to be a statement piece, and my water bottles will fulfill that role.

» **Promotion:** I will have periodic sales and bundle smaller bottles during special promotional periods to push sales. Through donations to clean water charities with every purchase, I intend to create positive media buzz and increase the exposure of my brand.

» **Placement:** My bottles will be available directly from my website, from select high-end retailers, and through an influencer program that compensates high-powered social influencers for sales they direct to my site. This placement strategy maintains and reinforces the premium nature of the product and contributes positively to my brand position as a luxury water bottle provider.

Traditional Marketing vs. Digital Marketing

Today, digital technology has become so ubiquitous that "digital marketing" may as well simply be called "marketing." What were formerly considered digital-only marketing tactics have become part of any savvy marketer's marketing plan.

When we discuss traditional marketing, we are usually referring to what is considered *old media*, generally defined as mass media technologies that predated the information age: printed matter, telephone, radio, television, etc. *New media* includes the digital space as we have come to understand it today. It refers to digital communication methods that have come about as a result of the information age—search engines, social media, streaming video, and mobile. The following are some of the disadvantages of old media:

Old Media Is Rigid

Digital ads can be changed (often quickly) with a few clicks of a mouse, whereas a physical roadside or rooftop billboard needs to be stripped and its vinyl faces re-hung. After a print ad is approved, it is effectively set in stone once the printer starts cranking out newspaper or magazine issues.

Because of its form, old media is inflexible and slower to respond to changing conditions. This rigidity makes it tough for marketers to try new approaches or to test out different market/media/message mixes on a budget. A powerful asset for digital marketers is the ability to endlessly test, confirm, and discard different approaches, enabling them to maximize effectiveness and keep budgets in check.

This isn't to say that digital marketers should change their campaigns on a whim. As with any other business activity, changes should be well planned and have a stated objective. Too many changes in too short a time can destroy marketing efficiency and effectiveness, not to mention obscuring your ability to glean information about what works and what doesn't.

Old Media Is Blind

Because it is impractical to print a separate ad for each individual reader of a magazine, marketers using print media have to make assumptions about the audiences they are speaking to, using a potentially outdated media kit to try to craft a market/media/message mix that resonates with the most people possible. Digital marketers, on the other hand, have access to a range of sophisticated and robust targeting capabilities that allow them to better understand exactly who they are speaking to and, therefore, what they should say.

Old Media Is Expensive

A national television spot is beyond the reach of many small-business marketing budgets. Digital marketing, on the other hand, has very low barriers to entry. Not only is it less expensive to get started, but digital marketing campaigns can also start delivering results right away, more quickly justifying costs.

Old Media Is Opaque

Clever marketers have come up with a variety of ways to track the effectiveness of traditional media campaigns, but nothing matches the wealth of data available, often in real time, to digital marketers.

Now that we have described the fundamental marketing concepts that drive strategy and inform campaign-building, let's take a look at major concepts in digital-specific marketing.

Chapter Recap

» Marketing is the business process responsible for identifying, anticipating, and satisfying customer requirements profitably.

» Marketing activities fulfill critical business needs. Marketing efforts reach customers and help decision makers understand exactly who their customers are. The conversation between brand or marketable entity and customer enables marketers to convey the benefits of their products or services more easily.

» Marketing activities are crucial brand builders and, together with a robust brand experience, move the buying process into an emotional space rather than a rational one.

» The marketing formula, or the relationship between market, media, and message, forms the foundation of marketing efforts in and out of digital spaces. It is a mix of who you are talking to, how you are reaching them, and what you are saying.

» Of the wide range of marketing perspectives and approaches, inbound marketing (pull), outbound marketing (push), direct response marketing (action-oriented), and conversion-based marketing (digital measurement) are the most relevant.

» The marketing mix, or the 4 Ps of marketing, brings together the most relevant details marketers should consider when deliberating their strategy. There are various interpretations of what exactly constitutes the marketing mix; the particular blend of important factors for your marketing efforts has to do with your target market, product, pricing strategy, distribution, and promotional efforts.

» Brand positioning is the deliberate strategy of cultivating a particular customer perception surrounding a business, its products, and its story. The brand positioning matrix is a visual tool that can be used to represent the range of brands competing in the same space.

| 2 |

Core Digital Marketing Concepts

Chapter Overview
>> CLV, AOV, and CAC—what they are and how to calculate them
>> Defining some key marketing concepts
>> Exploring the media mix

Now that we've introduced key foundational marketing principles all marketers need to know, let's change gears and discuss the principles that drive marketing campaigns, specifically in digital spaces.

It is a misstep to consider marketing product design, process design, and strategic pricing activities as separate and distinct from overall operations and business objectives. The flow of information that marketing efforts produce, both into and out of the business, is essential to many decision-making processes. Barriers between marketing and operations may seriously inhibit the best possible decision-making outcomes. Entrepreneurs, managers, and decision makers who ignore marketing insights are running their businesses blind.

Customer Lifetime Value (CLV)

It is often said that the best kind of customers are repeat customers, because they are less expensive to market to, they can provide valuable insights into your target market, they can validate (or encourage changes to) your customer profile, and they can bolster brand awareness through word of mouth. Decision makers have a tendency to look at customers in a transactional sense—meaning on a per-purchase basis—but that isn't really an accurate depiction of the relationship your customers have with your brand, which is more on a continuum.

A more holistic approach looks at the total value of a customer, or the sum of all transactions that a customer will have over the lifetime of their relationship with your brand, less the cost to acquire that customer. Expressed as a metric, this concept is known as ***customer lifetime value*** (CLV). Taking a more long-term perspective, through CLV, can have a tremendous effect on a company's operations and marketing strategy.

NOTE

You may also see customer lifetime value abbreviated as LTV for "lifetime value."

Companies that focus on the lifetime value of a customer have a much deeper understanding of what reasonable marketing budgets are and what constitutes a fair customer acquisition cost. Basing your marketing strategy solely on a customer's first transaction is an incomplete approach and can lead to overspending on one hand and a reluctance to take advantage of key marketing opportunities on the other. This is because that first transaction may or may not represent a customer's typical purchase amount or frequency.

When looking at the lifetime value of different customer segments, the CLV metric helps you identify which customer segments to allocate sales and marketing dollars toward for the best return. This metric also helps you uncover the appropriate amount to spend on customer service. Customer service can be costly, but if the prospect of losing customers means abandoning the remainder of their CLV, the cost can often be justified. Last but not least, a firm understanding of the lifetime value of your customers is a helpful tool when it comes to designing new products or expanding/ contracting existing product lines. With robust CLV tracking, less guesswork is needed for critical business decision making, such as identifying target profit margins and price points.

Calculating CLV

Let's take a look at an example that illustrates the importance of calculating CLV. A fictional meal prep service named "Home Fresh" offers weekly shipments of easy home recipes and the fresh ingredients to make them. The core Home Fresh offering provides three meals to feed two people at $59 per shipment. On average, Home Fresh customers use the service for twenty-one weeks before canceling their subscription. Based on this information, we can roughly calculate the lifetime value of these customers by simply multiplying the weekly rate they pay by the average number of transactions over the lifetime of the relationship. Were we to assume the numbers just stated are accurate, then the following calculation tells us that the total lifetime value of one new Home Fresh customer is $1,239:

AVERAGE TRANSACTION SIZE
x
LIFETIME AVERAGE # OF TRANSACTIONS

$$\$59$$
$$x \quad 21 \text{ weeks}$$
$$= \$1,239 \text{ Customer Lifetime Value (CLV)}$$

The example in figure 7 is missing one important factor, however. We know how much revenue Home Fresh can generally expect customers to bring in, but we haven't accounted for the marketing cost to acquire them—to get them to buy. A business's *customer acquisition cost* (CAC) is a simple but powerful metric that summarizes the cost (per customer) associated with converting members of a target market into paying customers.

If Home Fresh has a CAC of $290 per customer, a number that includes sales costs, marketing costs to acquire new customers, and any other relevant acquisition costs, then that CAC number is deducted from our CLV calculation of $1,239, resulting in a total of $949 per customer. With these marketing costs factored in, Home Fresh can expect $949 from each new subscriber.

As you can imagine, an incomplete CLV calculation that does not factor in customer acquisition costs (CAC) doesn't provide an accurate picture of the true value of your customers. Decision makers use CLV to determine marketing, customer service budgets, and more. Tracking CLV over time is also a baseline measurement of business performance. Most important, however, is that being aware of customer lifetime value helps business owners and other decision makers think in a new way about the relationship they have with their customers. Looking at the average amount spent by customers over the life of their relationship in our Home Fresh example, it becomes obvious that each customer is worth significantly more than their first week's purchase of just $59. Given that customers are really worth more than nine hundred dollars, marketers understand the true worth of acquiring new customers, spending money to retain current ones, and spending money to reactivate old ones who have unsubscribed from the Home Fresh service.

By basing calculations on this CAC number, rather than $1,239, a more accurate marketing and customer service budget can be determined. It is obvious that customers are worth much more than their first week's $59 purchase might suggest, which means that Home Fresh should be willing to spend much more than $59 to retain or reactivate old customers, given the long-term value of those relationships.

A general rule of thumb is that a company should spend no more than one third of its CLV to acquire a new customer. Or, said another way, a business should expect to make, over the lifetime of the relationship, at least three times what it paid to acquire that customer. In other words, for every dollar spent to acquire a new customer, the company should earn three dollars. As with any cost metric, the lower a company's CAC, the better. However, there may be times when a company strategically accepts a CLV-to-CAC ratio worse than 3:1, such as during new product launches or aggressive attempts to win market share.

In general, a subscription model produces revenue that is stable and predictable, based on number of subscribers. Additionally, a subscription model makes it easier to monitor exactly how much revenue each customer is worth and accurately attribute specific revenue to specific customers. For business models that don't rely on subscription pricing, customer lifetime value can be a little trickier to calculate with certainty.

Another approach to gauging CLV when purchases tend to vary by week or month is through the average order value (AOV).

CLV and Average Order Value

Out of the Box Gifts is a fictional upscale online gift retailer that sells luxury items suitable for men, women, and children. Because customers choose from a wide assortment of products with varying price points, it's difficult to link a specific product to a customer's lifetime value. In cases like this, it's more effective to use a common metric known as ***average order value*** (AOV). Average order value is sometimes referred to as "average cart value" and is simply the average order size—the total value of all orders in a given period divided by the number of customers who ordered.

Out of the Box Gifts has an average order value of $89. Using shopper account history data, it is discovered that 14 percent of customers are repeat customers, defined in this case as those who make more than one purchase in the same quarter. It costs Out of the Box Gifts $16.70, on average, to acquire a new customer. Based on this information, we can calculate Out of the Box Gifts' CLV on a quarterly basis using the following equation (figure 8):

fig. 8

CUSTOMER LIFETIME VALUE =
(FOR OUT OF THE BOX GIFTS)

$$\left[\frac{\text{AVERAGE ORDER VALUE}}{\text{(1 - REPEAT PURCHASE RATE)}} \right]$$

Plugging in the numbers from the sample above, we arrive at the following calculation (figure 9):

fig. 9

CUSTOMER LIFETIME VALUE =
(FOR OUT OF THE BOX GIFTS)

$$\left[\frac{\$89}{(1 - 0.14)} \right]$$

CUSTOMER LIFETIME VALUE = **$103.49**
(FOR OUT OF THE BOX GIFTS)

It is important to remember that metrics such as CLV, AOV, and CAC are signals that provide critical insights into your business and the direction in which it's headed. For example, if you calculate a CLV value on a quarterly basis for a product that is sold in quantities that are meant to be a year's supply, you will generate an indicator that's not useful. What is most important is that the CLV number can be recorded, tracked over time, and calculated with a reasonable degree of accuracy. In the case of Out of the Box Gifts, the CLV is much smaller because the order frequency is lower than Home Fresh's weekly subscription. Only 14 percent of Out of the Box Gifts' customers place a second order every three months.

Key Digital Marketing Concepts

Before we move on, it's worth pausing for a moment to define some important terms. These terms will come up time and time again in your digital marketing journey.

Channels and Platforms

Platforms and channels are two terms you will hear used often in the world of digital marketing. Although they are sometimes used interchangeably, they describe different things. *Channel* refers to the broad communications categories a marketer has to choose from to reach a customer. Channels can flow in one direction, from marketer to customer, or in two, enabling a back-and-forth dialogue between marketer and customer. Examples include digital advertising, email, and social media, as well as traditional channels like television, print media, and radio.

Within channels are platforms. A *platform* is a tool providing a means of communication, a way to share content or facilitate shared experiences. A marketer who is using Facebook to reach potential customers is using the Facebook platform—the servers, systems, and protocols—as a social media channel. That same marketer could also be using the Twitter, Quora, and Pinterest platforms in their social media channel.

fig. 10

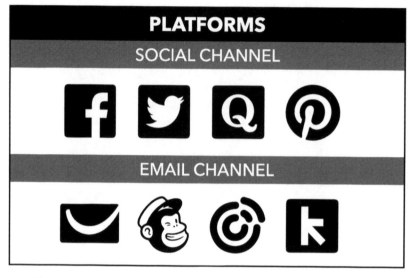

Channels are made up of the platforms that best suit the needs of marketers.

Traffic and Audiences

Just as the terms *platform* and *channel* are often used interchangeably, so too are *traffic* and *audience* (though it's not always wise to do so in either case). Online **traffic** is the stream of users who visit a website, web page, or online asset. Generally speaking, the more traffic you have, the better, but not all traffic is created equal.

Traffic that includes members of your target audience is much more valuable than traffic that does not. For our purposes, an **audience** is any clearly defined market segment, in or outside of digital space. Audiences come in all shapes and sizes, and the wealth of data that exists regarding our online personas—and which represents facets of our off-line lives—means that it's easier than ever to define an audience.

Reach and Impressions

Reach represents the total number of *people* who see your content. *Impression*, on the other hand, refers to the number of *times* your content was displayed. Think of reach as the unique individual people who saw your content, ad, or social media post and impressions as the total number of times that information was shown to someone, unique or not. For example, if someone looked at the same ad three times, that would count as three impressions, even though you reached only one person.

Engagement and Conversions

Engagement is a predictive measure that reflects the degree to which your audience interacted with your content, such as by liking or commenting on a blog post. *Conversion* describes when a member of your target audience takes an action that you've asked them to, such as signing up for your newsletter or leaving a product review. When this happens, you've converted them—meaning you've successfully persuaded them to do what you wanted them to do. A sales conversion is when a prospect becomes a customer by spending money.

A Review of the Media Mix

GRAPHIC

fig. 11

MEDIA MIX		
Paid Media	**Earned Media**	**Owned Media**
Advertisements or any kind of messaging with paid placement	Unpaid exposure that is a result of paid and owned media efforts	Messaging channels that you own and that directly reflect your brand's voice

The media mix consists of paid, earned, and owned media.

When we discuss the channels and media through which our target market can be reached, we are generally discussing the *media mix*, which consists of general classifications of all the channels that your business can use to initiate and maintain a dialogue with your target audience. The media mix consists of paid media, earned media, and owned media (figure 12). These categories hold true whether we're talking about traditional or digital media.

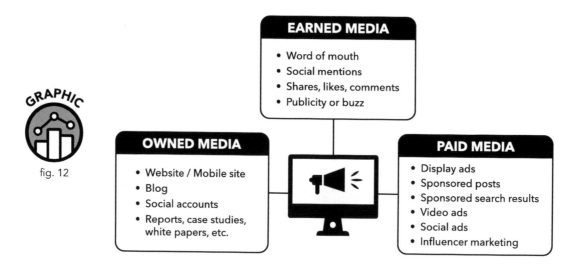

GRAPHIC

fig. 12

EARNED MEDIA
- Word of mouth
- Social mentions
- Shares, likes, comments
- Publicity or buzz

OWNED MEDIA
- Website / Mobile site
- Blog
- Social accounts
- Reports, case studies, white papers, etc.

PAID MEDIA
- Display ads
- Sponsored posts
- Sponsored search results
- Video ads
- Social ads
- Influencer marketing

Paid Media

Paid media is any message you want to share with an audience that you pay to present to them. The most common form of paid media is advertising. Marketers love paid media because it is highly scalable—when done effectively, the more money you spend, the more people you reach. Not only that, but there is no shortage of platforms, publishers, and other businesses offering ad space or promotional placement opportunities. And there are few restrictions on what your message can be; you generally control the content and the way it's presented.

Paid media is not without its drawbacks, however. The biggest obstacle is cost. As reach increases, so does cost, and campaigns that don't achieve their objectives can waste a lot of marketing dollars.

Paid media is a highly competitive environment. Marketers looking to capitalize on a paid media strategy must work harder and harder to stand out from the crowd. The laws of supply and demand work against marketers too, in the form of inflated costs for the most valuable placement opportunities. In addition, audiences across all media channels experience what is known as *ad fatigue*, a decline in interest or responsiveness the more often they are exposed to the same message. Nevertheless, these diminishing returns, coupled with the other paid media pitfalls, should not dissuade marketers from utilizing paid media. As you will see, it comprises an essential part of a robust marketing strategy—which is even more true when you're marketing in the digital space.

One final note regarding the potential drawbacks of paid media. While metrics such as cost, reach, and ad fatigue are straightforward to measure (and to work toward improving), there is one aspect of paid media that is much more elusive: credibility.

Consumers are generally wary of paid messaging, even though it influences over 90 percent of purchasing decisions. The messaging in advertisements and other paid media is often seen as compromised by the profit motive (meaning it's hard to believe because the primary focus is getting the sale). This high degree of consumer skepticism toward advertisements is not unjustified; we have all purchased an item or paid for a service that was woefully dissatisfying despite being advertised as the latest and greatest. For this reason, in order for a complete marketing strategy to achieve peak effectiveness, it *must* include both earned and owned media channels in addition to paid. Relying on paid media alone is expensive, inefficient, and self-limiting.

GRAPHIC

fig. 13

PAID MEDIA	
+ Benefits	**– Obstacles**
• Scalable • High degree of control • Lots of creative freedom • Numerous ways to reach your audience	• Diminishing returns • High-competition environments • Credibility

Are there ways to remove the credibility barrier in paid media? Yes! Savvy marketers have spent thousands of hours and millions of dollars trying to determine the best way to cement a relationship of trust between their brand and their customers. Personalizing messaging—especially paid messaging—helps to bridge the trust gap. Using earned and owned media channels to help develop a brand image as trustworthy and reliable is another way to improve the credibility of paid media. And lately, the tactic of ***native advertising*** has come to the forefront of digital marketing techniques.

Native advertising is a form of paid placement that is designed to look and feel like other surrounding content. Federal Communications

Commission (FCC) rules and general advertising ethics demand that advertisers disclose the paid nature of the material, but otherwise native ads are not immediately identifiable as ads or paid placement. This is a common tactic in online publishing venues such as news sites or blogs, which may publish advertising designed to resemble the "real" articles or features on the site.

Earned Media

Earned media encompasses all the conversations about your brand that you don't control. Typically, it's comprised of word of mouth, news coverage, and social media conversations that revolve around your brand or one of your products. In the age of viral content, earned media has the potential to be more impactful than ever before.

Marketers love earned media because it does not directly incur cost and it has a high degree of credibility. Additionally, strong positive earned media, in the form of social mentions, news coverage, product reviews, and satisfied customers sharing their outstanding experiences, helps boost the effectiveness of paid and owned media efforts. Each of these sources of earned media is seen as much more credible than a paid advertisement because the source is usually considered more impartial. When a journalistic source favorably covers your brand, the perceived conflict presented by profit motive is diminished and the message is seen as honest and transparent. There is just one big problem with earned media—you have no control over the message.

This lack of brand control in earned media is one of the main reasons consumers see it as more trustworthy, and it means that an impressive earned media presence is worth its weight in gold. All it takes is one satisfied customer with 10,000 Twitter followers to share their great experience, and suddenly your brand and your products are in front of all the people who follow that Twitter star. For this reason, despite the drawbacks, difficulties, and uncertainties associated with earned media, it is still worth a brand's time and effort to develop the earned portion of the media mix.

MY TAKE

While it is true that earned media generally does not directly incur cost, efforts to encourage earned media, such as public relations and other outreach activities, aren't free. However, those costs have the potential to be much lower than those of paid or owned media; earned is still much more cost-effective than the others.

The most frightening aspect of earned media is that it isn't always positive for your brand. Super-investor Warren Buffett is quoted as saying, "It takes twenty years to build a reputation and five minutes to ruin it. If you think about that, you'll do things differently." Buffett is right. Today's social media landscape is fertile ground for amplifying success as well as missteps—and the worse the news, the faster it seems to spread.

Now more than ever, it is essential that companies manage their earned media presence. The challenge with presenting a unified, cohesive brand is that earned media doesn't guarantee messaging that is consistent with your brand image. And there are other headaches associated with earned media. Because much of it is word of mouth that can't really be controlled, it's tough to create positive word-of-mouth conversations on a larger scale. And while software solutions do exist to track social mentions and collect brand sentiment data, earned media is still the hardest part of the media mix to measure and improve.

The biggest takeaway with respect to earned media is that if you don't pay attention to it, it can get away from you. Stay on top of monitoring your earned media by amplifying good coverage and responding to or working to mitigate any bad press; this is a winning strategy for using earned media to strengthen your brand. While it's true you can't control it, per se, you can try to integrate the good stuff into your brand and work to distance yourself from the bad.

One of the ways to balance the lack of control over earned media is to take advantage of controllable channels, including owned media.

GRAPHIC

fig. 14

EARNED MEDIA	
+ Benefits	**– Obstacles**
• Highest degree of credibility • Does not directly incur cost • Can convert customers into brand ambassadors	• No level of control • Difficult to scale • Can be damaging • Hard to measure and improve

Owned Media

Owned media represents the space between paid and earned media. It refers to the communication channels a brand or business directly owns, such as websites, blogs, email, and social followers. Owned media is much more cost-effective than paid media (though not always as easy to scale) and offers the highest amount of control over messaging, with no creative restrictions.

While paid media lasts as long as you continue to write checks, and earned media lasts as long as the conversation around your brand or product can be sustained, owned media is the longest-lived. Blog posts, web pages on your branded site, and your own social posts remain until you decide to take them down. This longevity, coupled with the low cost to produce owned media, makes it an excellent foundation for your marketing strategies. Owned media supports the effectiveness of paid media and encourages earned media.

The biggest drawback of owned media is that it has no inherent reach—and reach, in general, can be tough to scale. Unlike paid media that has instant reach as long as you're paying, and earned media that has unpredictable (but potentially large) reach, owned media's reach must be won one person at a time.

Reach is the number of people you can reach through an ad or offer. Scale is the capacity of your efforts. If you want to increase your reach, you will need to scale up spending or effort.

Owned media also suffers from the same crisis of credibility as paid media. There will always be an asterisk in the mind of your audience noting that the content and messaging that makes up owned media is motivated by profit. Lean in to earned media channels and demonstrate transparency and trustworthiness at every turn to combat this effect and maximize the efficiency of owned media.

In the world of digital marketing, it is extremely expensive to use paid media, such as advertising, to reach your existing customers all the time. Once you have converted a prospect into a paying customer, use owned media, such as email marketing, to nurture the relationship and encourage future purchases. The cost efficiency of owned media means one of your main goals as a digital marketer will be not only converting traffic into customers but shifting traffic from paid to owned media channels and transforming it into traffic you own.

GRAPHIC

fig. 15

OWNED MEDIA	
+ Benefits	**– Obstacles**
• Highest level of control • Cost-effective • Long-lived • Versatile • Highest level of creative opportunity	• Low level of credibility • Takes time to scale • Does not have inherent reach

Using the Media Mix to Best Effect

The components of the media mix aren't just abstract concepts that business students debate. Every marketing activity you undertake represents one or more of the elements of the media mix. Furthermore, no aspect of the media mix—or of your overall marketing strategy, for that matter—exists in a vacuum. All the pieces augment one another, leading to results that are larger than the sum of their parts.

To narrow the focus of the media mix to the digital space, think of it in terms of traffic and control (figure 16).

GRAPHIC

fig. 16

PAID MEDIA ⟶ **TRAFFIC YOU CONTROL**

EARNED MEDIA ⟶ **TRAFFIC YOU DON'T CONTROL**

OWNED MEDIA ⟶ **TRAFFIC YOU OWN**

Paid media is traffic you control. You "control" it because when you pay for an ad, you are paying to divert traffic from where it is currently—to control its flow and tell it where to go. When someone opens their Facebook app and starts scrolling through their news feed, they belong to the general traffic on Facebook. If they click or tap on your ad, you are controlling that traffic by directing it somewhere that will help you achieve your goals.

Earned media is traffic you *don't* control. You exert no influence over its behavior; it just "shows up" as a result of social buzz, mentions, word of mouth, etc.

Owned media is traffic you own. When your brand speaks, owned media listens. This is highly valuable and cost-effective. Owned media often consists of customers or traffic you have already provided value to in some form or another. Nurturing this traffic segment is crucial to your bottom line, so take care of the traffic you own so that it becomes loyal, long-term customers!

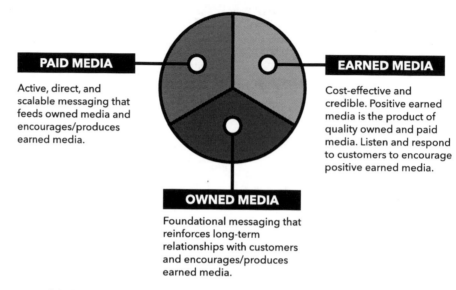

PAID MEDIA

Active, direct, and scalable messaging that feeds owned media and encourages/produces earned media.

EARNED MEDIA

Cost-effective and credible. Positive earned media is the product of quality owned and paid media. Listen and respond to customers to encourage positive earned media.

OWNED MEDIA

Foundational messaging that reinforces long-term relationships with customers and encourages/produces earned media.

fig. 17

Marketers find the most success when using all three aspects of the media mix.

Chapter Recap

» Customer lifetime value (CLV) is a measure of the total value a customer spends over the life of their relationship with a brand, which can extend far beyond the value of each individual transaction.

» Customer acquisition cost (CAC) represents what a business pays to acquire a new customer. Keeping this number in check is essential to maintaining a sustainable marketing budget.

» Average order value (AOV) is the average amount that all customers spend on a per-transaction basis. Together with CLV and CAC, AOV is used to determine the success and effectiveness of marketing campaigns.

» Although the terms are often used interchangeably, "channel" and "platform" refer to two different concepts. A channel is a broad communications vehicle, like social media or television, and a platform is a tool within a channel, such as Facebook or CBS.

» "Traffic" is a general term meaning internet users, and "audience" is a defined, targeted segment of traffic. "Reach" represents the total number of people who see your content. "Impression" refers to the number of times your content is displayed, regardless of who sees it.

» "Engagement" is a catch-all term for the ways in which people interact with your content online, generally on social media. A "conversion" occurs whenever a member of your target audience takes a desired marketing or business action.

» The media mix includes paid, earned, and owned media. These general categories of media have different broad applications, restrictions, strengths, weaknesses, and capacities for integration into campaigns.

» Paid and owned media are outlets that you control; paid media includes advertising, primarily, and owned media consists of your website and social media accounts. Earned media is out of your control and includes things such as publicity, word of mouth, and social media mentions.

| 3 |

Who Are You Selling To?

Chapter Overview

   »   Narrowing your total addressable market into something more useful

   »   Constructing and using your customer avatar

   »   Identifying and segmenting your target market

The first question you should ask yourself when deciding to undertake marketing efforts is, Who is my market? When we discuss "the market" we are discussing the people who have a need for the product or service you are selling. Even the largest corporations in the world don't have the resources to target everyone who could conceivably want or need their product. This problem is even more acute for smaller companies. To get the most out of their marketing dollars, and to approach the process of marketing from a realistic position, it becomes necessary for smaller businesses to narrow their markets and focus their efforts on prospects with the highest potential for converting.

Your Market

Described in its most general terms, the market for a given product or service is broken into three broad but distinct groups: the total addressable market (TAM), the serviceable available market (SAM), and the target market. Basically, your total addressable market is composed of all the people who could conceivably have a need for your product, anywhere in the world. For example, if you sold a car accessory, your TAM would consist of the more than 1.3 billion car owners worldwide. Your serviceable available market is made up of all the people you could potentially sell to. If you only sell your car accessory online, your SAM shrinks to car owners who have internet access, which is a smaller number. You can reach them, but they may not all be your ideal client. The third group, your target market, is made up of the people most likely to fit the mold of your "perfect customer." These are the people who potentially need your product or service and whom you can economically reach. In this example, that might consist of car owners with internet access in English-speaking countries.

Because the ***total addressable market (TAM)*** is the total number of potential customers for a given product or service, independent of a company's reach, it's often an enormous number. For that reason, the TAM is not often very helpful for marketers, since, without an unlimited budget, marketing efforts can reach only a portion of the TAM. And while your TAM could have a need for your product for service, it is generally assumed that you will be unable to reach every single individual in this group. Instead, your efforts should be devoted to reaching those people who are much more likely to have the problem that your product or service solves *and* who are reachable with conventional marketing methods.

Total addressable market calculations are most helpful for entrepreneurs, new ventures, or new product lines to use as a kind of shorthand to describe growth or revenue potential.

> Let's say you're developing a mobile app that is compatible with both iOS and Android systems worldwide. In this example, your TAM would be all iPhone and Android users in the world—quite a large market.

The ***serviceable available market (SAM)*** is the portion of the TAM that, all factors being equal, have a need for a product or service within the area that your service or product can cover. And given that nearly every business has some level of competition, it is assumed that no single company can own 100 percent of any given SAM—it is the market share that can be fulfilled by all companies that offer a solution to a customer problem.

> If the same mobile app from the example above is designed to help college students in the United States keep track of their assignments, monitor their grades, and communicate directly with professors, then your SAM would be all the college-age members of the total addressable market in the United States, rather than around the globe.

The ***target market*** is the portion of the serviceable available market at which your product or service is directly aimed. The members of a target market are the people who have a need for the solution your product or service provides and who are most likely to buy from you. *Members of your target market will be the focus of most of your marketing efforts.*

When marketing and selling to people who are a good fit for your product, your marketing dollars go farther. It's easier to cultivate customer loyalty as well as positive brand perception and awareness. Furthermore, the feedback you receive from customers in your target market will help you improve your products and services.

The target market of our mobile app for college students consists of iPhone and Android users in the US between the ages of eighteen and twenty-four who most closely resemble our ideal customer. This ideal customer is a college student at a school that has a high student-to-teacher ratio and a large student population. College students at smaller schools have more face-to-face time with instructors and therefore may not have as deep a need for a product that helps them stay organized and in contact with faculty. This doesn't mean that we will disregard these potential customers altogether; however, most of our efforts and marketing dollars will be spent trying to reach the members of our target market, because they most closely resemble our ideal customer. Those prospects within the target market are at larger schools.

As a marketer, assessing your TAM, then whittling it down to your SAM and eventually to your target market, is a good way to get a handle on the growth potential of your product or service. But it leaves out a few key details. We know that our marketing efforts will be most effective when our market, media, and message are all working in unison and are tailored to the needs of our ideal customer. But who, exactly, *is* our ideal customer? And just as important, where can we find them?

fig. 18

The Customer Avatar

In order to develop a clearer picture of your ideal customer, it's often useful to develop a customer avatar. A ***customer avatar***, which is also called a "buyer persona," is a helpful tool that acts as a placeholder for your real customers and helps you segment your target market. Many of the decisions that will be made with regard to your strategic marketing efforts will be based on the "ideal customer" criteria that you define during the customer avatar creation process.

Creating a customer avatar is a critical first step in achieving future marketing success.

While it is true that getting your customer avatar right will have a huge impact on the success of your marketing efforts, don't stress over it. Your customer avatar(s) will evolve as you learn more about exactly who your ideal customers are and as customer preferences naturally change over time. It's okay if your customer avatar isn't perfect right away. What is important is that you *don't skip this step* when undertaking marketing campaigns and *don't leave your customer avatar to collect dust* in a desk drawer or in a folder on your computer. Keep it handy and refer to it often to ensure that your marketing message is speaking directly to your customer avatar as you've identified him or her today.

The foundation of a solid customer avatar starts with the answers to two key questions:

> » **Who has the problem that my product or service solves?**
> A brainstormed list of these types of people or businesses is a great starting point. Not a literal list of names and addresses, but a list of the attributes that define these customers more broadly, such as age, gender, location, employment, interests, or disposable income—whatever makes the most sense for your product or service. If your product is geared toward businesses, then you want to know which industry, business size, brand attributes, location, etc., best suit your avatar.

> » **Who has already spent money on this product or similar products or services?**
> Who better to provide an example of the sort of person who is interested in buying this product than someone who has already bought it (or a similar product)? Gaining a better understanding

of who wants or needs the product they have for sale is one of the biggest reasons that companies collect copious amounts of information from their customers. Companies use surveys, reward programs, and other tactics to develop and improve customer avatars on an ongoing basis.

Building on these basic questions, a customer avatar begins to take shape. As more areas are explored and criteria added, the number of people who have attributes in common with the developing customer avatar decreases. By narrowing your focus to just the people who most closely match the customer avatar, you are effectively defining your target market. Consider these five areas when constructing your own customer avatar.

1. Demographic Information

Demographics are the aspects of your customer that describe personal details such as their age, occupation, marital status, gender, and location. Also consider any demographic information that is relevant to your product or service, such as job title, level of education, or number and age of children. You can even get as specific as the type of car they drive, whether they belong to a country club, or if they frequent a fitness club. These are the types of personal details that will help bring your avatar to life.

2. Goals and Values

What does a person who would buy your product want to accomplish? Where does your product fit into their ability to accomplish their goals? Is your product essential or merely tangential to their goal fulfillment? Are their values aligned with the values that are demonstrated by your brand?

Understanding the goals your customers have will allow you to design products and services that are indispensable to your target market. Better understanding the values of your target market will help you make a stronger emotional connection through your market, media, and message mix.

You'll want to make clear how your product or service can help your customers achieve their goals, whether it's to have an organized closet, a dog that is housebroken, or a higher return on investment in their portfolio. Along with that, you'll want to convey your brand's values, which confirms to your audience that your offering is the best fit for their needs and resonates with the things they deem important in their own lives. For instance, clients who are price-sensitive may not be a good match for your high-end custom cabinetry. Clients looking for a top-of-the-line inground pool won't be convinced to work with you if in your marketing you emphasize how inexpensive your products are. It's important to reflect your customers' values as you help them reach their goals. These two factors need to be in alignment to be effective.

3. Pain Points

The obstacles and challenges that push customers to buy are referred to as *pain points*. Pain points translate into a pressing need for a solution, and they are particularly useful to marketers. Not only is it helpful to know why someone is in the market for your products or services but drawing a customer's attention to their pain points makes it possible for you to agitate or emphasize these challenges—so that they can be brought to the forefront of customers' minds and encourage them to take action.

Think back to our discussion of features and benefits in the previous chapter. Another way to think of pain points is that they are the exact problems that the benefits of a product or service solve.

A challenge for many marketers, however, is identifying pain points. Members of your target market know they are seeking solutions to their problems, but they typically think of them in terms of the solutions that are available—not in the form of underlying pain points.

If I had asked people what they wanted, they would have said faster horses.
                                                                      – HENRY FORD

Though the preceding is generally regarded as being misattributed to Mr. Ford, the sentiment still rings true. The pain point being expressed is a need to quickly get from one place to another. Before the mass production of automobiles, horses were the solution to that problem. Ford's cars, at least in principle, alleviated this pain point by providing fast transport that never got tired and didn't need food or water. But no consumer would have been able to state a need for an automobile—they just wanted faster horses.

Similarly, no one who bought the initial MP3 players had expressly asked for them. Consumers were used to CD players, and if asked what they disliked about CDs, they might have responded that they took up too much space, they were inconvenient to carry around, they could only hold a certain number of tracks, etc. These are pain points that were alleviated by the first MP3 players (the solution).

As we know, digital music players can hold thousands of songs and do not skip or develop scratches that affect playback, and digital albums can be much more inexpensive than new-release CDs. This ability to provide a solution to distinct customer pain points rendered the previous solution (CDs) obsolete in much the same way that CDs had replaced tape cassettes and vinyl records. However, if any of the MP3 player designers had asked a customer what they needed, they would have suggested CDs with more storage space or perhaps CDs made of a more durable material. (Similarly, customers themselves would not have anticipated a subsequent switch to smartphones and streaming for music playback!)

NOTE

People will often flee from discomfort before they will pursue pleasure. In terms of marketing, this means that it is more effective to focus heavily on the ways in which a product or service eliminates or overcomes pain points. Remember, the buying process is more emotional than rational. Agitating or focusing on the ways in which pain points are unpleasant or challenging can help bring members of your target market closer to the point of affective override, where they are much more likely to purchase.

4. Behavior and Attributes

We all know that a person is much more than the sum of his or her demographic traits. It is not demographics but behaviors that reveal what truly interests a person and who they really are. For the marketer's purposes, behaviors and attributes resemble a window into the when, how, and why of spending. Identifying and speaking directly to these motivators can encourage sales and forge a stronger connection with your target market.

EXAMPLE

Some example behaviors might include the following: John always shops in the evenings after work. Wendy won't travel more than fifteen minutes from her home to work out. Sam only cooks meals that require minimal prep and cleanup. Mark checks in with social media before making a purchase.

Attributes are a little less concrete than behaviors but are similarly important for marketers to understand. Personal attributes are similar to personal preferences. They provide clues to the personality of an individual and serve to round out your customer avatar in a big way. Like behaviors, well-defined attributes can help forge a stronger connection to the target market.

Some example attributes might include the following: John is frugal. Wendy loves cats. Sam likes to travel. Mark likes meeting new people.

5. Media Diet

Where do members of your target market go for information? This can be a little tricky to nail down at first, because it's important to identify sources of information that your target market would rely on but that others may not. Remember, we are trying to *narrow* our market. Members of a target market that turn to online news sites for information could include just about anyone—the market has not been narrowed at all. The insight that "my target market watches the news" is also not very helpful. Instead, pick sources of information that are relevant to your product or service—and if they're sources that your customer avatar would consume *but that no one else would*, all the better.

If you are selling golf equipment, your customer avatar will be a golfer. Many people have heard of the most popular golfers and popular golf publications, like *Golf Digest*. Dig deeper and select publications that your customer avatar would read *but that others would not*. That means listing more obscure golfers, more obscure golf publications and very niche golf websites. Similarly, anyone who enjoys gardening would likely read *Better Homes & Gardens* magazine, but so would a lot of people who read it for some of the other topics the magazine covers. On the other hand, the readers of the more niche magazine *Container Gardening* would likely be much more interested in the topic of gardening specifically. The goal is to find the most concentrated aspect of your target market and work outward from there.

As you can see, quite a bit of thought and research goes into crafting your customer avatar. When the finished product comes together, it paints a picture of a person who is an ideal fit for your business. It describes the life aspects that motivate and define this person, and it provides a groundwork for where these people might congregate (in the real world or online).

Even though your customer avatar will be a list of attributes on paper, it is important to treat it as though it's a living person. Imagine your avatar as a person who could really buy your product or service. It may seem silly, but go so far as to name your avatar, and it doesn't hurt to use a stock photo of a generic person as a reference point. Really imagine who your ideal customer is, what they look like, where they live, what they wear, and how they make purchasing decisions.

Andrea Avatar, our example customer avatar.

Meet Andrea Avatar, as depicted by the marketing geniuses at Finesse Yoga Studio. Both the avatar and its creators are purely fictitious (figure 19).

Andrea is thirty-two years old and is married. She and her husband live within a thirty-mile radius of my yoga studio in a suburban home in Southern California. Combined, their household income is more than $100,000. Andrea works in an office setting and is looking for ways to unwind before or after work, as well as wanting to be a little more active after sitting at a desk all day.

Andrea enjoys fitness activities but doesn't want to commit to an intense workout. She is smart with her money but isn't afraid to spend on something she finds worthwhile. She relies on mobile and other smart devices in her life and has a high level of digital fluency. She doesn't like to go too far out of her way when driving to and from work, and she has free time outside of normal business hours only. She doesn't subscribe to a restrictive diet, but she is health conscious.

Andrea likes yoga and low-intensity fitness activities but has trouble finding suitable venues and feels she does not get the same results when practicing at home, although she isn't always interested in hands-on instruction either. A venue that allows her to participate in classes or just "do her own thing" in a dedicated space would be a perfect fit.

Q: What if I have more than one product?

So far, we have only discussed customer avatars as they relate to a single product or single market segment, but what if you have many of each? Right away it should be apparent that the hyper-focused customer avatar for one product won't be useful in defining the target market for a different product. If you have several products, then each one requires a customer avatar. If you have different market segments (market segments are explained in detail in the next section) then each segment requires a different customer avatar.

A good rule of thumb is that for every type of person you can think of who has a problem your product solves, that market segment should be represented with an avatar. You may not end up using every one of these avatars to zero in on your target market; some may represent market segments that are too small or too difficult to reach with targeted marketing efforts. Nonetheless, every marketing approach should begin with an avatar.

Don't forget to take advantage of the Digital Assets included with your purchase of this book. Among other supplemental material, you will find resources like a Step-by-Step Avatar Builder. Access this and all the other Digital Asset files for this title at www.clydebankmedia.com/digitalmarketing-assets.

Not every business will have extensive historical data about who their customers are and the ways they behave, and that's okay. Reverse-engineering the market, media, and message mix that your competitors are using can tell you a significant amount about who their target customer is for that specific campaign. Industry trade groups and other business resources can also offer valuable information to help new businesses develop their customer avatar and identify their target market.

Developing your avatar is an important step in clarifying who, exactly, your ideal customer is. And now that you're crystal clear on that point, you're ready to do some market segmentation.

Narrowing Your Market through Segmentation

Market segmentation is the process of dividing a large, homogenous market—meaning people in the market are fairly alike—into smaller subdivisions or niches based on shared characteristics. For example, within a total market of automobile owners in the US, you have market segments of people who own SUVs, minivans, sedans, and trucks, to name a few. That would be one way to segment the market—by the type of auto a person has purchased. Or you could break up that same market by the car manufacturer, such as Honda, Chevy, Cadillac, Kia, or Mercedes. As these different segmentation categories are layered on top of one another, you are creating smaller and smaller segments of people.

Market segmentation is critically important because no one company is large enough or has sufficient resources to fulfill the diverse needs of an entire market (think total addressable market). Instead, they segment the market into smaller sections and strategically target the highest-impact segments. Segments could be deemed "high impact" because they have a specific problem (incentivizing them to seek solutions), because they have sufficient disposable income to purchase a specific product or service, or because of the geographic area they're in, among other reasons.

When crafting your customer avatar(s), remember that the *distinct avatars you create represent different segments*. To be considered effective or useful, segments must meet the following criteria:

> » **Segments must be clearly identifiable and distinct**
> If a segment can't be clearly identified, then it might not be a segment at all. If two customer avatars are basically representing the same ideal customer, then the distinction might not be a significant one. The topic of distinction among market segments is a nuanced one. On one hand, the more granular a level of distinction your marketing efforts can achieve, the more success you will see. On the other, marketers have to consider cost. Developing, creating, and executing a unique market, media, and message for a plethora of segments that are very similar is not particularly cost-effective.
>
> For example, within the market for coffee drinkers, there is likely a lot of crossover between segments based on preferred brand. People

who like Starbucks probably also like Peet's or Green Mountain Coffee Roasters. Those segments may not be distinct enough, because they blend together. Whereas within the total market of college or university grads, you can segment consumers by the school they attended. That's more of an either/or proposition, since the vast majority of students graduate from only one undergraduate institution.

» **Segments must have a reasonable reachable size**
The size, and more importantly the *reachable size*, of a market segment is a crucial factor in deciding whether that segment is worth committing resources to. A segment's reachable size is the portion of that target market that can be shown specific messages or advertisements in a cost-effective manner. Segments that are overly large or consist of people who are very resistant to media exposure are likely not a good fit for a sophisticated, targeted campaign.

» **Segments must be a good fit for the business and its resources**
Is this a market segment that makes sense for the brand? Is it a market segment that is in line with your mission and vision? Does it fit with your strategy? Can you reach the segment with the resources you have available, and will it be profitable enough to meet your financial goals? Does the segment align with your firm's values? Could there be backlash on social media, etc., for working with this group? These are all important questions with no easy, quantifiable answers, but they are questions that should be considered when assessing the fitness of a segment for your marketing efforts.

Some of the factors to consider in evaluating this question include the following:

Demographics and Location

Demographic segmentation is the process of dividing a market based on the personal attributes of your potential customers. These demographic attributes include age, gender, income level, and occupation, to name a few. While a market will, of course, include a variety of people with different and unique needs, grouping these people together based on similar characteristics (relevant to your product or service) helps you get the most out of your marketing efforts. It cuts straight through the total addressable market and groups people together based on characteristics that are easily defined and measured. This is all the more true for digital marketers who enjoy access to a wealth of information about vast swaths of the online population.

The ease and accessibility of demographic segmentation is not without its drawbacks, however. It is a gross oversimplification to say that any two men, any two children, or any two thirty-three-year-olds have the same wants and needs simply because they share one or more demographic characteristics. For example, a forty-five-year-old woman might be a mother or a grandmother, might be working full-time or enrolled in college, might be planning for retirement or reentering the workforce as her children head off to college. Demographics can be a unifier or a tool for further segmentation. As with the construction of a customer avatar earlier in this chapter, demographic information is a strong foundation on which to build an accurate account of the members of your target market, but it doesn't paint the whole picture.

Location-based segmentation—also known as *geographical segmentation*—groups potential customers together based on where they are physically located. Geographical segmentation can be as large or as small as is useful to marketers. A yoga studio might be interested in reaching potential customers within a radius of only two or three miles if they are in an urban area. A pool installation and servicing company might be willing to drive much farther to reach their customers. In some cases, the pool company might even be interested in reaching customers across an entire state or region.

On the flip side, casting too wide a net with geographical segmentation isn't always helpful. Remember, a segment must be reachable to be useful. For this reason, geographical segmentation is often combined with other forms of market segmentation to provide useful results.

EXAMPLE

Geographical segmentation helps companies invest their marketing dollars more wisely by using location as the primary filter for choosing which potential customers to target. The key is identifying where those high-potential customers live or work or vacation. A resort on the outer banks of North Carolina may focus its efforts on vacationers within a day's drive, for example. Or it could divide its customer database by region and market to areas of the country where its most loyal customers live. That approach might yield prospects that are thousands of miles away. Even online businesses, which can service customers across the country, could benefit from knowing where a greater share of their market segment resides.

Behavior

Segmenting members of a market into groups based on how they act as consumers while making purchasing decisions is known as behavioral segmentation. This type of segmentation is designed to understand, predict, and target the following:

» The purchasing habits of your customers and target market—how often they buy your product.

» The benefits sought from your product is another characteristic; this is the pain point customers are responding to when they make a purchase.

» The usage habits of your customers and target market, or when, why, and how they use your product. How often do customers seek out your product, or similar alternatives?

» The timing, or occasion, when your customer makes a purchase is another approach. What triggers a purchase?

» The spending habits of your customers and target market, which is a more general view of how your customers use their money. Do they save up for big purchases and pay cash? Do they rely heavily on credit cards? Are they sensitive to high prices or will they pay the asking price without too much thought?

» The level of loyalty customers feel to your brand is another aspect. How often do customers purchase from you? Do they divide their loyalties between your product and a competitor's?

Effective behavioral segmentation helps businesses understand the ways in which their product or service captivates different market segments (think customer avatars). Additionally, businesses can tailor their marketing efforts to reach customers at times when they are most likely to purchase. Finally, behavioral segmentation data gathering is a useful way to better understand the likes, dislikes, and general preferences of your target market. Behavioral data doesn't exist independently of other customer data; it is better described as an extension of existing segmentation data and often correlates with demographic data.

NOTE

Behavioral and demographic data often intersect. That is, you generally see them together. For example, a suburban teen who buys makeup at the mall on the weekend with her friends provides both demographic data (suburban teen) and behavioral data (buying makeup at the mall on the weekend).

When it comes to figuring out who your potential customers are, behavior segmentation provides unique insight, but it isn't foolproof. Gathering behavioral data risks providing marketers with "false positives" in the sense that one potential customer may exhibit a key behavior, but he or she may not necessarily be destined to become an actual customer. However, the more behavioral information marketers have, the deeper the level of targeting they can exercise and the more personalized the message becomes.

EXAMPLE

If you have ever received an email containing a coupon to a store you just left, then you have firsthand experience with marketing based on behavioral segmentation. Post-purchase coupons are an effective example of encouraging customer loyalty while increasing repeat business. Similarly, any time you have provided your email address in exchange for a special report, summary, or similar PDF download, you are responding to behavioral-segment–based marketing. Customer behavior is easiest to record and act on in digital spaces, but the principles are nothing new. Have you ever wondered why grocery stores offer club cards or other free membership discount programs? These programs turn otherwise anonymous grocery transactions into a record of customer behaviors, including visit frequency, average spend per visit, and brand preference, which are linked to the demographic information you provided when signing up.

Psychographics

Psychographic segmentation divides a market into segments based on emotional, values-based, or interest-based characteristics. This classifies consumers within a market into groups based on the way they think and the way they want to live. These characteristics are far softer than demographics, which are based on more tangible aspects, such as age or education level. Psychographic segmentation is based on five general personal characteristics:

» Lifestyle
» Social status
» Activities, interests, and opinions (AIO)
» Values, attitudes, and beliefs
» Personality traits

As you can see, psychographic segmentation, when layered on other segmentation methods, reduces a large and diverse portion of a market down to a very specific, focused group of people. Marketing—whether traditional or digital—that focuses on a very specific psychographic profile is generally referred to as *lifestyle marketing*. Lifestyle marketing connects a brand with its target market through the promise of enhancing a certain lifestyle—one that is defined by psychographic elements as described in the preceding list.

In an industry where margins can be thin and customer preferences are always changing, clothing brands often lean heavily on lifestyle marketing tactics to differentiate themselves from their competitors, often combining more than one personal psychographic characteristic. High-end sports and "athleisure" clothing companies use values-based messaging that reinforces the idea that there is no substitute for hard work, focus on customer segments with activities that include frequenting the gym, and sell products that spare no expense to deliver performance, speaking to lifestyle and social status preferences.

On the other hand, a clothing store that sells men's, women's, and children's clothing all under one roof might focus on customers with families (lifestyle) and use messaging that conveys the comfort and economy of their clothing (values, attitudes, and beliefs).

The downside to the extreme level of personalization that psychographic information yields is that it has the potential to be much harder to gather than demographic or behavioral data, because it's more complicated information that isn't as easily acquired as age, income, and so on. Not only can the process of acquiring psychographic data be time-consuming, but the data that it yields is almost entirely qualitative (which is to say, non-numerical). Quantitative data, like household income, frequency of product usage, and other demographic and behavioral characteristics, *are* easy to sort and endlessly model, but qualitative data can be a little trickier to handle and understand in a meaningful way. As a result, psychographic segmentation can be a mixture of art and science.

QUESTION

Q: How do I know which type of market segmentation works best for defining my target market?

The segmentation process begins with defining your customer avatar. Since your customer avatar is a template for the kind of person who would make the perfect customer for your product or service, building a market segment around people who share attributes with your customer avatar is an excellent next step. One useful source of intel on the kinds of segmentation methods that work best are your competitors. Reverse-engineering the segmentation methods they are using is a great way to generate ideas for your own segmentation methods. This isn't always straightforward at first, but as you become more fluent in digital marketing concepts and the needs of your target audience, it will become much easier to gain an understanding of the thinking of other marketers by looking at their messaging to customers.

B2B Segmentation Methods

Businesses who themselves have businesses as customers can't rely on the same segmentation methods that their B2C counterparts enjoy. **B2B** stands for business-to-business or brand-to-brand and references businesses that sell to other businesses rather than to consumers. The market segmentation methods we've covered so far revolve around businesses that have consumers as their customers. These businesses can be referred to as **B2C** businesses, or business/brand-to-consumer.

B2B businesses use two basic methods of segmenting their target markets of business customers. **Firmographic segmentation** is essentially demographic segmentation, but for businesses; it segments business customers into groups based on shared qualities. Instead of age, gender, or income, firmographic data looks at qualities such as annual revenue, number of employees, or location.

Firmographic data is easy and inexpensive to collect, but it has the same shortcomings that plague demographic data for B2C businesses. Just as we can't assume that every member of a demographic group thinks or feels the same way, we can't assume that all businesses that have been opened in the last four years, or have fewer than fifty employees, have the same needs.

The other popular form of B2B market segmentation is known as tiering. *Tiering* is a method that classifies business customers into different segments known as tiers. These tiers are organized by the potential value the customer has to the business, often in terms of CLV, as well as the effort required to win the business. Tiering is generally combined with firmographic data to refine target segments and is most useful to B2B marketers because of the higher value and longer sales cycles typical of B2B purchases. B2B sales can take months or years to finalize, such as with a major technology contract, for example, and be worth millions of dollars. Sales teams are responsible for determining the best allocation of effort and resources to improve the odds of eventually making a sale. The highest-value opportunities should receive the highest level of sales contact and resource investment, whereas lower-value business opportunities should receive a commensurate level of attention, meaning much lower. A B2B organization's goal is to avoid wasting resources and this is done by pursuing the highest value business and avoiding devoting resources to businesses that might not be a good fit.

In contrast, B2C purchases can be spur-of-the-moment and, as with impulse purchases at the grocery store, unplanned and immediate. B2C purchases are also more frequent, in many cases. For that reason, tiering as a segmentation strategy isn't as relevant or effective in B2C; the sales cycle is short and the purchase value potentially much smaller.

A graphical representation of customers who are segmented based on tiers looks like a pyramid. The highest-value customers, which are a smaller group, are at the top, with the larger pool of lower-value customers at the bottom. The more valuable the customer is, the more effort is devoted to closing a sale with that customer (figure 20).

The core concept here is that companies should match the level of effort and resource dedication to the value of the customer. In early-stage or startup ventures, this tiering concept can be much simpler. Companies just starting out often create a hot list, or a list of the companies they would most like to land as customers. The companies on that list are their biggest priority and, as result, they receive the highest level of attention.

GRAPHIC

fig. 20

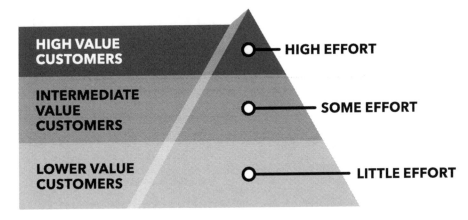

HIGH VALUE CUSTOMERS — HIGH EFFORT

INTERMEDIATE VALUE CUSTOMERS — SOME EFFORT

LOWER VALUE CUSTOMERS — LITTLE EFFORT

The tiering method of segmentation matches the value of potential customers with the appropriate effort to reach and convert those customers

The Customer Journey

The *customer journey* refers to the process a customer goes through from the first time they come across your business or brand to the time they take action and make a purchase. Stops along that journey are the touchpoints—the opportunities they have to connect with your company, such as by visiting your website, asking a question on chat, or taking to heart the opinion of a trusted friend, family member, or celebrity influencer. Sometimes the customer journey is just that simple and straightforward. Other times it has more twists and turns.

In the B2B world, potential business customers often gather quotes from potential suppliers as the start of a business's customer journey. As a supplier, you may be alerted to a bid opportunity by email, or you might see an announcement in the news. That's your first touchpoint with your potential customer. As you put together your proposal to the company, you might reach out to the contracting agent to ask a question and do your own research to better understand their needs. Your formal proposal or bid is your opportunity to present your capabilities and offerings in the best possible light. And the awarding of the contract is the conclusion of the customer journey, whether the bid goes to you or not.

For B2C customers, the customer journey might look something like the progression shown in figure 21. After discovering a brand, a person might check out its website or social media presence. As they learn more about the ways that brand can solve problems they face, potential customers might explore reviews or the opinions of others about their experiences before committing to a purchase.

A B2C CUSTOMER JOURNEY

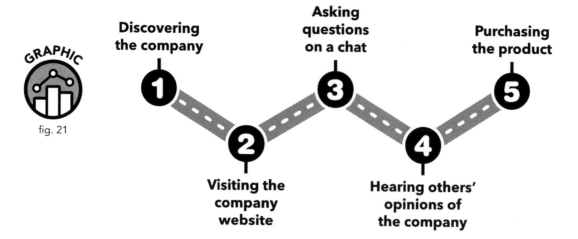

GRAPHIC

fig. 21

Discovering the company — 1

Visiting the company website — 2

Asking questions on a chat — 3

Hearing others' opinions of the company — 4

Purchasing the product — 5

Generally, from the marketer's perspective, you want to check in with your potential customer as often as possible during their customer journey. You want to make sure they know that you're available to serve them. This is true whether you're a brick-and-mortar retailer, a banker, or an online coach. Staying in touch improves your odds of persuading them to buy from you, eventually. We take a look at some exact strategies for doing this in part III of this book.

There tends to be a directly proportionate relationship between the price of a product or service and the length of the customer journey. The decision about whether to buy a bottle of water may take five minutes as a consumer scans the shelves of water at the store and then pays the cashier. But the decision regarding choosing a wedding gown can take months of researching various styles and designers, consulting magazines, talking with friends and family members, going for fittings, placing the order, and staying in touch with the retailer until the dress is finally delivered for the big day.

MY TAKE

Mapping out a customer journey can be a useful exercise for marketers because the process forces you to get into your customer's head to figure out what's important to them, which features and benefits are affecting their choices, and what they'll likely need to know along the way.

Chapter Recap

» The total market for a good or service is much larger than any one company can target. It is necessary for marketers to narrow their focus from the TAM—total addressable market—to a subset of the serviceable available market (SAM) that is most likely to purchase. This subset is the target market and will be the focus of marketing efforts.

» A customer avatar is a template or placeholder for your ideal customer. It is used to refine marketing efforts and to better develop your understanding of people who are in your target market. The best customer avatars are facsimiles of real people. They are made up of demographic information, goals and values, key pain points, behaviors, and other personal attributes.

» Market segmentation is the method of breaking smaller groups of people out of a homogenous target market to better appeal to their individual wants and needs. To be useful, a market segment must be clearly identifiable and distinct. It must have a reasonable, reachable size, and it must be a good fit for the business and its resources.

» People can be segmented through a variety of methods: demographic segmentation, geographic segmentation, behavioral segmentation, and psychographic segmentation.

» B2B companies—businesses that have other businesses as customers—use different forms of segmentation to cut to the heart of their target markets. Firmographic segmentation groups potential customers together based on their business characteristics, such as number of employees or net annual revenue. Firmographic segmentation is demographic segmentation but for businesses.

» The segmentation process of tiering matches potential customers with their value to the business and the amount of effort expected to be necessary to convert them. These groups of customers are broken into tiers based on their potential value to the company so that the appropriate level of marketing effort can be exerted.

| 4 |

What Are You Selling?

As you build the foundation of your marketing program, in addition to being clear about who you're selling to—that is, who your target market is and why they'd prefer your product or service over the competition's—you also need to be able to convey *what* you're selling. What, exactly, does it do for your customer? What problem does it solve? In what ways is it superior to other alternatives? Why do they need it? Or even, why should they want it?

The Value Ladder

There is an age-old adage in the business world that states, "There are only two ways to increase your revenue from customers—increase the amount of money each customer gives you or increase the number of customers who give you money." Many marketing activities are concerned solely with reaching more people to convince and convert them into customers, but that's not the only way to grow your business.

The concept of a "value ladder" illustrates that strengthening your company's relationship with customers can lead them to increase the value and frequency of their purchases over time, resulting in higher revenue for your company. A *value ladder* is a map that organizes several related products or services into a sequence. As customers climb the ladder, moving up step by step, or "ascending," the offerings they are presented with increase in price, frequency, and value (figure 22).

If the value ladder is correctly constructed and each rung of the ladder focuses on a result or benefit, then the ascension process is a natural one. With each step taken or rung climbed, customers buy more and receive more benefit from their relationship with the company. Customers who have already received value are open to receiving even more value, especially if it continues to meet and exceed their needs. When used correctly, a value ladder can shatter what was once the ceiling of revenue that would have been possible with only sales of the core product. Never forget, however, that the entire reason a value ladder is an effective tool is that it continues to provide value (benefits) at every rung. A value ladder that only serves the needs of the business and fails to deliver value to customers will break down very quickly, as customers will rarely progress beyond the first step.

GRAPHIC

fig. 22

A visual representation of a value ladder. As a customer ascends the ladder, they should be offered more value at a correspondingly increasing price.

If you have ever downloaded a free report, a checklist, a worksheet, or some other file in exchange for your email address—often part of the behavior segmentation process we mentioned in chapter 3—then chances are good that you were ascending the first rung of a value ladder. In that case, the company offering the free download is using it as a type of "ethical bribe" to capture your contact information. Once they have permission to contact you, the company will work to move you further along their value ladder by uncovering your needs and presenting you with offers that increase in value and price. This is an effective marketing practice.

EXAMPLE

Most of us have already interacted with value ladders as consumers, in the off-line spaces as well as online. Chiropractors, mechanics, dentists, coaches, gyms, and more are all businesses that lean heavily into the value ladder model. A gym client may join because they value their health and want a place where they can regularly work out. Their basic membership provides access to the facility and workout equipment, but that's all. A salesperson might reach out and offer a spinning class once a week at a special rate, to supplement their weightlifting. If they accept, they've just ascended a rung on the ladder. Then they might inquire about two classes a week, or about personal training or a customized diet plan, all of which move them further and further along the value ladder.

Nearly all the tools and strategies outlined in this book are directly or indirectly concerned with acquiring new customers and ascending them along the value ladder. It is impossible to understate the importance of the value ladder concept in the world of digital marketing. Keep the concept in your mind and think of ways that the offerings of your own business (or soon-to-be business) can be organized into a progression of increasing value and commensurate price.

Once companies fully embrace the value ladder model, many find that the ladder can become the backbone of their business. With an effective ladder in place, the focus of the business becomes bringing customers to the ladder and moving them up.

Upselling

An *upsell* is an offer that increases the value and price of an order. It is the easiest and fastest way to improve average order value and is a digital marketer's staple when it comes to offsetting the cost of paid promotions. One of the key aspects of crafting an upsell that works and makes sense for your customers is to offer an add-on purchase that doesn't invalidate their original order but improves it (provides value). Perhaps the most well-known upsell in history—"Do you want fries with that?"—is also the best example of an expertly crafted upsell.

Hamburger restaurants would love to sell each customer as many hamburgers as possible, though they know realistically that their average dine-in customer will likely eat only one or two burgers per visit. Asking customers "Would you like another burger at a discount?" won't do much to increase their sales. Even with the enticement of a discount, the average customer isn't interested in more burgers than they need or want. Instead, "completing the meal" with fries and a soft drink is a value-added upsell and a great way for a burger joint to increase its average order value.

A general rule of thumb is that customers are most motivated by upsells that help them overcome their pain points the fastest. If they want more food for better value, fries and a drink accomplish this much easier than another burger. Or, to use an example from outside the fast-food industry, a florist could offer a greeting card, balloons, or stuffed animals as ways to fulfill their customer's need to express themselves to a loved one. Here, suggesting that a customer purchase more flowers won't have the same success rate—once you have the bouquet you came for, additional flowers aren't as desirable, but a greeting card is a good way to complete your purchase.

Downselling

A *downsell* is an offer that is presented to customers who, for whatever reason, decide to pass on your main offer. This may take the form of a lower price on the featured product. Or it may be the offer of a different product altogether: so you won't shell out a hundred dollars for my complete online cooking course; will you consider buying my *Book of 35 Amazing 15–Minute Recipes* for twenty dollars?

At a glance, downselling may seem like no more than a last-ditch attempt to salvage a potential lost sale. In some ways, that is true, and yes, making money you would not have otherwise made is always preferred. But something else, more subtle, is at play in the midst of a successfully executed downsell. A person who may never have become a customer is now a customer. And an individual who gives you money and receives something of value from you—even if it's not your main offer—is generally more likely to do business with you again, especially if they end up very satisfied with what they gain from the initial transaction.

Have you ever received follow-up discount offers from retailers for products that you once put in your shopping cart but then clicked away from? That's downselling. The retailer is trying to salvage that potential purchase by offering you a better deal on the product, lowering their profit margin but potentially generating some revenue and critically capturing you as a customer.

Similarly, have you ever called or emailed to cancel a service, such as satellite radio or a subscription box, and been offered the chance to continue at a lower price than you had been paying? That's another downsell. The company doesn't want to end up earning $0 from you, so they offer a compromise in the hopes of keeping you as a customer, even if you are less profitable than you were originally. Figure 23 demonstrates the upsell/downsell concept using the sale of a hamburger as an example.

Digital marketers have the opportunity to continue selling not just a burger but an entire series of products to their customers, moving them along the value ladder even if the customer–merchant relationship originated with a successful downsell. Hence, the value of a downsell versus no sale at all must not be overlooked; it's the difference between making nothing and making something.

Crafting an Offer

The term "offer" is used extensively in the world of marketing and sales, and it is relevant to just about every chapter in this book. Despite this frequency of usage, offers are an often-overlooked aspect of truly successful digital marketing campaigns. A well-crafted offer dovetails perfectly onto the market/media/message triangle and benefits immensely from the development of compelling customer avatars.

Before we explore the contours of what a perfect offer looks like, let's break down an offer into the simplest possible terms. For our purposes, an *offer* is an instance of a marketable entity—a brand, a person, etc.—presenting a promise of a value exchange to another party. This is a broad definition and intentionally so. You may also notice that this definition bears a striking similarity to our definition of marketing in general. Marketing and sales efforts are built on offers.

We generally think of offers as explicit quid pro quo situations. For example, if you give me two dollars, then I will give you a soda. The exchange of a soda for cash is certainly an example of an offer, but as digital marketers we should be thinking about offers in much more inclusive terms.

Anytime a brand asks that its audience take action is an instance of that brand presenting an offer. All calls to action are offers, even if they aren't explicitly asking for a purchase. All advertising, even awareness advertising, is a kind of offer. Though most offers are explicit, in the case of awareness advertising, the *implicit* offer is that if you give us some of your time and attention to learn more about who we are and what we do or how our products or services can solve a problem for you, you will benefit, at a minimum, by becoming more educated and informed.

Pivoting into the digital space, we can point to numerous examples of value exchanges that do not involve purchases. Facebook, for example, is a platform that is free to use. Facebook's core offer is that you can connect with friends, family members, and strangers alike in exchange for your attention in the form of ads.

The Anatomy of an Offer

As with any other marketing function, offers are structured, goal-based, and targeted. At its core, an offer is defined by the answers to four key questions:

1. **What are you hoping to achieve with this offer?**
   All marketing efforts start with a goal. Is your intent to drive sales with new customers or with existing ones? Is this offer designed to encourage customers to hand over their contact information and join your mailing list, or is it designed to help customers ascend up your value ladder?

2. **To whom will you be presenting this offer?**
   Will this offer be presented to an existing customer avatar, or will you be creating a new avatar specifically for this offer? Will the people this offer is presented to be aware of your brand, or will this be their first exposure? Are they aware of the solution you provide to their pain points, or are they only problem-aware at this point? Or are they yet to confront the fact that they have a problem at all (think life insurance)?

3. **What are you offering?**
   What, specifically, is the "thing" you will be offering? Is it a product that you already have for sale, or will it need to be developed? Is it a core product, an add-on, or maybe a free product aimed at introducing new customers to your value ladder? How does this product relate to your overall goal and to the pain points that your audience experiences?

4. **What does ideal customer ascension from this offer look like?**
   Where is this product in your value ladder? Is it an upsell to an

existing product? What is an appropriate upsell from this point on the ladder? Can this product be bundled with other existing products?

Let's quickly dissect an offer to illustrate this point. Tim is a business coach who specializes in helping startups increase their sales. He sets up a landing page (simply put, a web platform for information about a company) to make an offer, using the four questions as his guide:

1. (What he's hoping to achieve) To build up his mailing list

2. (Who he will be presenting his offer to) Entrepreneurs and aspiring startups

3. (What he's offering) The first module of his popular course for free

4. (What ideal customer ascension looks like) After providing an email address, new subscribers will receive email messages about products and services he offers that may be of interest and that will move them up his value ladder

What Many Entrepreneurs Fail to Understand about Offers

Asking yourself these four questions at the start of every campaign, at the start of every promotion, and while planning your business is not challenging. In fact, it has the potential to produce superior, repeatable results. The challenge is that many entrepreneurs do not give the construction of offers and the development of a robust value ladder the appropriate level of consideration when they are planning their products and services. Granted, the process is more involved than simply creating and running a splashy ad, but taking the time to set up offers using the four-question process will help to reduce wasted energy and expense. It will also improve your odds of generating sales.

Here's the way many people tackle building their business. They have a product or service that they believe can be the center of a successful venture. They dive into that part of things headfirst—somewhere along the line they were told that "stuff like marketing" comes later in the process. What this ultimately means is that later down the line many entrepreneurs are cobbling together a value ladder out of products or services that weren't designed with this arrangement in mind.

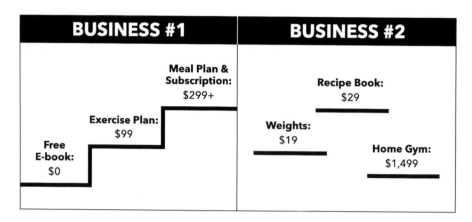

| BUSINESS #1 | BUSINESS #2 |

Meal Plan & Subscription: $299+

Exercise Plan: $99

Free E-book: $0

Recipe Book: $29

Weights: $19

Home Gym: $1,499

A well-organized value ladder will produce a more repeatable—and more profitable—customer experience.

Looking at the value ladder example in figure 24, we can see two businesses that are both working to help customers lose weight. The business on the left is using a value ladder to urge customers to ascend toward higher-ticket, higher-value products. The business on the right is selling products that may solve customer problems, but their presentation doesn't follow a value ladder model. For the business depicted on the left, the customer's path is clear. After receiving the free e-book—a product that is free yet still provides value—the customer is offered an exercise plan. Once they've started the exercise plan, a meal plan and subscription will help them complete their goals. After that, the value ladder could extend on to home gym equipment, personalized coaching, and more.

The business on the right doesn't have a clear path for its customers. There is no clear offer—if you don't want weights, we also have a recipe book for sale, or you can get out your wallet for a complete home gym. While there may be people who purchase one, some, or none of these items, there is no logical succession or path designed to extract the maximum value out of the customer. Going back to the business on the left, everyone who is offered the exercise plan (second rung of the ladder) has already received value in the form of a free e-book. Not everyone who is offered the exercise plan is a guaranteed sale, but the business on the left can be confident that they are in the best possible position to make a sale. Plus, with a clear CLV in mind, they know how much money they should be spending to attempt to ascend their customers while maintaining a profit margin.

To be clear, building your business in the same way as the business on the right without a clearly defined value ladder isn't a guarantee of failure. But what it does mean is that there will likely be gaps in the business's value ladder, and marketing efforts—both traditional and digital—will face numerous inefficiencies and obstacles. The most important thing to remember about your offer is that your goals, your target audience, the product or service you're offering, and your ascension plan are all integral parts of a larger strategic structure.

Crafting a Hyper-Compelling Offer

The amount of work you have done as a marketer constructing and honing your offers is put to the test once you present that offer to your audience. A *hyper-compelling offer* is one that is such a perfect fit for the audience it's presented to that it becomes totally irresistible. Of course, there is no such thing as a guaranteed sale, but the more puzzle pieces we have in place, the more sales we can generate and the more value we can deliver to customers. Ideally, a hyper-compelling offer provides such an overwhelming amount of value that your target market would be missing out by not taking advantage as soon as possible. Savvy marketers use the following techniques to increase the desirability of their offers.

Urgency

The last thing you want your audience to ask is, What's the rush? In a personal selling environment, salespeople have numerous tactics to keep their audience captive and to push a sale. In digital environments, your audience can always navigate away. They can also postpone taking action. When customers decide not to take action right away, not only is the burden on you to follow up, but the chances of those customers committing is greatly reduced.

On one hand, creating a sense of urgency—among other techniques—is a way for digital marketers to encourage customers to take action and to take action right away. The most popular method of injecting offers with urgency is to put a clock on the terms. Everyone has seen ads on TV that promise bonuses or discounts for people who call "in the next ten minutes." This is a perfect example of an offer that is enhanced with urgency, but it also breaks one of the cardinal rules of creating a compelling offer—every aspect must be authentic.

We all know that, in reality, everyone who calls receives the same bonus if they mention the "next fifteen minutes" call to action, even if they call three days after seeing the ad. This undermines the urgency of the offer and ultimately tells the audience that they can always postpone their order. Why order now? What's the rush? There is no incentive to take action, and the marketer who spent money and effort to reach that person has now lost momentum and potentially lost a sale. There is no greater barrier to cold sales like this than the phrase, "Maybe I'll do it tomorrow." To maintain the trust of your audience, it is important that the conditions that produce urgency in your offer are authentic, or at least appear to be.

On the other hand, if the urgency dial is turned up to the max, the offer can come across as pushy, untrustworthy, or even desperate. Say you're browsing the internet and an advertisement tells you there is a 90 percent discount for the next ninety seconds; you are probably not interested in hurriedly putting in your credit card information without really understanding what the product or service does. The stereotypical unscrupulous car salesman comes to mind—if there's nothing wrong with the car, then why are you being rushed through the sale?

NOTE

Understanding exactly how much urgency to add to an offer can be tricky. As always, an excellent source of information is your competition and other digital marketers. When you are presented with an offer, dissect each of the elements that you're seeing. How urgent is the offer? How does the messaging associated with the offer make you feel? Don't be afraid to test your own offers with different combinations of deadlines, expiration dates, timers, or other urgency-inducing tactics.

Scarcity

Scarcity is urgency's older sibling. Scarcity is a very specific way to induce urgency in an offer. After all, as human beings we intrinsically understand that if something is rare, then it is potentially valuable. Limited quantities, one-time offers, special editions, flash sales, and closeouts are some of the most common ways that offers are made into vehicles of scarcity to the benefit of marketers.

FOMO, the fear of missing out, is a distinctly twenty-first-century term for an age-old human emotion. FOMO is best described as feelings of envy, insecurity, or anxiety that stem from the prospect of others having fun, enjoying themselves, or otherwise gaining access to something that you won't have access to unless you take immediate action. FOMO-focused marketing heightens urgency and scarcity to their peaks and is particularly well suited to the digital environment. For example, automated systems can do a very good job of displaying not only popular products, but the number of customers who have purchased within the last twenty-four hours, the dwindling levels of stock ("only six left at this price"), and the time remaining to take advantage of a special deal ("only one hour until the price increases").

The Power of FREE

Is there anything better than getting something for nothing? To marketers, the answer is no. The bottom line is that people like free things. One small caveat, here and throughout this text: the term "free" should be understood as "a visible cost of $0." Despite the word "FREE" appearing in all caps in sales letters and on just about every landing page, nothing is truly free. This is an especially important concept for you as a digital marketer to understand; "free" means that no money is changing hands, but free offers pay for themselves in other ways.

An easy way to capitalize on the power of free is to stack value on your offer to the extent that the value provided far surpasses the purchase price. If a juicer costs $79, that's one thing. But if the juicer is $79 with a recipe book, glassware, multiple blades, and a trial subscription to a juice blending service, all listed as free, isn't that a much more compelling offer? Instead of presenting the offer—juicer plus accessories—as a single $79 product, present it as the juicer for the sticker price with numerous free add-ons "included" in the price, which makes the product much more attractive as a whole. Of course, the cost of the "free" items is included in the overall purchase price, but listing them as complimentary harnesses the power of free.

Q: What do I give away for free?

Savvy marketers look for ways to add value and list items as free to encourage customers to ascend their value ladders—the more value the better. Like the value ladder itself, however, the more thought put into these products, the better. The free products shouldn't just be whatever you have lying around. These products are designed to entice customers and convince them to spend more money. Digital products are an excellent way to enhance a product as a free add-on, and marketers love them for their low cost. Pay once to produce them, and give them away for a lifetime. Digital products don't incur shipping costs and don't take up space in a warehouse.

The best free add-ons complement the purchase they come with and truly provide value. Bought a new juicer? A recipe book will help you get the most out of it right away. Trying to lose weight? A meal-planning sheet, a calorie-counting companion worksheet, or other add-ons will not only help you get the most out of the product but will help you meet your goals. A word of warning, however—you have to deliver on the value you promise. A flimsy one-page PDF or a grainy YouTube video won't cut it and will lead to dissatisfied customers.

Free is often seen written as "FREE" for several reasons. First and foremost, advertisers are seeking to grab the attention of their audiences. This was as true in the days predating TV, radio, and color printing as it is now. As English readers, we're trained to recognize the prominence of capital letters, and their presence in any text immediately draws our eye. More recently, using capital letters online has become synonymous with "shouting" via text. According to "netiquette," the informal rules of online etiquette, text that is overly capitalized is considered loud or intrusive—two words that could also be used to describe the attention-grabbing tactics that many advertisers rely on.

Getting offers right takes time, practice, and a high degree of familiarity with your target audience. If you are feeling overwhelmed at this point, that's okay. Spend time dissecting the offers you're being shown as you travel across the internet. What is the promised value? What hyper-compelling tactics are being used? Is anything free? If so, how does it promise to help you achieve your goals? Take note, too, of the way different aspects of the offer are presented. What is the main focus? Is it price? The results promised? The free add-ons? How do each of these aspects subtly change the audience the offer is speaking to? Don't be afraid to screenshot offers that convinced you to buy, and store them for inspiration later—use the best parts of the offers you see around you every day and make them your own, to help grow your business and deliver the most value possible to your customers!

Chapter Recap

» A value ladder is a visual representation of a company's efforts to entice its customers to buy more from it, moving prospects from the lowest rung on the ladder, which might be a free digital download, all the way up to a high-priced one-on-one coaching package, for example. Each rung offers a different feature or result. Moving up the ladder is called "ascending."

» The three major ways to generate more revenue are 1) to increase the amount of money each customer spends, 2) to increase the number of customers who buy from you, and 3) to increase the frequency with which your customers buy from you.

» Upselling is the act of presenting an offer that increases both the price and the value of an order. Downselling is a method of saving a sale and introducing customers to your value ladder even if they aren't open to your initial offer, by making an alternative, less expensive offer. Together, these two methods help increase average order value and customer lifetime value while ascending customers along your value ladder.

» An offer is made when a business or brand asks a potential or existing customer to exchange items of value with them. It may be an exchange of money for new tires, or it may be an exchange of a useful checklist for the prospect's contact information.

» Think about four key questions as you design your offer: 1) What are you hoping to achieve? 2) To whom will you present the offer? 3) What thing are you offering? 4) What does customer ascension on your value ladder look like? That is, where does this offer fit on your value ladder?

» A hyper-compelling offer is one that is such a perfect fit for the audience it's presented to that it becomes totally irresistible. Hyper-compelling offers have urgency and scarcity that help entice buyers to act.

| 5 |

What Are Your Objectives?

Chapter Overview

- » Deciding on objectives
- » Being flexible and adaptable
- » Planning for success
- » Budgeting basics

Now that you have a solid marketing foundation, you've clarified who your best potential customers are, and you've zeroed in on your product or service offerings, it's time to start setting objectives. Just like any other business function, digital marketing activities must be carried out with a concrete goal in mind. And, as with other business functions, they must also be measured and evaluated. Objective setting is a crucial process; the objectives you choose will determine the components of your market/media/message mix as well as the tools that will deliver the best results. Failure to set objectives at the beginning of your campaigns can result in wasted effort, wasted ad spending, and missed opportunities to connect with the members of your target audience.

What Do You Want to Achieve?

The range of digital marketing tools and methods at your disposal can be used in many different ways to achieve many different goals. Your marketing goals inform your methodology and tool selection. For example, a new product may benefit from market education or awareness-building. With a mature product, one that is farther along in its product lifecycle, you might aim for repositioning it in the marketplace to target an entirely new customer segment. And for a hot product facing new competition, your focus might be squarely on protecting your sales and improving the loyalty of your customer base.

Here are some common high-level business objectives:
- » Increasing sales
- » Increasing profits
- » Growing market share
- » Launching new products or services
- » Targeting new customers
- » Entering new markets
- » Enhancing customer relationships
- » Generating more leads

It is important, however, not to focus exclusively on these higher-level objectives but to learn to see them as composed of smaller, tactical goals that can be achieved through digital marketing tools and strategies. As we will discuss, broad, nonspecific goals don't help us be better marketers, and they don't help us achieve our business goals. By identifying each of the steps that come together to make up these broader goals, we can tackle them one by one and truly understand what steps we will need to take to accomplish them. Famed inventor and former head of research for General Motors in the early half of the twentieth century put it best:

A problem well stated is a problem half solved.

– CHARLES KETTERING

Head of Research at General Motors

Let's reframe each of those overarching goals by defining them using their smaller tactical goals.

Increasing sales
- » To increase sales, we have to increase traffic to our online store.
- » To increase sales from our online store, we must ensure that our store looks good and is easy to navigate.
- » We can increase traffic to our online store through ads.
- » We can increase traffic to our online store by contacting our current customers.

Increasing profits
- » To increase profits, we must lower our customer acquisition cost (CAC).

> » To increase profits, we must increase the average order value or the number of products each customer buys.
> » To increase profits, we must test new pricing options and bundle different products together.

Enhancing customer relationships
> » To stay in the forefront of our customers' minds, we will need to contact them more often and in more ways.
> » To forge a stronger connection with our customers, we will have to learn more about them.
> » To earn the trust and positive opinion of our customers, we will have to find ways to deliver more value to them.

Launching a product/service
> » We need to learn more about the people who have a problem we can solve and how many of these people are out there.
> » We need to develop a comprehensive customer avatar for our ideal customer to direct our marketing efforts.

With these smaller, tactical goals uncovered, marketers can start selecting the tools and methodologies they will use to achieve them and, in turn, the higher-level business goals they pertain to. In this way, objective-setting is the critical first step in any digital marketing undertaking.

SMART Goals

Useful as it would be, unfortunately there is no such thing as a "make more money" button. Therefore, your goal setting needs to be explicit, useful, and helpful. The *SMART goal setting framework* is a good way to whittle down overarching business goals into manageable and actionable steps. SMART stands for Specific, Measurable, Actionable, Relevant, and Time-bound (figure 26). Put another way, what are you trying to achieve, how will you know when you have achieved it, is it something you can achieve, will achieving it solve a problem you are facing, and in what time frame is it reasonable to complete this achievement?

When they're translated into digital marketing terms, we can see vague, unhelpful goals transformed into actionable steps. Our fictional home meal delivery company, Home Fresh, from chapter 2, like any business, wants to increase sales. A SMART goal—or series of goals—will be much more actionable than writing "sales" on a whiteboard and circling it several times.

SPECIFIC
What exactly are you trying to achieve?

MEASURABLE
How will you measure your progress and your results, and how will you know when you are done?

ACTIONABLE
Is this something you can act on? Is the result achievable?

RELEVANT
Will completing this goal solve a problem you are facing?

TIME-BOUND
What is the deadline for completing this goal? What is a reasonable time frame for this goal to be completed in?

GRAPHIC

fig. 26

Compare:

» Home Fresh needs more sales. We need to sell more subscriptions.

» We want to increase the number of new meal plan subscriptions by at least 15 percent by the end of the year without increasing the cost to acquire those by more than 5 percent.

The former, while true, is so vague as to be unhelpful. The latter describes not only the desired outcome, but the time frame in which the goal should be completed to be effective and some of the parameters that help make the goal actionable. And it's expressed in measurable, achievable terms. Expressing your goals using the SMART framework not only helps focus and direct your efforts toward the business outcomes you are seeking but also makes your objectives easy to communicate to colleagues, partners, contractors, and other business stakeholders.

Digital Marketing SERVEs

QUESTION

Q: Why spend so much time on goal setting and objectives when there are sales to make and customers to convert?

Any carpenter will tell you that the right tool for the job makes all the difference. Any marketer will tell you the same thing. In the coming chapters we will be discussing the strengths, weaknesses, and uses of a wide array of digital marketing tools. The "right tool for the job," so to speak, is the one that is best equipped to help you meet your business objectives and marketing goals. Without a clear goal to aid in selecting the right tool, you may find yourself hammering a nail with a screwdriver. Digital marketing efforts fall broadly into one of five categories: increasing sales, fostering an exchange of communication between marketer and customer, reducing overall marketing costs, increasing the value conveyed to customers, and extending the reach of the brand in digital space and beyond. Collectively, these categories can be remembered with the acronym **SERVE** (figure 27).

SALES
Increase sales to new and existing customers

EXCHANGE
Foster a two-way channel of communication between marketers and their audience

REDUCE
Reduce the overall marketing cost through optimization and reduced customer acquisition costs (CAC)

VALUE
Increase the value conveyed to customers to ascend them along the value ladder

EXTEND
Extend the reach of the brand across digital space and beyond

GRAPHIC

fig. 27

Sales

This is the primary goal of most marketers. Whether using email, direct messaging, social media, or other channels, marketers want to make sales to new or existing customers. Ideally, the sales that marketing efforts produce will be explicitly tied to those efforts so marketers can justify the expense of campaigns and ensure that costs aren't spiraling out of control.

Exchange

Digital marketing—and marketing broadly—thrives on data. At a time when consumers have an unprecedented level of access to the brands in their lives and an expectation that their voice will be heard, it's easier than ever not only to connect with customers but also to collect data about their pain points and preferences.

Reduce

All businesses are concerned with keeping costs in check, and effective marketers are obsessed with maximizing the efficiency of their spending. Capitalizing on the scope and scale of digital communications while relentlessly finding ways to reduce spending, increase customer lifetime value, and reduce the cost to acquire new customers is not only a process that continues to yield results over time but one that can be tracked at even the smallest scale.

Value

The root of any business is its value proposition—the ways in which it sets itself apart from the competition and convinces customers they should choose it over other options—and digital marketing tools and strategies are uniquely positioned to enhance this value proposition. Think back to the concept of the value ladder; the overarching objective for marketers is to create a customer journey that ascends the customer up the ladder by providing more value at a commensurate price at each "rung." Being able to present this value at the precise time the customer is most receptive and ready to make a purchase makes a huge difference for businesses of all sizes and strengthens customer relationships.

Extend

In the age of viral marketing, with devices that are always online providing a constant stream of information, it should be readily apparent that the scale and reach of digital marketing tools mean that your brand can be put in front of more people than ever before. Viral marketing is a digital marketing tactic designed to propagate a message or content asset around the internet by encouraging people to share it with their own social circles in digital space.

The ALS Ice Bucket Challenge is an example of a highly effective viral marketing campaign that took place in the summer of 2014. Celebrities, media personalities, and ordinary people would film themselves pouring a bucket of ice water over their own heads and share it with their friends to raise awareness of ALS (amyotrophic lateral sclerosis, or Lou Gehrig's disease) and to solicit donations in the fight to find a cure. This unique blend of competitiveness, social media fervor, low cost using everyday materials, and supporting a good cause led to more than 2.4 million videos being tagged as participating in the challenge and a whopping $220 million raised for ALS research worldwide. There have been numerous revivals in past years. The staggering success of the ALS Ice Bucket Challenge created a cottage industry of internet-based challenges designed to capitalize on the same competitive and highly sharable concept, to varying degrees of success.

Your marketing objectives aren't static—they'll change as your business or product matures, as you develop new offerings to roll out, or even as the economy or customer preferences shift. Keeping the SERVE digital marketing functions in mind when reassessing your goals ultimately means that tool selection and strategy will always be aligned with your goals.

SERVE and Effective Goal Setting in Action

Objectives can and should change over time, especially as your value ladder becomes more sophisticated and your business grows. As your business and your target market evolve, so, too, should your marketing objectives and approach; you need to remain adaptable, which means being willing to test different marketing methods. Don't fall in love with one tool, one ad, or one approach and refuse to see if you can get better results with a different one. Use extensive testing and measure your results to understand which methods are working and which should be scrapped. Use industry-wide best practices as a guide to get started, and craft your own approach that is tailored to your target market and your unique value proposition. We'll cover testing in greater detail in chapter 9, but the takeaway here is that you shouldn't think of failure as a dead end. In fact, in the world of digital marketing, as in the world of entrepreneurship, a "failure" is a jumping-off point—you have eliminated an approach that doesn't work, which puts you one step closer to finding one that does!

The fluid nature of marketing in digital spaces leads some new marketers to resist taking time to create a plan. But planning is an important tool in your digital marketing toolbox, *especially* if you are working with a team. Your marketing plan—the details of which will be filled in as you read through this book—is a communication tool, a discovery tool, a yardstick, and a road map all rolled into one.

Marketing plans are excellent communication tools to convey your vision to colleagues, subordinates, or contractors. Having a "single source of truth" when it comes to marketing decisions means that people who weren't in the room when goals and processes were determined (or people who haven't read this book!) can get on the same page faster and make decisions with a tool that helps them see the bigger picture. A marketing plan is also a discovery tool in that it can help you spot stuff you may have missed. Once you have completed your marketing plan and you take a step back to admire your handiwork, the completed plan can act as a checklist to bring your attention to gaps or areas you've overlooked in the marketing process.

A common mistake that even sophisticated marketing teams make is putting too many resources into a single high-investment activity. If an opportunity looks really promising, it can be tempting to allocate a lot of money and resources to it. This could pay off, but if it's an untested opportunity it could also end up siphoning away more money and effort than you were anticipating.

A marketing plan acts as a yardstick and a way to check your results as you move forward. Are you sticking to your budgets? What have you learned from the data you've been gathering? What have you learned about your customers that you didn't know before? In this way, your marketing plan acts as a benchmark, or a snapshot in time, that can be measured against when determining marketing goals and efforts down the road. Speaking of roads, your marketing plan can also act as a road map that keeps you focused and on track. *Shiny object syndrome* is the somewhat facetious name for the very real issue of business owners and marketers changing course with every new product or tool that is offered to them.

For every marketer, it seems that there are four companies attempting to sell the latest and greatest tools that do more and make more money. While it is absolutely true that every marketer should be on the lookout for new ways of reaching new people, changing tools and tactics at the drop of a hat can cause lots of headaches, redundant effort, and ballooning costs that can be hard to spot. A robust marketing plan that keeps you focused on collecting data and delivering value to your customers can cut through the noise.

All of that being said, it is important to remember that a marketing plan is a living document and that planning in digital spaces is a fluid process. Don't be afraid to change course if the situation calls for it, and always be ready to make decisions based on the data you're collecting.

Potential Obstacles

Most anything worth doing in life will involve encountering obstacles, and digital marketing is no exception. Marketing obstacles may be technological, resource-related, legislative (for instance, a new law pertaining to information collection or retention), or something you never expected. Obstacles are something to be aware of when thinking about your own marketing, but don't let them scare you off—in digital spaces there is always a way to reach people.

Competitors

Other marketers that sell products similar to yours or that offer a substitute solution to your target audience are examples of competitors. Competitors are a fact of the business world—you can't get rid of them, so you may as well embrace them. In the world of digital marketing, competitors can increase costs by driving up the cost of ad placement and by siphoning customers away from your business. The good news is that competitors are an excellent source of inspiration. You can learn a lot about what is working for your competitors by purchasing their products and consuming their marketing materials. In fact, some seasoned digital marketers recommend buying one of everything your competition has for sale, to see exactly how they work to ascend their customers along their value ladder, what offers they use, and what products they sell.

Obsolescence

New best practices and technology are always emerging, but that doesn't mean that your basic marketing strategies will stop working. Stay open to pivoting as new technologies, new solutions, and new platforms emerge, but don't fall prey to shiny object syndrome. When evaluating a new offering, ask yourself, Does this help me deliver more value to my customers? Does it help me deliver more value to my business? Does it solve a burning need that I have to take my business to the next level? In some cases, the answers will be yes, and it might be worth considering a change.

Lack of Money

The simple truth is that marketing incurs cost. For some small businesses, this is a very real obstacle. However, no matter what your budget is, most digital marketing solutions grow with you and costs scale as your needs grow. The results you get from spending $10 a day on Facebook ads pale in comparison to the results of spending $1,000 a day, but the ability to tightly control your spending and ensure you aren't throwing away money is a feature of many digital marketing solutions. And remember, digital marketing is one of the most cost-effective methods out there when it comes to reaching people and making sales. Starting small and reinvesting gains from small wins will help you grow at an appropriate pace without overextending yourself. The tactics and techniques in this book speak to the very real need that marketers have to keep costs in check—you will be well armed!

MY TAKE

Business owners who maintain an abundance mindset—that is, a belief that there is enough business out there for everyone and that spending money will help generate more—are the individuals who will spot the new opportunities as they appear. Business owners who harbor a scarcity mentality—being focused on penny-pinching and not spending money but holding on to everything they currently have—miss out on the chance to generate even more revenue. Stay focused on all the opportunities around you, and work to cultivate an abundance mindset in your business and your marketing activities.

Lack of Time

Every entrepreneur who is holding this book knows the very real pain of having only twenty-four hours in each day. Marketing with plans, campaigns, and message after message to put out into the world can feel overwhelming, and it is natural to panic while scrambling to find time in your schedule to set aside for marketing efforts. But there's good news: automation is here to save your time. Many digital marketing activities and tasks can be automated, meaning once they're set up, they run on their own. This set-it-and-forget-it functionality can amplify your efforts and allow you to focus on the other aspects of your business that matter. The key is to automate as much as possible. Automate welcome messages to new customers. Marketing emails, responses, upsells, downsells, and just about every other aspect of your marketing can be put on autopilot to an extent, so that once the initial work is done you can spend less and less time doing repetitive and time-consuming tasks.

Lack of Familiarity

If you're new to digital marketing, or marketing period, then you may feel as if there's just too much to learn. Not only that, but the uncertainty of committing your hard-earned dollars to untested marketing approaches can be an obstacle in its own right. The upside here is that marketing in the digital space can be very forgiving. Not only is it possible to keep a close eye on your spending, but campaigns and ads can be turned on and off with just a few mouse clicks. Besides, armed with the knowledge in this book, you will have the confidence (and your own marketing plan) to run your first campaigns and get your feet wet. Advertisers and advertising partners want to make it as easy as possible to spend money on their platforms, and as a result, many digital marketing tools are very easy to use, with responsive support and extensive documentation.

On Budgeting

As with most things, it's quite possible that your marketing plan requires money your business doesn't have—yet. Fortunately, you don't have to spend thousands of dollars to see results. If you are starting your marketing efforts while strapped for cash, it is not only possible but advisable to build on small successes to generate revenue to reinvest in your marketing efforts and slowly build your budget over time.

The exact amount that you spend on marketing depends on several factors, including but not limited to the following:

» The lifecycle stage your business is currently in. Are you a startup or have you been around for decades?

» Your target markets. If your customers are hard to reach, that will mean more of a marketing investment.

» The competitive nature of your industry. If you are in a highly competitive industry with established competitors, you will need to spend more money to stand out and cut through the noise.

» The price of your product. Higher-priced offerings often have a longer sales cycle and can require more marketing input to produce a sale.

» Where your selling happens. Purely online businesses can cut out many costs that brick-and-mortar businesses have to absorb.

» The amount of money you have in the bank.

One basic rule of thumb is that, for established businesses, 5 percent of sales—based on last year's numbers or on this year's projected sales—should be set aside for marketing. Established businesses enjoy a considerable amount of brand recognition and an active customer base. If your business is a startup, on the other hand, 10 to 15 percent for your first year of marketing is a healthier target as a starting point for spending. These numbers are fine jumping-off points. The more data you can use to inform your decision, the better your results will be.

A data-based approach to budgeting is based on customer lifetime value (CLV). Using this method, take approximately one third of a customer's CLV and multiply it by the forecast number of customer purchases in a given period. For instance, say a CLV is $200; then 33 percent would be $67. If you're trying to calculate an advertising budget for a month, then multiply 67 times the number of unique customers you anticipate over a month's time.

Another option is to start with a zero-based budget and do some calculating. How many contacts do you need to make to get a lead? If you divide your number of leads by your number of contacts, you can figure out the rough percentage of contacts that become leads. Then, how many of those leads typically become customers? You can calculate that percentage too. From there, you can figure out about how many contacts you need to start with in order to reach your desired number of customers. And then estimate how much it would cost to drive that amount of traffic to your website, or into your store, or onto your phone lines.

Another source of information to help you judge how much you should invest in marketing is industry statistics. Turn to your industry trade association or professional society to gather details regarding how much companies in your sector budget for marketing. Deloitte's CMO Survey is another potential starting point for a better understanding of what industry players are spending.

There's no hard-and-fast rule for how much you should spend, but, as with everything else in marketing, you'd be smart to test different approaches and choose the method or methods that generate the most leads for the least amount of money.

Chapter Recap

» Digital marketing tools can be used to achieve virtually any business objective, but you need to decide up front what you want to have happen as a result of your investment.

» Your objectives for digital marketing may include building awareness, generating leads, boosting engagement, and getting sales. The more targeted your marketing activities are on one of these objectives—rather than more than one—the more successful you'll be. As your business or product matures, your marketing program should adapt and evolve with it.

» One of the best ways to remain flexible and adaptable is to constantly be testing your different marketing activities to see which are performing the best, and then shifting more money to those activities and away from those that are delivering suboptimal results.

» To increase the effectiveness of your digital marketing tactics, you'll want to create a plan that links your products and services with specific marketing methods that help you achieve your objectives.

» Potential obstacles you may encounter include competition, obsolescence, lack of money, lack of time, and lack of familiarity. All can be overcome, but they may impact the results you're able to achieve.

» Many businesses set a marketing budget based on sales percentages. Looking at the typical marketing expense for your industry and size of business can be a great starting point, but keep in mind that newer businesses may need to invest more in marketing to gain traction.

PART II

TOOLS OF THE TRADE

| 6 |

Coming In for a Landing

Chapter Overview

» Big picture: the role your website plays
» The strategic role of landing pages
» Effective sales pages
» Generating leads and opt-ins

Flashy tools and the latest trends get the lion's share of attention in the realm of digital marketing tactics and strategies. While it is true that purpose-built tools can be valuable assets in your digital marketing toolbox, the humble landing page is both a digital marketing workhorse and a versatile tool that is featured in nearly every digital marketing campaign. Landing pages are (usually) hosted on your website, and they are the stop on your customer's journey where they first take action. Before we dive into what landing pages are and how they work, let's examine the role your website plays in your overall digital strategy and why it is essential to have one.

Smart digital marketers take advantage of tried-and-true tools that make their jobs easier and help them achieve their goals. We've included recommendations for some of these tools, from our preferred email marketing platforms to web page analytic utilities, in a brief called the Digital Marketing Tool Kit. Look for this along with a lot of other supplemental material by visiting www.clydebankmedia.com/digitalmarketing-assets.

Thinking about Your Website as a Tool

One of your most important online marketing tools is your business's website. Whether it consists of just a single page or several, it will play a large role in your digital marketing efforts. Even a simple website that acts as a source of information for online traffic has value for a modern business. Your customers will expect that you have a website no matter what industry you're in. Companies without websites send the message that they have stopped operating or, perhaps worse, are out of touch with customers. Let's review some principal functions of a business's website.

A Point of Contact

We have already discussed the ways in which new media tools produce a two-way conversation between brands and their customers. To this end, a contact page or other contact capability on a website is an essential function. Your customers expect to be able to reach you, and the more avenues of communication you provide for them, the better. Email addresses for information or support, a mailing address, and links to social media accounts are a minimum. Relevant phone numbers and fillable forms for questions and feedback are preferred, as is 24/7 live chat capability.

Modern customers have high expectations when it comes to their online experiences. They expect speedy and frictionless usability and prompt resolution of any problem. Of course, as service levels increase in responsiveness and complexity, so does cost. When planning the functionality of your website with respect to customer contact, think about your product and your customer avatar(s). Do you expect your customers to be tech-savvy? Do they regularly make phone calls, or do they prefer email or instant messaging? Would they find the lack of an email or chat function frustrating?

Anticipate common questions, or note questions that come in regularly, and make answers readily available using a frequently answered questions (FAQ) page or section. Not only is this a convenient feature for your customers, but it can produce time savings on your end—the lower the volume of customer inquiries, the more time you and your staff can devote to building the business. As with many aspects of your business, it is much better to be proactive than reactive.

An Informational Resource

It is also important that your website serves as a source of information for customers. If someone wants to know something about your business, they will reach for their phone and Google it. In order for Google to return the information, it must exist somewhere on the internet. To be an effective resource (and an effective business asset) your website should include easily accessible answers to your customers' questions. Basic details about the company's operations—hours, service area, contact info, and address, to name a few—must be easy to find and crystal clear. Failing to make this information easily available can frustrate potential customers.

An Owned Media Asset

As we touched on in our discussion of the media mix, your website represents a digital property over which you have complete control, because you own it. This means that in addition to basic information about your business, there is no limit to the content, messaging, and general narrative components your site can showcase. The most ubiquitous example of this is the "our story" or "about us" pages that can be found on nearly any business's website. Consider using your site to feature your brand accomplishments or flex your creative muscles. Use it to make a great first impression, and don't pass up any opportunities to convey your expertise and build credibility. When it comes to using your site as an owned media asset, the sky is the limit.

A Dedicated Sales Environment

In addition to being a virtual storefront, your website represents a dedicated sales environment. Digital space is crowded. Nearly every business in operation right now is vying for eyeballs online. Ultimately, this means that attention is currency and if your business is going to thrive, you've got to grab the attention of individuals online. Unless there's a strong incentive for someone to stop and focus on what you have to offer, they are likely to scroll right past your message, ad, or offer and keep looking for the next cute cat photo. Your goal must be to make your message and offer compelling enough to convince people to leave whatever site they are on and navigate to yours, which represents a dedicated sales environment. Once they're on your site, you will have much more freedom to encourage conversions via pages, prompts, and pop-ups that aren't available on external sites or social media platforms.

NOTE

The concept of changing the sales environment is nothing new. A street vendor knows their first challenge is simply to get passersby to stop and check out what they're selling. Once a pedestrian has stopped, the vendor can deliver their sales pitch, give out samples, and hopefully close a deal. This same concept is at work in digital sales environments. When traffic on social media, search engine result pages, or other digital spaces is enticed to stop scrolling and "visit your street vendor cart," the possibility of a sale increases dramatically.

A Home for Your Landing Pages

A *landing page* is a stand-alone web page created specifically to fulfill a digital marketing need or objective. It's the page that someone "lands on" after clicking on an ad or link in an email, on a website, or on social media. Landing pages form the backbone of digital marketing campaigns because they represent an important environmental change—from a browsing environment to an action-oriented one. To be most effective, entrepreneurs, small business owners, and freelance digital marketers need to devote time to building campaigns around specific offers on landing pages. When preparing one, you'll need to consider your goals, target market, budget, execution strategy, creative message, and copy.

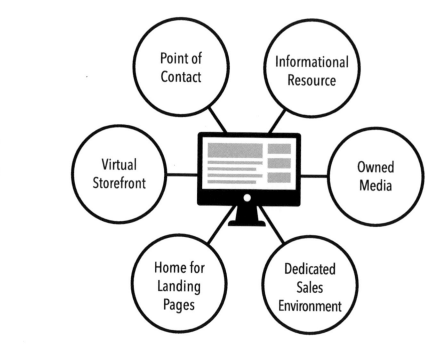

GRAPHIC

fig. 28

Exploring the Role of Landing Pages

A digital marketing campaign that uses paid media in the form of advertisements first attracts potential customers with compelling ads. When an ad inspires people to click through, they are sent to an associated landing page. If the landing page doesn't connect with the ad in message and appearance, visitors can become disoriented and are likely to navigate away. The same is likely to happen if information on the landing page is hard to understand, spammy, or otherwise intrusive or untrustworthy.

The groundwork for matching your landing pages with a receptive audience is laid long before you even begin building the landing page elements. Accurate identification of your customer avatar, the goals of your offer, and the market/media/message mix all contribute to sending the right traffic to your landing page. Just as campaigns are built around offers, landing pages are built around objectives. The specific contents of the page reflect the value you are delivering to your audience, the nature of the offer (a sale, a free product, a sample), and the results you are hoping to achieve.

Just about any marketing goal you can imagine calls for a landing page. Selling tickets to your event? A modified sales landing page is in order. Want sign-ups for your free webinar? A landing page is a good fit. Nonprofit organizations seeking donations, volunteers, or sponsors all put their own minor tweaks on common landing page configurations.

GRAPHIC

fig. 29

LANDING PAGE FEATURES	
HEADLINE	Summarizes the content of the page, acts as a reader hook, and encourages page visitors to continue reading.
COPY	Sales or marketing text that accompanies a call to action. Used to communicate the value and benefit the page visitor will receive if they take action.
CTA BUTTON OR FORM	The literal action you want the page visitor to take. Use a button to navigate to a purchase page, enter personal information into a checkout form, or opt in to your mailing list—whatever action will deliver value to them and help you achieve your goals.
GRAPHICS, IMAGES, AND VIDEOS	Used to increase the visual appeal of your landing page and entice page visitors. Video is the holy grail of engagement, but it is also pricy and can backfire if poorly executed.
SOCIAL PROOF	Used to convince page visitors they should take action to avoid missing out on the value others have already received. This can be communicated with social proof from a number of sources such as experts, celebrities, or customers.
OPT-IN FORM	Used on squeeze pages to collect contact information from your audience. This information is used to ascend your new contacts along your value ladder and convert them into customers.

Opt-In Pages

An opt-in page, also known as a *squeeze page*, is a type of landing page specifically designed to entice visitors to exchange their contact information for something of value that you offer (you're "squeezing" the contact information out of them with something they want). This "something," called a *lead magnet*, should be highly relevant to visitors' pain points. It promises tremendous value and is often provided with a visible cost of zero dollars—meaning it's free. Many marketers have found that a digital download in the form of an actionable executive summary, worksheet, how-to guide, or white paper often works as an effective lead magnet. The sky is the limit when it comes to designing your own lead magnets, but generally they should have the following attributes: be immediately available to visitors who opt in, be at very low cost to you, be valuable and actionable for your landing page visitors, and, above all, be relevant to the problems your visitors face.

GRAPHIC

fig. 30

QUESTION

Q: **Why go to the trouble of developing a great lead magnet when all you're asking for in return is your prospect's contact info?**

It all comes back to the value ladder. The lead magnets digital marketers use often represent the lowest rung of the value ladder. In exchange for contact information, your audience receives value from you. This value is proportionate to the price paid—zero dollars. However, with this contact information, smart digital marketers can now send messages to keep these customers engaged and ascend them along the value ladder. Moreover, modern communication methods and digital marketing tools can automate just about every aspect of the process, meaning once all the pieces are in place, this process can run on near autopilot.

The defining aspect of a squeeze page is the opt-in form. In fact, the most effective squeeze pages feature an opt-in form and little to nothing else. Visitors to your squeeze page are presented with two options: follow through with the call to action or navigate away from the page. Excessive copy, other offers, or pages that try to be too many things to too many different people are confusing to users and will produce inferior results. Figure 30 depicts a squeeze page that uses minimal elements to focus on the call to action included in the opt-in form.

WHEN UTILIZING OPT-IN FORMS:

Make sure the headline and other elements of the form focus on the value of your lead magnet. Limit the amount of information you request to just what is essential. Not only will this increase conversions, but in today's climate of increasingly restrictive digital privacy legislation, minimal collection may be mandated by regulators. Many marketers find that all they need is a first name and an email address. When designing your capture forms, less is more.

Sales Pages

Sales pages are a type of landing page designed to convert traffic into customers. Opt-in and lead-generation pages are geared toward getting potential customers onto the value ladder so they eventually become customers, but a sales page is much more direct. It's all about getting the sale right then and there.

A *sales page* is a stand-alone page with the express goal of generating sales. It's the digital equivalent of the classic sales letter. The length of the page may vary, but all sales pages should feature persuasive language, speak to the benefits of a product or service, and include a sales-oriented CTA (call to action). An empty sales page is a blank canvas—if you can dream it, you can build it. There are, however, some best practices and some common elements that effective sales pages share.

Headline

A headline, or header, on a sales page acts just as it does in the world of journalism. It grabs attention, summarizes the content of the page, and encourages visitors to continue reading.

WHEN WRITING HEADLINES:

Be specific, be snappy, and be persuasive. Ideally, headlines are *continuity interrupters*, meaning they are so different, surprising, or amazing that they demand the attention of the reader. When done well, these headlines are irresistible. To pique the reader's curiosity, ask a question, promise you'll share a secret, or tease with a little-known fact.

While a great headline is priceless, we all know what it looks like when continuity interrupters are poorly executed. Commonly known as *clickbait*, the internet is littered with spammy, overly sensationalized, and outright misleading headlines.

To differentiate yourself from the rising tide of clickbait, be sure to deliver on any promises contained in your headline. Be specific with exact numbers (the larger and odder the better—like "817 Ways to Save Money") and use digits and symbols where possible in lieu of writing out numbers or words like "and." The fewer words used, the better. Create a sense of urgency whenever possible and lay out exactly what value the page delivers.

> » How to [achieve critical, specific goal] in less than [specific, short time period] WITHOUT [pain point].
>
> » Your [specific relevant topic] is [producing detrimental effect]. Here's how to fix it.
>
> » Join [specific number] of other [group members] who said goodbye to their [pain point] and achieved [valuable outcome].
>
> » Still [doing conventional approach]? You don't have to keep [suffering from pain point]. Here's how.

Notice how these headlines speak directly to specific customer avatars. The more specific and tailored headlines are, the more success they will generate.

Plugging some specifics into our templates above, we can see that the following headlines are interesting, specific, and compelling to a laser-focused customer avatar:

» How to shave 9 strokes off your golf game in just 14 days WITHOUT spending a fortune on new equipment

» Your small business is bleeding profit. Here's how to stop the flow.

» Join 4,679 other medical professionals and cut your administrative workload in half.

» Still going to the gym to lose weight? You don't have to keep sweating with strangers and failing to shed pounds – here's how...

Copy

Copy is the sales and marketing text that accompanies a call to action. Marketing copy is distinct from text contained in a book or a newspaper, in that it is always produced with a desired marketing action expected of the reader. It doesn't just share interesting facts; each sentence—every word, for that matter—has a purpose. The field of copywriting is equal parts art and science and is a defined career path for writers and marketers who choose to specialize in it.

Do your research when writing copy. As you browse the web and read copy from other brands, competitors, and general ads you see, start saving snippets. Copywriters call these collections of snippets *swipe files*, because they were "swiped" from copy that works for them. As your swipe file grows, it can be used as inspiration for your own copywriting efforts or as a resource to help convey your vision to a copywriter you hire. Obviously, you cannot duplicate other companies' material word for word, but do use it as inspiration for your own take on a topic or message.

Tried-and-true copywriting formulas will help you shape your message, which you can then make more specific for your target audience. Ultimately, the characteristics of your customer avatar (chapter 3) should guide your copy—the more personalized and avatar-tailored your copy is, the more successful it will be.

If you hire a copywriter, be sure they know about and understand the customer avatars you've created. Above all, realize this: good copy can make or break a sales page or an offer, but even great copy can't save a bad offer. At the end of the day, crafting a strong offer built specifically for your target audience is the single best step you can take to develop an effective sales page.

A full exploration of the world of copywriting is beyond the scope of this book; however, we've included a summary of some time-tested, popular copywriting formulas in our Copywriting Success Blueprint, free to download with your purchase of this book. Visit www.clydebankmedia.com/digitalmarketing-assets.

CTA Button/Form

No sales page would be complete without a call to action that encourages page visitors to take the next step and become customers. All the page elements should lead your visitors to this critical point. This means the CTA should reflect the claim made in the headline (see figure 31). The copy should reinforce the value of the offer and lead readers to the CTA, and any images should support the CTA.

A common best practice is to make the call to action a button. This draws attention and makes it impossible to miss. In the case of CTA buttons on sales pages, they generally link to checkout pages or order forms. Some marketers have experimented with putting the order form directly on the page. In this case, rather than customers being sent to a separate checkout page, the general components of the order form are displayed directly on the landing page, with the payment options populating once the name and email address are entered, or the order form displaying as a new field on the page once the CTA button is clicked.

fig. 31

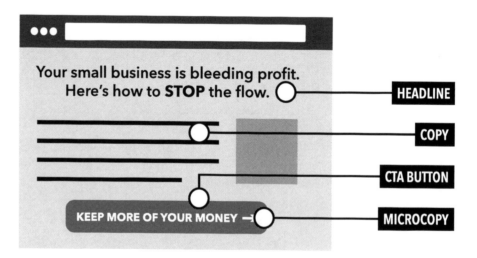

An example of a CTA form

Notice how in figure 31 the copy on the button (keep more of your money) complements the attention-grabbing headline. This is superior to vanilla copy such as "Buy Now" or "Check Out Now."

Collectively, the copy on CTA buttons, along with other single lines of copy or stand-alone single sentences, is known as *microcopy*. As with other copy, the best inspiration for your own microcopy might come from a well-curated swipe file.

WHEN DESIGNING CTA BUTTONS:

Keep the microcopy relevant to the benefit the customer will achieve. As you read earlier, the button should be impossible to miss, and customers should know what to expect when they click on it. Most important, follow through on any promises you make. Nothing derails a sale like an unfulfilled promise or a shady bait-and-switch tactic.

Graphics and Images

Traffic arriving on a landing page expects the "trip" to be worth it. When someone decides to cut short their Facebook browsing to check out your landing page, they expect to find value on that page that equals or exceeds the value of their browsing. If they land on your sales page and find an overwhelming wall of text, it's a safe bet they'll hit the back button—no one wants a reading assignment.

That's why you should depend on attractive and engaging graphics to break up the text and help clarify your offer. Graphics can shift the selling environment into emotional space and act as hooks to keep your visitors on the page. Digital audiences expect pages to be useful, attractive, and easy to navigate; high-quality images are a big part of what makes a page attractive and engaging.

When developing and choosing graphics and images, keep utility in mind. High-quality stock images are widely available online and are often free or inexpensive. Images including human faces are generally recommended, especially ones that align with your customer avatar's segmentation information.

Graphics and images are far more likely to keep traffic on your page and encourage conversions than a page filled with text, but nothing beats compelling video content. Video is by far the best way to connect with your audience and keep them on the page, but it can be a double-edged sword. Professional-quality video that looks great and gets your point across can be expensive to produce and edit. Lower-quality video is inexpensive and easy to produce, but, in this case, you get what you pay for. Cheap video makes a landing page cheap by extension, whereas professional, visually attractive video creates a wow factor and is a better representation of the brand you've spent time and energy crafting. A general rule of thumb is that no video is better than bad video.

Video Sales Pages

Video sales pages are another variation on the landing page, with the distinguishing factor of having most of the page devoted to showcasing a video. The video window is the largest element on that page, which is typically sparse in terms of other pieces of information. The focus should be front and center on a crystal-clear video, ideally with high production value.

fig. 32

An example of a video sales page

Really, the only elements on a video sales page should be:
» Headline
» Subhead
» Video
» Buy button (or order form)

Video sales pages can be extremely effective when done well, especially when they feature a product that can be demonstrated—think kitchen appliance, snowboard, tool, or piece of software.

Webinar Registration Landing Pages

Whether the goal of a digital marketer is to attract attendees to a future webinar or deliver a webinar on demand, a landing page is a great tool for doing either one. Webinar registration landing pages are laser-focused on one goal: getting visitors to sign up to attend a webinar.

To convince prospective attendees that a webinar is a good use of their time, most hosts include a headline stating its purpose, a short amount of copy explaining its value—what's in it for attendees—and some details such as where and when the webinar will be held. You could include a brief video featuring the host of the event or rely on persuasive and engaging copy to convince people to sign up. Every webinar registration page should have a sign-up window that captures the names, email addresses, and other information of attendees. Once you've got that information, you can add those attendees to your marketing funnel—the series of steps your audience will take toward achieving a desired goal like making a purchase.

An example of a webinar registration form

Best Practices

In addition to keeping squeeze pages sparse and headlines compelling, what other best practices can digital marketers take advantage of to make their landing pages shine? The answer can be found in traditional marketing practices, sometimes referred to as marketing or sales psychology. Use these tools on landing pages as well as across your campaigns to increase conversions and accomplish your digital marketing goals.

Social Proof

Somewhat paradoxically, the internet has created a truly global community of individuals who are more connected than ever, while simultaneously forcing users to be naturally suspicious of others online. A free and open internet has been a wondrous thing, but it has also enabled scammers, phishers, shoddy merchants, and other digital predators. This has caused some members of your audience to develop understandable hesitation over patronizing unfamiliar businesses—there are many incredible claims on the internet, after all! To ease the reluctance of consumers, marketers (digital and otherwise) have leveraged the psychological phenomenon known as *social proof*.

Social proof is defined as the phenomenon of people taking on the actions of others in an attempt to reflect correct behavior for a given situation. In other words, it involves people looking to *other* people for cues on how to behave. There are five distinct ways that this phenomenon manifests, each of which is presented differently in marketing efforts.

fig. 34

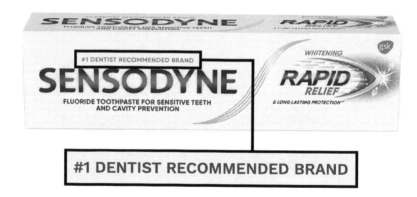

Source: www.sensodyne.com
An example of expert proof

> » **Expert Proof:** We rely on the recommendations of experts on a regular basis because, generally speaking, expert opinion is considered weightier and more trustworthy than others. The overall assumption is that if an expert, such as an industry leader or health care professional, considers a particular product or service the best on the market, that recommendation is well informed and

therefore powerful. One of the most prevalent examples of expert proof can be seen in advertisements for toothpaste, mouthwash, and other oral care products. Nearly all of these products are "dentist recommended" or accepted by the American Dental Association (as seen in figure 34). Depending on the product, the expert does not necessarily have to be a medical professional, because different products and services lend themselves to different kinds of experts.

» **Celebrity Proof:** Celebrities may not be experts in all areas, but their recommendations are often treated with just as much reverence. Celebrity culture revolves around current trends, social status, and high visibility—the perfect combination for social proof. Thanks to brand partnerships with actors, musicians, social media influencers, and others, celebrity proof has become more common than ever, and more accessible to marketers. The evolving world of influencer marketing provides affordable access to a wide array of digital personalities with their own focused celebrity status and dedicated fan base.

fig. 35

Source: www.coca-cola.com

Musician Taylor Swift lends celebrity proof to Diet Coke.

NOTE

If you choose to employ celebrity proof, locate an influencer who is both influential and affordable. The biggest celebrity names charge big bucks for endorsements of products and services. In 2013 singer Taylor Swift signed a long-term deal with Coca-Cola, agreeing to be a brand ambassador for Diet Coke. Her price tag was reportedly $26 million.

» **User Proof:** For many consumers, expert proof and celebrity endorsement are viewed with a bit of the same skepticism that accompanies overt advertising in general. On the other hand, people who have paid money for the product are considered to be unmotivated by profit, and therefore their feedback is authentic, unbiased, and trustworthy. In digital spaces, this feedback often comes in the form of reviews or testimonials. Amazon reviews that verify the user purchased the product are one example of user proof.

fig. 36

A fictionalized Amazon review of snowboarding boots

User proof is a form of earned media. As we discussed in chapter 2, brands have no control over where or how earned media pops up. This means brands should do what they can to amplify positive reviews and testimonials and stay on top of critical or negative reviews for best effect.

» **Proof in the Wisdom of the Crowd:** This form of social proof is the opposite of expert endorsement. Instead of relying on the authority and experience of a single person, social proof using the wisdom of the crowd highlights the endorsement of large groups of people. The angle here is that if hundreds, thousands, or even millions of people have already decided to become customers, they must know something that others don't. This form of social proof also works to create feelings of FOMO (fear of missing out). If thousands of other people who have the same pain points as you have already found a solution in a product or service, isn't it worth checking out so you can get in on the solution, too?

fig. 37

A classic example of the "proof in the wisdom of the crowd" style of social proof

» **Proof through Certification**: In the case of proof through expert recommendation, a brand is relying on the perceived authority of an individual. In the case of proof through the wisdom of the crowd, a brand is relying on the perceived authority of large numbers of people. When using proof through certification, a brand is relying on the authority of esteemed institutions. Better Business Bureau (BBB) accreditation, Underwriters Laboratories (UL) certification, and the USDA Organic seal are common certifications that brands use to tap into the authority and trust conveyed by an institution (figure 38). As another form of proof, some companies post images of the logos of media outlets in which their business or product has been mentioned.

Regardless of what form it takes, social proof requires work. You've got to earn the five-star customer reviews or find an influencer willing to speak on behalf of your brand. You can't claim that the Department of Agriculture has certified your eggs organic if it has not done so. The fact that it's not easy is part of what makes social proof valuable. If you've earned it, don't be afraid to flaunt it.

Source: www.peteandgerrys.com

Proof through certification example of eggs bearing the
"certified organic" and "certified humane" seals

How you flaunt it effectively depends on the type of social proof you're employing. If you've got an expert or a celebrity endorsing your product or service, make sure to put the focus on them with video, or at least good images. Let people see who they are, and make sure their message comes through loud and clear. If your product has been featured in a popular publication, get that publication's masthead pasted onto your page. Good reviews can be prominently featured, along with enviable partnerships. Seeking out the best social proof you can find and using it to your advantage will not only go a long way in developing effective landing pages but can be used in other aspects of your marketing strategy.

A landing page is the first page traffic is sent to after interacting with an ad or a link from elsewhere on the web. This means that all landing pages, and especially sales pages, should be constructed to truly stand alone with regard to the rest of your site, messaging, and branding. In the case of landing pages, you have only one chance to make a first impression.

Scarcity and Urgency

As mentioned in chapter 4, people understand that rare things are valuable. And as rarity and value increase, so too do the levels of desirability and exclusivity surrounding the product. Marketers have long tapped into this feeling to encourage on-the-fence shoppers to take action and get out their wallets. Increasing the urgency of an offer is another way to encourage customers to take action in cases where they might otherwise not. The idea is to construct an offer that is so compelling that if a shopper—or internet browser—does anything else other than take action, they will miss out on an opportunity, and they won't be offered the same deal again. The scarcer an item, the more people will want it, and the more urgent the need for them to take action, the sooner they will act on their perceived need.

Digital marketers have access to a wide range of tools and tactics to harness the power of scarcity and urgency, but the savvy ones know not to overdo it. A sales page that comes on too strong with urgency comes off as spammy or untrustworthy. On the other hand, if there is no urgency or scarcity to an offer or an item, what's the rush? Why buy today when you can buy tomorrow? The bottom line is that introducing scarcity and urgency tactics to your landing pages and sales campaigns means more conversions and more revenue. Let's take a look at some of the most common tools digital marketers use to encourage their audiences to take action.

fig. 39

Source: www.oatsovernight.com

A limited-time promotion from food subscription company Oats Overnight.
New members save 10% on their first order, but only for a limited time.

Pop-Ins

Intrusive and distracting pop-up windows have gone the way of AOL, but the basic need for a way to interrupt the browsing experience with an offer or message is here to stay. Modern pop-ups—perhaps more accurately referred to as "pop-ins"—can slide onto the screen from any direction, float from the top or bottom of content, stay with the viewer as they scroll through your content or landing page, or cover the entire screen when someone brings their cursor toward the "back" or browser exit button. If you can imagine it, someone has probably programmed it. In figure 39, you can see Oats Overnight driving home the point that the 10% off your first order is a limited offer. A pop-in like this should be a bright, eye-catching color and should clearly present the value it's offering. A messy or overly intrusive pop-in that has a muddled message can frustrate traffic to your site and turn people away instead of compelling them to take action.

Diminishing Inventory

Would knowing that there are just a few items left impact your purchase decision? Using visible and diminishing inventory on an offer is a great way to encourage people to take action. Displaying the number of seats available at a concert or presentation, the number of hotel rooms still available at the price advertised, or the stock levels of sale items are all examples of using visibly diminishing inventory to encourage visitors on your site, landing pages, or sales pages to take action.

Countdown Timers

As we discussed in chapter 4, "putting a clock" on a deal is a tried-and-true method of pushing people toward making a decision, especially if the customer feels like they're being offered something extra rather than being pressured into acting fast. These could be offers like free shipping if you order before midnight, flash sales that offer discounts for a very limited amount of time, or offering an incentive like an upgrade, only if an order is completed within a certain short period of time. Figure 40 shows an effective use of a countdown timer in conjunction with a discount to entice customers to take action. This pop-in, with the timer starting at thirty minutes, appears when you attempt to navigate away from the site.

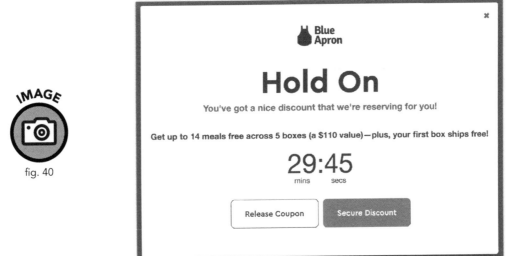

A pop-in from Blue Apron that very effectively pairs a
countdown timer with a compelling discount

Metrics to Measure

To gauge the success of your landing pages, you'll need to track the results of their performance. Without employing this process, it will be difficult to gauge what's working and what's not, which makes it hard to justify your budget or make plans for future spending.

Let's have a look at some of the tools used to measure the effectiveness of landing pages.

Conversion Rate

The *conversion rate* is a measure of the percentage of page visitors who complete a desired action during their visit. If sixty out of one hundred visitors to your landing page handed over their names and email addresses to sign up for your newsletter, for instance, you'd have a 60 percent conversion rate. Conversion rate applies to any action you hope to achieve. It could be newsletter sign-ups, purchases, free trial enrollments, webinar registrations, you name it.

fig. 41

$$\text{CONVERSION RATE} = \frac{\text{CONVERSIONS}}{\text{TOTAL VISITORS}} \times 100$$

Regardless of the desired action, the conversion rate is an important metric in measuring the overall effectiveness of a page. If conversion rates are dropping, it's a sign that something is wrong and there is need for corrective action. If conversion rates increase as adjustments are made, it signals that the changes represent steps in the right direction.

So what's a good conversion rate?

The short answer is "one that is trending upward." The longer answer is that, while it's true that rising conversion rates are almost always better, it's hard to nail down a "good" conversion rate that applies to every situation. Conversion rates depend on a number of factors, and the design of a landing page is only a portion of what triggers visitors to convert and take the desired action. Factors that have little to do with the landing page, such as the fitness of an offer for the audience, page load times, traffic sources, and whether the audience is problem-aware and/or solution-aware, can also impact conversion rate.

A good place to start when contextualizing your conversion rate is to set benchmarks for your performance and compare them to similar industry benchmarks. Once you have a picture of your performance as it roughly compares to that of your competitors, it becomes easier to evaluate your efforts.

Bounce Rate

The conversion rate of a page is a concrete measurement of the portion of visitors who accomplished a specific action. A page's *bounce rate*, on the other hand, can be less telling and harder to gauge. The bounce rate indicates how many people arrived at the page and decided they weren't interested in completing whatever action you were seeking on the landing page or navigating to another part of your website. Essentially, it's the percentage of total visits to a page that result in the visitor leaving the site without exploring further.

Average Time on Page

Average time on page measures exactly what it says: the average amount of time a visitor spends on your pages. It's hard to gauge what is a "good" average time-on-page number, but, generally, the longer you keep your audience engaged with your pages, the better.

When used in conjunction with other metrics like bounce rate and conversion rate, average time on page helps paint a picture of how visitors use the pages on your site. If your bounce rate is very high and average time on page is very low, it indicates a lot of visitors to your page are quickly deciding that it's not their cup of tea and quickly leaving. That's a problem for you as the site owner, but as with most problems, it's probably one that can be addressed and improved.

Form Abandonment Rate

Form abandonment rate is an advanced conversion metric that can offer good insights into your lead capture, opt-in, or checkout forms. If a potential customer starts to fill out a form but doesn't complete it, it's valuable for you to know how and why that happened. Was the form too long? Was the information sought too personal? Did the customer decide at the last minute that the item being checked out was too expensive?

Paying attention to this metric will help you understand the point at which people are giving up on a form, the point at which they are no longer willing to interact with it. If you have a form that asks users to enter their gender, for instance, and users consistently abandon the form at that point, it should be clear that many people do not care to share that information. And, unless there's a compelling reason that you need it, it's a quick fix. Whenever possible, stick to asking for only the most basic information, remembering that once you've got a name and email address you can work from there to obtain more.

As more businesses explore their options in the world of digital marketing, the number of tools and services likewise grows. Leadpages, ClickFunnels, Unbounce, and many, many others are standing by to provide you with a comprehensive set of landing page creation tools that integrate your landing pages into a broader suite of digital marketing tools. Much like Apple's 2011 slogan "there's an app for that," in the world of digital marketing "there's a software solution for that." Digital marketers, even novice ones, don't have to go it alone.

Compliance

Compliance is certainly not the most interesting aspect of digital marketing, but it is an important topic to be aware of. A best practice when thinking about compliance issues is to bake them into your systems from the start. The important thing to remember is that while compliance issues may be an annoyance, they ultimately create trust between consumers and marketers and help keep unscrupulous actors from taking advantage of their customers. This section is by no means an exhaustive summary of the legislation that may impact you as a marketer, but keep these broad strokes in mind when designing your own digital marketing systems.

California Legislation

There are hundreds of data privacy laws among US states and localities, but California recently enacted comprehensive legislation regarding data privacy. This broad legislation has far-reaching import and may very well signal what we can expect on a national level in the future. The California Consumer Privacy Act, cross-sector legislation that became law on the first day of 2020, gives consumers more control over the information businesses collect about them. Major components of the law include these consumer rights:

» The right to know about personal information a business collects and how it is used and shared
» The right to delete personal information that has been collected from them (with some exceptions)
» The right to opt out of a company's ability to sell their information
» The right to nondiscrimination for exercising their rights under the CCPA

Any business that collects information about a California resident, including companies not located in California, must include information in their privacy policies about when and how data is collected and how consumers can access, correct, and delete their private information. Failing to do so can result in big fines—as much as $2,500 per instance—so be sure to pay attention to whether your business may be affected by this legislation.

In a sign that the state is taking this legislation seriously, California recently removed regulation and enforcement of the CCPA away from the state's attorney general and formed a new, independent agency to take over those duties. Also, state residents voted in the November 2020 election to replace the CCPA with another law, the California Privacy Rights Act (CPRA), which places additional responsibility on businesses regarding the handling of personal data. The CPRA is set to go into effect in January 2023. It is the most comprehensive state data privacy legislation enacted to date in the US.

Guidelines for the European Union

Europe has a history of protecting the privacy of individuals that goes back to the 1950 European Convention on Human Rights, which released a statement saying, "Everyone has the right to respect for his private and family life, his home, and his correspondence." The General Data Protection Regulation (GDPR), however, took Europe's privacy concerns to a new level. Put into effect in Europe in 2018, the GDPR was billed as the world's strictest legislature regulating digital privacy. Promising costly fines for both small and large businesses that did not comply, the guidelines captured the attention of marketers across the continent.

The GDPR requires marketers and publishers to request and receive consumer consent before collecting data. At its onset, many feared that it would negatively affect data companies' and businesses' digital marketing efforts. However, the law has had less of an effect than anticipated on how data is collected and used. It turns out that plenty of consumers do provide the consent to share their data if they believe that your brand has something of value to offer.

What this means in practice—among other legal nuances not covered in this text—is that landing pages must do the following:

» Request permission to collect contact information for marketing purposes from people in the European Union. This can be done with a checkbox that provides a clear description of how the contact information will be used and a clear request for permission to collect that information.

» Not "assume consent" by pre-checking any boxes requesting contact information. Traffic must provide positive consent or, put another way, users have to opt in on their own.

Any conversation surrounding compliance and penalties can be scary, especially given the global nature of internet traffic. After all, traffic coming to your landing pages could be from anywhere in the world, including countries in the EU, even if you don't have customers there.

Now that GDPR has been on the books for a few years, solutions have emerged. Tools that help identify and segregate or divert EU users are readily available, and many popular digital marketing solutions have GDPR and other compliance features baked into their service offerings.

Chapter Recap

» A business's website fills a wide variety of roles; an effective site serves as point of contact, an informational resource, a home for owned media, a sales environment, and more.

» A landing page is constructed with a single goal in mind. Although the exact features and content will vary from campaign to campaign, landing pages are single pages with little functionality beyond getting visitors to complete a specific action.

» Headlines, copy, and visual elements work to help keep traffic on your landing page. Social proof helps convert traffic, and a CTA button or form is used to complete the conversion action.

» Opt-in pages, aka squeeze pages, are landing pages dedicated to collecting customer contact information. These pages are most effective when they contain minimal elements and focus on the opt-in conversion action with a simple form that only collects information necessary to deliver value.

» Video sales pages and webinar registration pages are more geared toward prompting an action, including making a purchase.

» Digital marketers need to be aware of compliance issues, legislation, and regulation that governs their actions in digital spaces.

| 7 |

Capturing Traffic

Chapter Overview

- » Effectively using earned media
- » Leveraging SEO to attract traffic
- » When and how to use content as a digital marketer
- » Building traffic through social media

To be a successful digital marketer, you need to be able to connect with potential customers efficiently and cost-effectively. You'll want to create reasons for visitors to check out your products and services. You also should provide opportunities for them to identify themselves so you can begin a conversation. Building or tapping into digital spaces where your prospects are active gets your offerings in front of them for consideration. That's the first step in making a sale—building awareness.

The four best ways to attract and capture traffic are through earned media, SEO, content, and social media.

Attracting Traffic through Earned Media

As you read in chapter 2, earned media, or publicity, is free media coverage. It is content created about your company by those outside your company, and featured in media outlets such as news and current events websites, social media, and podcasts. It is arguably the most valuable form of marketing because it sparks discussions about your brand and the products or services you offer—also known as word of mouth. When media outlets rave about your products or mention your services, consumers learn more about your business and are likely to be motivated to pay you a visit.

That's how you get traffic. Free traffic! Earned media carries some risks, like the lack of control you have over the exact content of the discussions or coverage, but the payoff can be big when the content is positive.

One of the easiest ways to attract earned media is to learn about stories reporters and writers are working on. What are they interested in for which you might be a source, or a quoted expert? To connect with journalists, you can monitor source requests they distribute. Many use online platforms to announce their information needs and ask that qualified sources get in touch. Let's look at some of the most popular platforms used by journalists:

> » **Help a Reporter Out (HARO), helpareporter.com**
> This free service disseminates three emails daily, Monday through Friday, often offering dozens of opportunities to be quoted. Respond when your background or experience matches what the journalist or writer is requesting, and you could earn some positive media mentions.

> » **ProfNet, profnet.com**
> This service is geared more for public relations firms and a corporate audience and, consequently, there is a sizeable fee to get into the game. But the basic service rendered is similar to others, in that subscribers receive emails containing lists of sources journalists are seeking.

> » **Qwoted, qwoted.com**
> This relatively new service has a free version, like HARO, but allows a wider variety of requests from media outlets.

> » **Twitter, twitter.com**
> Twitter offers a wealth of insight into current events. So much so that it can be overwhelming. As a resource for finding earned media opportunities, you can often find journalists or other content creators searching for sources by using the hashtag #source or #jouralisticsource or #journalistquote. The results may not always be a perfect fit for your earned media needs, but it can be a great way to start a conversation.

This approach is reactive—waiting until a reporter expresses a need. But you can also be more proactive, sending out information to reporters in the hope they will take the bait and write about you or your business. This approach has a lower return on investment (ROI), because your success often involves getting the timing right and it can take a significant amount of time on your part.

Below are some of the most popular tools for issuing promotional messages about your business:

- » Press releases
- » Press or media kits
- » Tip sheets
- » Media alerts

Not sure when to create media materials? Normally, news is shared when there is something notable to announce. Some newsworthy reasons include the following:

- » Your business earns an honor or award
- » An employee wins a professional honor or award
- » You hire a new employee
- » You've moved your offices
- » You've created a new free report
- » You've landed a new round of financing

You can even opt to pay a wire service to disseminate your news, which increases the odds that it will appear somewhere online. Here are a few of the best wire services:

- » eReleases
- » PRWeb
- » PR Newswire
- » Business Wire

Earned media can help get your name in the news, giving you an opportunity to build on the coverage. If you can develop a good relationship with a reporter or editor, your releases may be more enthusiastically received than those from someone unknown to them. Learn about the publishing guidelines of various news or feature outlets. The less work a reporter has to do to make your story compatible with publishing guidelines, the more likely it is that your press release will appear. Use an earned media win to spark more coverage or more media opportunities, which can increase your visibility online. And *that* can help you capture more traffic.

NOTE

With many news organizations around the country in decline and facing significant staff cuts, the opportunity for getting your news out has, in many cases, expanded. With less staff available to seek out and cover stories, publications are relying more heavily on submitted news, which includes press releases and other sources.

Search Engine Optimization (SEO)

Earned media strategies require a significant amount of work on the part of marketers. From crafting media materials and press releases to pounding the digital pavement, every instance of earned media is hard won. SEO practices, on the other hand, have the ultimate goal of capturing traffic at scale. When someone enters a query into Google's search bar, they are looking for a solution. The content of their question also identifies their wants and needs in the moment. A person indicating their wants and needs? This scenario presents a perfect opportunity for digital marketers to provide value. If a marketer can indicate to Google that they have the best solution to the searcher's problem, that marketer will be rewarded with prominent placement in the search results that Google returns.

A complete exploration of the topic of SEO is beyond the scope of this book. An entire book could be written about the intricacies of a sophisticated SEO strategy. Indeed, SEO has become so integral to the marketing ambitions of modern businesses that major brands have dedicated SEO managers, and "SEO professional" has emerged as a lucrative career path for web developers and marketers who specialize in the discipline. Consider the material in this chapter an SEO crash course that will set you and your brand up for success. The fundamentals and best practices covered here are the foundation of successful SEO efforts now and for years to come.

Appearing on the first page of search results or, better yet, in the number one result spot, without paying for ad placement is a cost-effective way to capture a large share of highly relevant search volume. With a robust strategy in place, this source of traffic from Google and other search engines can be converted into paying customers using methods that run nearly on autopilot.

No website or organization is simply handed the coveted number one spot, however. Competition is fierce, especially for search topics that experience a high volume of searches. *Search engine optimization* (SEO) is the practice of using a combination of technical and nontechnical methods to encourage search engines to organically rank your content higher in specific search results.

SEO specialist organization Moz estimates that first-page results can capture as much as 91 percent of search traffic for a given term. Results on the second page capture just 6 percent.

The pages that return search results once a query has been submitted are referred to as **SERPs** (search engine result pages) and there are two ways marketers can achieve high SERP visibility: organic and paid. When we talk about organic results, we are referring to those the search engine has determined to be a perfect response to whatever search was entered. Organic results are not ads, so you do not pay for them.

NOTE

A sophisticated digital strategy reflects both paid and unpaid SERP placement; however, unpaid organic results can significantly stretch marketing dollars and have the added benefit of perceived authenticity over sponsored or paid results.

QUESTION

Q: How do digital marketers create and distribute content that gets organically ranked?

In the early days of the internet, search engines relied primarily on keywords. If a keyword in the search query was present on the page (along with some other indicators), it was likely some degree of a match for the search query. That relatively simple process made it easy for search marketers to find ways to make the search engine think their site should appear at the top of the search—regardless of whether it really was related to the query entered in the search box. Today's search engines are substantially more sophisticated and much smarter about identifying which content is of high quality and relevant to the solution a searcher is seeking.

To retain its lion's share of the internet search market, Google faces a complicated task. Its systems must interpret the query that is put into the search bar, sift through the mind-bogglingly vast library—known as a *search index*—of web pages and sites Google has compiled, and return only the most relevant results. This last step is particularly important because a search engine that returns results that are unhelpful or irrelevant will fall into obscurity in short order.

Search intent is the umbrella term that describes the ultimate goal of a search engine user, or the solution they're looking for by searching with the particular phrase they used. Since the only window a search engine has into a person's search intent is the phrase entered into the search bar, search intent is sometimes referred to as "keyword intent."

For example, a search query of "cheap hotels in Philadelphia" has clear search intent to us as humans, but Google's engineers have the unenviable task of crafting an algorithm that picks the perfect result and places it first. The next most perfect result is placed second, and so on. With the sheer size and scope of today's content-packed internet, it is no longer enough to simply produce a list of sites that are related to a few choice keywords in the search query. This means that as digital marketers attempting to optimize for search results, we live and die by search algorithms.

To this end, *search engines reward content that responds to search intent.* Search engines like Google are largely indifferent to exactly which sites end up in the SERPs. The company uses a complex system of search and ranking algorithms, which are constantly updated and changed. The exact machinations that power these algorithms are closely guarded secrets to protect the integrity of the product. If just anyone can game the SEO system, then Google instantly loses its credibility as an impartial source of information, loses users, and loses revenue. If someone figures out how to get around the algorithms, low-quality websites and unrelated, spammy content can appear in more prominent positions of the organic content than they should, making for a not-so-great user experience. That's why Google tweaks—in both large and small ways—their algorithms an estimated 500-600 times per year.

These algorithm changes drive the SEO crowd crazy, but it's important to understand that, regardless of the specific SEO best practices in play, Google encourages and rewards high-quality sites that perform well on its search engine. If a search engine, Google or otherwise, lets you know that SEO tactics used in the past no longer work or that different factors now have different weights, take this guidance to heart.

There is no shortage of resources for the aspiring DIY SEO expert, and there's an army of freelancers standing by to lend a hand if you have the budget available. Start with the basic stuff and work your way up as you gain knowledge and experience about how to improve rankings. Nobody is born understanding SEO, but most of us can learn the fundamentals pretty easily.

Q: Do search and SEO really matter outside of Google? What about Google alternatives?

In this book and in SEO circles, Google is usually the search engine that receives the most focus. Google is far and away the leader in online searches, and this appears unlikely to change. Some sharp-elbowed competitors have carved out their own spaces in the search engine marketplace, however. These Google alternatives come and go—think Ask Jeeves—and some have managed to hold their own, like Microsoft's Bing. At the time of writing, emergent privacy-focused engine DuckDuckGo, which does not track search history and blocks advertising trackers, has gained a dedicated following.

Together, Google alternatives have a presence that should not be dismissed. Generally speaking, however, these search engines will mimic the aspects of Google that make it useful and successful. This means that best practices for Google will often translate into best practices for their competitors. This can be confirmed through testing and experimentation, but for the sake of simplicity, in this book we will often refer to Google in place of the variety of available search engines.

SEO for Two Sets of Readers

For sites that want to tackle their own SEO efforts, it's important to remember that content is produced for two sets of "readers." The first is search engines. They read your site so its contents can be added to their site index. Making your site easy to read and catalog for search engines is the first step toward obtaining high SERP ranking. The other set of readers is humans. They are the people entering the search terms, demonstrating search intent, and actively consuming the content that you produce.

As you just read, whether you are attempting SEO yourself or outsourcing your efforts to an agency or freelancer, it's important to stay in touch with the latest insights from the industry, as things change often and quickly. The basic concepts of responding to search intent, for example, or producing content that provides value and is easily consumable, are not likely to change anytime soon.

Optimizing for Machine Readers

Search engines don't have eyes (for the foreseeable future anyway). For this reason, the way they "read" sites is a little different than the way you and I do; search engines return their results from a compiled search index. This index is a massive catalog of everything on the surface web with a web address. This means sites, pages, videos, images—you name it. The *surface web* is the part of the internet that can be indexed by search engines. This is distinct from the *deep web* and the *dark web*. Pages on the deep web mostly consist of dynamically created pages (such as payment confirmation pages) or pages that exist behind passwords. The deep web is a function of today's web-enabled society. It would be a privacy disaster if, for example, the contents of your bank account would simply appear in a Google search. The same goes for other sensitive information or content that sites put behind a paywall.

The dark web, on the other hand, is on an entirely different network from the publicly accessible internet, though it works in much the same way. It has its own sites, pages, and even search engines, but does not integrate with the surface web directly. A surface search engine attempting to index a site on the dark web is like a person attempting to walk from the United States to Europe. You may know the address of your destination, but you can't simply stroll over there. At the time of writing, the dark web has a fraction of a fraction of the number of sites and pages the surface web has indexed. It is generally much slower than the surface web, and many consumers don't have browsers that allow them to access the dark web network in the first place.

Before we dive into the ways you can make your site and its content search engine friendly, it's important to understand the ways in which search engines like Google actually go about indexing your site.

Spiders

Tasking humans with indexing the internet is obviously out of the question. Search engines use **web crawlers**, which are internet bots that systematically browse and explore the internet and report their findings with index entries. Because these bots "crawl the web" they are often referred to as spiders (figure 42). When indexing, a spider will start by accessing a site. As it browses all the files in the site directory, it records the contents of each page, excluding pages that are disallowed for indexing or pages it cannot access. It also takes note of all the links on each page, what the link text says, and the link's destination.

A spider at work!

GRAPHIC

fig. 42

With this information recorded, the bot begins following the links that are available for indexing, and the process starts over when it reaches a new site. This ongoing protocol produces a map of the indexable surface web—the contents of web pages, how they relate to one another via links, and key information that will later be used to determine which results belong where in SERPs.

With an understanding of how machines read sites and their contents, let's dive into how you can optimize your site for machine readers (bots). Google doesn't index the surface web as a hobby. The results returned by Google spiders inform their index, which, in turn, is essential to Google's business objective of returning the perfect result for every possible query.

SEO efforts are broken into three general categories: technical, on page, and off page. *Technical SEO* refers to sitewide efforts designed to make the entire domain more accessible to search engine spiders, including site structure, site load speed, internal linking, and other factors. *On-page SEO* refers to content optimization on individual pages of a site. This generally consists of keyword optimization (researching and choosing the best keywords for your page) and user-experience-related best practices. *Off-page SEO* consists of SEO efforts to drive traffic to a site and generate a variety of backlinks. Each of these types of SEO is covered separately in this chapter.

Technical SEO

Technical SEO efforts are largely comprised of the steps that site owners take to make their sites more technically robust. If that's something that sounds daunting or out of your wheelhouse, there is no shortage of tools that can help close the knowledge gap and bring your site up to snuff. Let's take a look at some of the core aspects of technical SEO.

Rock-Solid Page Structure

From a bot's perspective, your website exists as a directory of files, resources, and, in many cases, a database on a server. Now that we've reviewed the way bots record your site, you can understand how sites with poor structure, dead ends, or other technical issues can make it tough for bots to do their job. Site issues such as broken links and poor loading times are logged by indexing bots and reflected in that site's index entry. In some cases, these types of issues can even prohibit bots from completely indexing a site—meaning portions of it that the owner *wants* to appear in search results will be omitted. If a site has a complicated or nonsensical design as opposed to a hierarchal, topic-based design, spiders can get confused or fail to make the right connections between different site topics. URLs with nonsensical numbers, hashtags, or symbols may be ignored or at least present additional challenges for indexing bots.

This is important because any site structure issues will be logged and will cause points to be deducted from the site's quality score, which is rated on a scale of 1 to 10 and takes a large number of factors into account. Consequently, when it comes time for Google's algorithm to match search results to a query, entries with low quality scores will be passed over. Low-quality results appear much deeper in the SERPs, or perhaps not at all.

For this reason, sound site structure is a fundamental aspect of technical SEO. Fortunately, contemporary content management platforms like WordPress, Squarespace, Wix, and just about any other site builder out there are designed to produce technically sound sites and pages in a no code / low code environment. If you are working with a developer, ensure that they understand your SEO needs. Getting things built the right way the first time around can save you a considerable amount of work down the road.

Site Speed

For better or worse, today's internet users are impatient. The simple truth is that users aren't willing to wait for your content, no matter how good it might be. To this end, Google and other search engines prioritize search results that load quickly—especially results that load quickly on phones and tablets. If internet users want content as fast as they can click or tap on the link to it, then that's what search engines will strive to provide. This is a clear example of how efforts to optimize your site for machine readers also optimize it for human readers. Site load speed is recorded by the search engine's spider as it crawls the web and is tested every time a user attempts to access your site. If the site takes too long to load, the user will simply abandon their attempt and look for an answer to their question elsewhere.

NOTE

This may not apply across the board, but it's estimated that the attention span of an average website user falls somewhere around eight seconds. If there's not a solution to their problem in eight seconds, they're looking elsewhere. Keep in mind, this eight-second window includes page load times. Every second your page takes to load eats into those eight seconds of attention. In fact, recent data suggests that as much as 40 percent of the people who access your site will expect it to load in two seconds or less.

Site speed is an eternal struggle. On one hand, conventional best practices dictate that the most engaging and effective sites are packed with video and high-resolution images. On the other hand, if mismanaged, these elements can drag down page delivery times and result in significant speed losses. These speed losses are even more acute when users attempt to access data-heavy sites via mobile devices. For many digital marketers, site speed issues can seem like an inscrutable black hole of technical expertise. Content management software (CMS) platforms can provide the answer.

As CMS platforms have become more robust and developed into sophisticated solutions for organizations of all sizes, so too have the ways in which websites are stored and presented. A quality CMS will draw on the latest and greatest web design techniques to help you build a site that looks great but doesn't sacrifice speed. Additionally, because of the immense importance placed on site speed as an SEO ranking factor—and the downside of lost traffic that results from poor site speed—freelance developers and designers are specializing in speed-focused services. The bottom line? The tools exist for you to succeed as a digital marketer even if coding isn't your strong suit.

Even Google wants to help you succeed. While the company is protective of specific details regarding its algorithms, at time of writing it offers the Google speed test and page optimizer tools that will crawl a URL you provide and return page diagnostics along with recommendations to improve your score. As noted earlier, it's in Google's best interests to have an internet brimming with high-quality web pages—their bots can better catalog the surface web and their SERPs will include fewer low-quality sites. It's a win-win-win proposition for Google, website owners, and people using Google to find solutions to their problems.

Q: What can you do to make your site faster?

Considering the rate of change affecting online technology, it's hard to be prescriptive without immediately dating this text. It is my opinion, however, that every little effort you make can help improve your site. Simply compressing images you upload, something that can be done easily using free tools, is a good start. Hosting video on third-party platforms such as YouTube, Vimeo, or Wistia can reduce the weight of data your page sends while ensuring that videos remain high in quality and responsive to users' devices.

Some digital marketers don't think as much as they should about the **web hosting company** they use. A web host or hosting service provider owns and rents out space on their servers to businesses or individuals that own a website. The directory files, images, video, and databases that power a website must exist on a server somewhere in order to be accessible to internet users, but not all servers (and not all hosting services) are created equal. Pairing technical speed upgrades with a speed-oriented host is a solid foundation upon which to build your SEO efforts.

Mobile First

A decade ago, most of the internet traffic occurred on desktops or laptops, with relatively little happening on phones or other devices. In today's age of internet-enabled refrigerators, televisions, and voice-activated home assistants, the share of web traffic that comes from traditional computers (desktops and laptops) has significantly decreased. It has decreased so much, in fact, that in the summer of 2019 Google announced it would begin indexing all new sites from a "mobile-first" perspective.

Mobile-first indexing means Google's bots will first analyze site pages as they'll appear on a phone or tablet before analyzing how they'll look on a desktop or laptop. This means that if your site is not optimized for mobile, claiming the coveted number one spot in Google's SERPs will be an uphill battle. We have all seen pages not optimized for mobile and know how frustrating they can be. Text size can be so small you have to squint to read it, or so large only a few words fill a line of text and cause endless scrolling. Images get cut off, squashed, stretched, or abruptly pop in and disrupt the text. Video can be slow to load, and playback is interrupted by frequent buffering.

Currently, the two main methods used to optimize sites and pages for mobile are responsive design and mobile-specific sites.

Responsive design is a method of web design that uses flexible layouts, flexible image sizes, and other flexible elements to render a web page based on the page visitor's screen size and device rather than on a set, static page. Responsive design comes standard with today's CMS platforms and is a favorite among digital marketers. Essentially, you just build a page once and publish it. Once live, it can be accessed on virtually any screen and always scales correctly to ensure that images, text, and general page layout are easy to read, easy to navigate, and never look ugly or unprofessional.

An alternative to responsive design is to build a mobile-specific version of a site. As a user navigates to the site, a snippet of code identifies what kind of device they're using and serves either a desktop site or a mobile site. This method requires more work, but sophisticated developers often prefer it. It allows a highly refined design approach that controls every aspect of the mobile experience instead of relying on responsive design to output what it "thinks" is the best experience. In either case, Google's bots take the overall mobile experience into account when indexing, so a page that delivers a subpar mobile experience will be penalized.

TECHNICAL SEO	
SITE STRUCTURE	• Working internal links • URL structures that make sense • Hierarchal site structure
SITE SPEED	• Compressed images • Optimized hosting • Video hosting services
MOBILE EXPERIENCE	• Pages load quickly • Responsive design provides flexible layouts • Text is readable and the overall experience is smooth

GRAPHIC

fig. 43

On-Page SEO

As mentioned earlier, on-page SEO is the practice of optimizing content on a page-by-page basis. These efforts mostly have to do with keyword optimization, readability, and content depth. ***Content depth*** refers to the length and quality of the content on a page. A page with one hundred words, three dozen links to unrelated topics, and no images is considered thin or shallow content. If you were searching for information and a thin page was returned as the first result, you would be pretty disappointed—the page would likely be useless.

Content Depth

Thin or shallow content goes against every pillar of the value-forward thinking that should be core to your digital marketing strategy. It provides little to no value for its audience. It does not provide answers and is unappealing, unengaging, and possibly completely unrelated to search intent. In short, it's spam (or worse).

As you develop your own SEO and content strategies and test different approaches, you'll notice that a value-forward mindset produces the most successes, time and again. Yet thin content persists on the internet—why? The biggest reason is that it's cheap. It is almost always cheaper to cut corners and sacrifice quality than to take the time needed to provide value to your audience. Thin content operates by following the law of large numbers. If enough people are directed to cheap, thin content, even a couple of people who convert can pay for the content and produce a trickle of revenue.

Thin content can also be produced by novice digital marketers who are unaware of best practices; who overextend their budgets, which forces them to sacrifice quality; or who are simply lazy. Search engines classify content as thin for a number of reasons:

» The page contains mainly links to other content, with little other text (this is considered highly suspicious).

» The list of links likely doesn't correspond to a user's search intent (the page is probably spam).

» There is duplicate content, content that is nonsensical, content that exists simply to house **affiliate links**, and content that is too short to provide a helpful response to search intent.

» The page contains a range of disparate topics that don't provide answers to any one question.

NOTE

Affiliate links are promotional links that point to a product or service. Embedded in each link is a tracking number. If a visitor clicks on a link containing an affiliate's tracking number and makes a purchase, that affiliate receives a percentage of the sale or a flat fee, depending on the nature of the arrangement. Needless to say, a page filled only with spammy affiliate links likely does not respond to search intent or provide value to the visitor.

Thin content doesn't need to be a problem if you simply start producing content with search intent in mind. If your content addresses the questions and concerns of those visiting your site, you won't need to spend hours worrying about SEO in general and thin content in particular. Another way to keep your content from being labeled as thin is to adhere to content length best practices.

Content Length

Content length has been the subject of spirited debate in the content marketing community. Let's start with the basics. Current guidelines dictate that every page on your site that you want to rank should contain a minimum of three hundred words. Any less, and search engines (understandably) are skeptical that the page can adequately respond to user search intent. Common sense might then indicate the longer the page content, the better. However, some tests from content marketing companies suggest otherwise. Finding a balance between content that speaks to search intent and content that solves a problem for your audience while not overwhelming them with a wall of text or too many details is an ongoing challenge for digital marketers.

Start by ensuring that you have, in fact, solved a problem in your content, and go from there. Who is this content for? By building content around search intent, digital marketers can better understand an appropriate length for it and be assured that it solves any problems users might encounter.

EXAMPLE

When writing content designed to speak to the key phrase "best wireless earbuds," you might start by outlining some criteria readers should use when shopping around, and then profile some popular brands and their pros and cons. Once this has been achieved, you might very well find you had no trouble meeting the content length minimum. On the other hand, if the key phrase was "how do wireless earbuds work," more content might be required to sufficiently answer the implicit search intent, with discussions of audio fidelity, wireless data transfer, and ergonomics.

Multimedia-Rich Content

People respond to images and video. The more multimedia you can pack into your pages, the better, though there is a limit. It is still important to keep load speed and minimum length parameters in mind. Search engines see content that features numerous images, video, and other multimedia as more engaging, and so will your site visitors. Of course, images or other multimedia that are unrelated to page content, are offensive or inappropriate, or contain missing or broken links can count against you when your pages are crawled by indexing bots.

Think about sites that you trust and visit on a regular basis. In what ways do they creatively express their brand? In what ways do they enticingly convey their message? How do they ask you to take action? For those who aren't confident creatives, digital solutions abound. Stock photo libraries offer high-quality, professional images to enhance content, lead magnets, and site pages. Freelance designers are standing by on marketplaces such as Upwork and Fiverr. And for DIY digital marketers, simplified image editors such as Canva can be indispensable. Canva is part stock photo library, part editor, and part template service designed specifically for image creation needs, with professional results for today's content-driven internet.

One of the most overlooked SEO aspects of images is undefined alt text (alternative text). ***Alt text*** is descriptive text attached to images for vision-impaired site visitors. This text is embedded in the code that makes up your web page and is not normally rendered on the page. It's there for screen-reader software, which processes and reads aloud the text of a website for the vision-impaired. Screen-reader software is not yet sophisticated enough to recognize and describe images without explicit descriptions, which are what alt text provides.

MY TAKE

Not only is the inclusion of alt text looked upon favorably by search engines, it is simply the right thing to do. Vision-impaired users should be able to experience all the content the internet has to offer, just like any other internet user. Your CMS probably has an easy step-by-step walk-through for adding alt text to your images.

Off-Page SEO (Links)

Links are the circulatory system—the veins and arteries—of the internet. They transport traffic from site to site and page to page. As Google and other search engines see it, links play another important role. If I own a website and I know I'm able to earn traffic only if my audience finds my site and its content valuable, then any links I make to other content are seen as endorsements of that content. This is the thinking behind Google's focus on links—the more links that point to a page or a site, theoretically, the more value that page or site has to offer.

Gary's Great Golf Shop is my business, and I own and maintain its website. I know that my customers frequent the website to check out and purchase the excellent equipment I sell at discount prices, but they also visit because I provide a curated collection of links to golfing advice from top pros, schedules for upcoming PGA and LPGA events, weather reports for tournament sites, and other valuable information. By providing links to those particular sources, I am, effectively, endorsing the sites users are directed to.

However, not all links are created equal. Links from reputable sites are more valuable than links from sites that Google has identified as being of poor quality. In fact, links from websites that are considered spammy or of otherwise low quality can detract from your site's overall score. Because linking is such an integral part of achieving a high SERP result, there is no shortage of digital tools to help you analyze the links pointing to your site, the links within your site, and links on your site that point to other sites. These tools help identify linking opportunities, help you acquire high-quality links, and help you sniff out low-quality links that may be hurting your site's reputation in the eyes of Google.

fig. 44

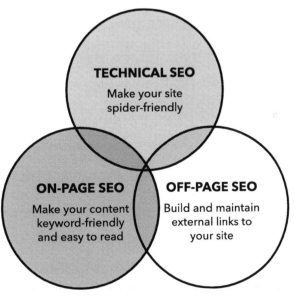

Optimizing for Human Readers

Providing content your audience wants to read, watch, listen to, or interact with is your main focus when optimizing for those visiting your web pages.

Readability

Content that is easily readable on a variety of device screens is a must, but readability goes deeper than selecting a font that is smooth or not too crowded. Using brief paragraphs, writing economically, and focusing on a single topic means visitors to your page will more likely find the information they were looking for quickly. Use clear headings and present information in a logical progression. Avoid jargon and try to present everything in the simplest terms possible, preferably at a high school reading level.

NOTE

Keeping content at a reading level users understand is important and often overlooked. Consider that *USA Today* is written at a tenth-grade reading level. More startling is that The Joint Commission, an organization that accredits medical facilities, recommends that the readability of all patient education materials be kept to a fifth-grade level or below.

Responding to Search Intent

When creating content for human audiences, it's important to consider search intent, or what information people are hoping to find in response to their search queries. The closer you can come to answering their questions or delivering the information they're after, the more effective your website is in the eyes of Google, and your target audience.

Encouraging Action

Content is meant to both help individuals find the information they're after and persuade them to act on what they read. When writing for human readers, your goal should be to draw them toward a call to action that converts, whether that's downloading a report, requesting a quote, or clicking on the Shop or Buy button.

A difference between human readers and indexing bots is that humans typically want to do something with information they've searched for, while bots just want to figure out what's on your site. To make life easier for human readers, give them the information they're after *and* make it easy for them to use that information to take the next step, such as making a reservation or a purchase—whatever makes the most sense for the topic at hand.

Keywords

In the early days of search-based marketing, unscrupulous site owners would jam as many instances as possible of their targeted keyword into the text of a page, whether it belonged there—or even made sense—or not. This is known as keyword stuffing and engaging in this practice today is a good way to get your site penalized by search engines. Nonetheless, keywords are still one of the most important signals search engines use to determine what a site or page is about and whether it's a good fit for a particular search intent query.

Long Tail vs. Fat Head

Keyword popularity is generally determined by how frequently a word or phrase is used in searches. For example, the word "baseball" is very likely searched more frequently than "curling," just as a general word like "cake" is probably more popular than "pumpkin chocolate chip cookies." More specific keywords and phrases, which are searched for less frequently than popular, more general search terms, are referred to as "long-tail" keywords.

Because long-tails are much more specific, the likelihood of a search resulting in conversion is much higher. That is to say that the individual searching for a long-tail keyword is probably closer to an action, such as a purchase. Someone who types "women's cotton cable-knit sweater" has narrowed her search, knows what she wants, and is probably much closer to making a purchase than someone searching for "sweater." As you can see in figure 45, long-tail keywords make up the majority of searches overall, even though each one attracts less traffic on an individual basis than a fat-head keyword.

A fat-head keyword is, essentially, the opposite of a long-tail. Fat-head keywords are very popular and prevalent, typically because they are very general. "University" is a fat-head keyword, "University of North Carolina Wilmington" is a longer tail, and "University of North Carolina Wilmington Computer Science Department" is even more so. Although fat-head keywords get vast amounts of search traffic, the SERP results for those terms don't always contain the information the person's looking for. Someone who searches for "university," for instance, could be looking for a job, tuition rates, an idea of how hard it is to gain admission, or directions to a campus. The search intent is difficult to determine because the keyword is so broad and vague.

THE SEARCH DEMAND CURVE

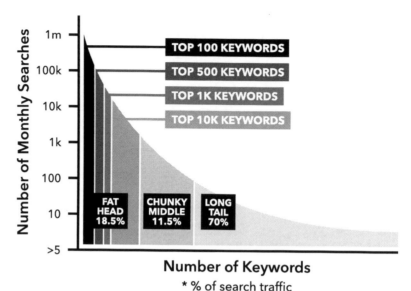

fig. 45

Source: BrightLocal.com

What Does It Take to "Own" a Keyword?

"Owning" a keyword means your content reliably appears near the top of the SERPs for a specific search query. Truly owning a keyword—or key phrase—means that the top several results for that search query point to your content—an enviable position for any brand to be in. Search for "houses for sale" and it's a good bet the first sites you'll see are Zillow, realtor.com, and Trulia. And yes, those are all big companies, but there is room near the top of the SERPs for your business as well. Owning a keyword or key phrase should be your long-term goal and is achievable if you continue to publish content related to the keyword or phrase while also adhering to technical, on-page, and off-page SEO best practices. Focus on long-tail keywords that relate to your product or service. This is where you can outmaneuver larger sites and grow the number of keywords you reliably rank highly for.

Content Is King

In a 1996 essay, Microsoft cofounder Bill Gates predicted that content delivery would become one of the most lucrative and widespread uses of the internet. He wrote from the perspective of Microsoft's participation in the content delivery aspects of the internet, but he also made an astute observation regarding the scale of opportunity afforded by an interconnected world. "No company," Gates asserted, "is too small to participate." Looking back more than two decades later, Gates's prediction has come true many times over.

As defined in chapter 1, content marketing is the practice of creating, publishing, and distributing specific content for targeted online audiences. It is a form of inbound marketing that is a soft sell—never overly promotional. Due to its success and wide adoption by digital marketers in every industry, content marketing is so prevalent in the online space that digital consumers now *expect* your brand to offer helpful and valuable content.

Content marketing is extremely cost-effective and wildly versatile. It's the first rung of the value ladder, it can generate leads and drive opt-ins, it informs and powers SEO, and it helps to develop and refine the customer avatar.

What Is Content?

So much online material can be considered content that it might be more productive to ask, What *isn't* content? Each individual piece of content, whether a blog post or a YouTube video, is referred to as a **content asset**. Before we discuss what is *not* content, let's look at the high-level categories of content.

- » **Written Content:** Written content commonly includes e-books, blog posts, and other types of posts, articles, and transcriptions of interviews. Interviews may rely primarily on audio or visual components, but it is currently an SEO best practice to include text-based transcripts of interviews. Doing so not only adds keywords to your page, but it reduces the chances of your page being labeled as thin content.

- » **High-Value Content:** This kind of written content is usually reserved for use as lead magnets due to its perceived higher value. Longer or more sophisticated e-books, robust case studies, relevant reports on an issue, helpful checklists, and actionable executive summaries all constitute high-value content.

- » **Images:** Generally speaking, the more images used, the better. Internet users expect instant gratification and maximum value for a minimal amount of work. An image-rich web page is far more appealing than a static wall of text, and value-added images such as infographics and visual step-by-step instructions are great uses of visual media. Some playful brands can get away with using memes or other humorous images to augment their content as well, but those won't work for everyone and if incorrectly deployed can be a brand liability. Moving images in the form of GIFs (short for graphics interchange format) can be a great way to liven up content. GIFs can be easily created from existing video files or from a sequence of images. They take considerably less time to load than most video content, but as video players and online environments continue to develop, that could change.

» **Video**: As you've read numerous times already, video is the holy grail of content, because it's highly engaging and plays to the instant gratification experience your users expect. Today's online video players are fast, responsive (they shrink and grow to fit a variety of screens), and deliver crystal-clear playback. Popular formats include how-to videos, "explainers" that break down complicated topics, interviews, animated shorts, long- and short-form advertisements, faux newscasts or semi-journalistic presentations, and product demos. A major component of video content is cost. Bigger-budget video content that bigger companies can afford to bankroll, which can include celebrities or paid actors, is eye-catching and popular, but the cost of a single video can surpass multiple annual content budgets of smaller businesses. So for smaller companies, video needs to be deployed as strategically as possible. When incorporating video into your content strategy, think long and hard about how to get the most bang for your buck.

Q: What about physical content?

Most digital marketers stick with digital content because it costs a lot less than physical content to produce, maintain, and deliver. Once a case study has been researched and written, for instance, you can make it available for download at no additional cost. There are no printing or shipping costs associated with delivery, and the entire process can be put on autopilot.

Physical content, on the other hand, needs to be shipped as members of your audience request it. They'll have to wait for the case study to be delivered instead of downloading it immediately. Physical content can cost a lot to prepare and deliver. That doesn't mean, however, that there is never a place for it. Colleges spend good money producing and mailing alumni magazines to graduates because it helps keep recipients interested in and loyal to their alma maters, which encourages donations and legacy applications in ways that a digital download likely never could. Books are another example of a valuable marketing tool. If your competition is only offering a PDF download and you are offering to send a whole book, who do you think seems to be presenting a better offer? Often, a physical product you can touch and hold has a higher perceived value than a PDF. This discussion about content leads us back to the question posed at the beginning of this section—what isn't content? The answer is short and simple: content marketing!

Content and content marketing are not synonymous. Content assets such as blog posts and product demo videos are not inherently strategic. The strategy lies in the ways these assets are used to achieve business goals. In the next section we take a closer look at the foundations of a content strategy and how it fits into a larger conversation surrounding your overall digital marketing strategy.

The Strategic Role of Content

From a strategic perspective, content serves as a means to an end. Unless you are selling your content as a membership site, books, courses, or presentations, it plays a very specific role in converting your audience into customers and ascending them along your value ladder.

Smart Content Starts with Why

As with any other business asset, content assets should be created with an objective in mind. This is not only true of the content asset itself—an article needs to get to the point where it delivers value—but content assets should also fill strategic roles in your marketing strategy. The more strategic roles a single content asset can fill, the better. That doesn't mean that any one content asset is a silver bullet. It's never a bad idea to think creatively to get the most out of your content assets, but trying to accomplish a goal with content that wasn't purpose-built for it can lead to underperformance.

Let's say you own an online sporting goods store and, as always, you're looking to increase sales. A creative way to do so might be to come up with alternative uses for items in your inventory that will enable you to reach new customers. Physical therapists use lacrosse balls, tennis balls, and squash balls for massage and to assist patients with stretching exercises, a technique that can be employed at home. An article explaining how this is done, accompanied by instructional images (or better yet, video) of stretches anyone can do at home would serve as a content asset geared toward a specific goal.

More Is Better

Building a good content inventory is fundamental to achieving content marketing success. There's a limit, but, generally speaking, you can't have too many content assets. Having a sizable quantity of varied content on hand increases the size of your digital dragnet. Plus, the more content you have, the more choices you'll have when starting a new campaign. Of course, more content translates to increased costs. If you're creating content yourself or relying on one or two others, it may take some time to build up a large library.

While a healthy inventory of content assets is good, it's important to keep two best practices in mind.

1. Quantity should never trump quality. Low-quality content assets, even if you have an entire library of them, will ultimately undermine your content marketing strategy and cannibalize your efforts. This is true even in cases where low-quality content produces results in the short term.

2. When producing content assets, specialization is the name of the game. Producing multiple assets that seek to fill the same role will often split the difference regarding performance. Each content asset should be built to fill a specific role in your digital marketing strategy. In most cases you'll get better results when you build new content assets tailored to new goals instead of stretching existing content toward those goals.

Content Should Be Mapped to Journeys

For digital marketers, content is key to content marketing success. From the perspective of your audience and customers, however, content is created to speak to their pain points, their search intent, and other aspects of their customer avatars. That becomes especially relevant when the message of the content matches your audience's stage of the buying process. That measure of awareness is often referred to as the "temperature" of your audience.

Content and Audience Temperature

Audience temperature is a loose estimation of the level of awareness your audience has regarding their own pain points, the solutions to those pain points, and the solution you offer. Very cold audiences are not only completely unaware of your brand or the products you offer, but they're unaware of *any* products or services that could solve their problem. They can even be problem-unaware, meaning they don't have the problem you are able to solve or they are experiencing it but don't know it. In other words, cold audiences have no need for your product or are not aware of their need.

Q: How can someone be unaware of a problem in their lives?

Think back to our discussion of pain points in chapter 3 and how they often must be coaxed out of people. Before the invention of digital music players, people didn't realize they wanted an MP3 player—CDs were just the way things were. Those folks were a very cold audience to MP3 players, and early on they needed to know more about what MP3 players did, or how they were superior to CDs. As more competitive products emerged, advertising and messaging changed to acknowledge that audiences understood what a digital music player was, and the focus was shifted to brand differentiators or other selling points.

Hot audiences are your existing customers or people who are about to become your customers. They are acutely aware of their problem and of the solutions available. They understand exactly who you are and how your products or services can provide a solution to their problem.

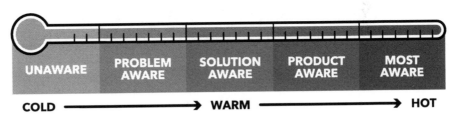

fig. 46

Customers advance across a continuum of awareness as audience
temperature—and product or solution awareness—increases

Everyone your marketing efforts reach falls somewhere on this scale. Between hot and cold, the customer journey exists in degrees of awareness. Audience members who have warmed a bit from being completely unaware may now be problem-aware and realize they need a solution to the problem, but not aware of the specific solutions that exist.

Using our earlier example of a sporting goods store attempting to sell lacrosse balls as stretching and massage aids, we can see how the messaging might change based on audience temperature.

> » **For a cold audience**: "Did you know that common sports balls can be used as deep-tissue massage aids?"

> » **For a warmer audience**: "Degree of stiffness and size are deciding factors when using lacrosse balls as stretching aids for shoulders and back."

> » **For a hot audience**: "Roll away tension and knots with these premium stiff lacrosse balls."

The third sentence might not make any sense to a cold audience, who only associates lacrosse balls with the sport of lacrosse, but a hot audience who is aware of the problem and the solution associated with using lacrosse balls as a massage aid will instantly understand the meaning.

Social Content

Social content is a distinct form of content in a category all its own. When we use our personal social media accounts on our own time, we are free to explore, scroll, and engage. As a brand, and specifically as a digital marketer, the opposite is true—every post, picture, and engagement is calculated. In social media spaces, communication isn't just about what you want to say, but about the way that users of a specific social platform want to hear it.

With regard to social media, it can often be the case that the medium is the message. Social media marketing is covered in detail in chapter 9, but here we will focus on the broad content strokes that companies use to communicate with their social media audiences.

The Five Types of Social Content

Social content can be loosely divided into five categories. For you as a digital marketer, each of these categories has a specific purpose. For the members of your audience, each category provides a different value. As with all other forms of content marketing, the value your content provides to your audience is absolutely critical to the success of your content marketing efforts.

Figure 47 shows the social content marketing matrix, a visual representation of the interconnected relationship between each of the five forms of content and the loose associations these content forms have with the buying process.

GRAPHIC

fig. 47

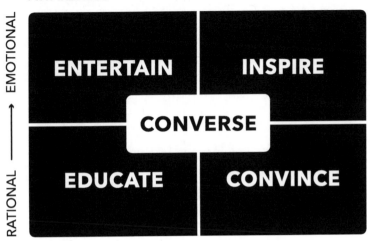

Entertain

One of the things we all love about content that's entertaining is that it asks nothing of us. Savvy social marketers have embraced the entertaining aspects of social media and used them to their own advantage. It's safe to say that when you see any kind of entertaining content on social media that comes from a brand, it isn't made just to make you laugh. Content that is entertaining is more likely to be shared organically by users among their friends and followers. Organic shares represent traffic you don't control—earned media. While you can't control the *rate* of organic shares, you also don't have to pay for them, so getting the most out of entertaining social content online can be a great way to keep digital marketing costs low while keeping success rates high.

As you can see in figure 47, entertaining social content corresponds to the awareness portion of the customer journey. This content is likely to be shared by friends, there's an expectation that the content will not ask anything of you, and it has a general participatory or fun nature—all of this means that members of your audience will be much more open to the message contained within the media. Everyone likes to be entertained, but entertaining content works best when connecting with audiences that have a lower temperature. Engaging with your entertaining content could mean that they move from being problem-unaware to considering the problem seriously or even becoming solution-aware.

Entertaining content most commonly consists of social content that's fun. Viral videos and branded videos with humorous or engaging content are popular, but they are also everywhere online. More outside-the-box content, such as quizzes, games, competitions, trending event tie-ins, or creative social stunts, have seen mixed success since social media's inception. Challenges, like the previously mentioned Ice Bucket Challenge to raise money and awareness for ALS, blend together some of the most powerful aspects of social media, entertaining content, and the awareness aspect they attempt to cultivate.

A prominent and effective example of entertaining content comes from high-end blender producer Blendtec, with their "Will it blend?" series. To demonstrate the power of their professional-grade blenders, they attempted to destroy a range of tough and durable materials. Videos of a person in a lab coat and safety goggles stuffing a golf club into a blender, breaking up loose pieces of concrete in a shower of sparks, and shredding a cell phone to ribbons not only helped the brand stand out but produced compelling content to boot.

Educate

Entertaining content asks nothing of you; educational content makes an implicit promise: when you're done consuming this content you will have learned something. We often turn to the wealth of information that can be found online to solve our immediate problems. Software demos, cooking tutorials, even instructions for how to wire a light switch are literally just a click away. Educational content is a great way to raise the temperature of an audience. With the promise of teaching your audience something they didn't already know, you can often entice social media users (and general web traffic, for that matter) to consume your educational content.

Well-crafted educational content delivers on its promise, but it also works to raise the temperature of the audience members that consume it. Using content that educates is the easiest and most suitable method of making audience members problem-aware, solution-aware, and familiar with your brand. Content such as press releases, how-to manuals or videos, guides, infographics, reports, and educational articles are all examples of content that educates. This type of content typically costs a bit more money to produce and usually "lives" somewhere other than on social media.

Inspire

It can be hard to nail down an exact definition of what it means to be inspired. But for our purposes here, think of inspiration as positive feelings toward a future state. Social content that inspires shows your audience that such a positive future exists—specifically, one in which their problem is solved. As any sales and marketing guru will tell you, one of the steps to convincing your prospect to get out their wallet is to make them believe or buy into the fact that their life will truly improve once they go through with the purchase. And we know that for many consumers, the decision to purchase is an emotional one, not a rational one. For this reason, inspirational social content often blurs the line between being "salesy" and being entertaining. It isn't an outright sales pitch, but unlike content that *only* entertains, it does ask you to emotionally invest in the story that is being told.

Content that inspires focuses on good feelings and generally pertains to **YMYL** topics. YMYL stands for "your money or your life" and describes the focus content creators place on the two elements that are most important to their audiences. Celebrity or spokesperson endorsements, reviews and testimonials, quotes, and success stories make up the bulk of content that inspires. Outside-the-box thinking works here too. A company that makes healthy shakes sharing a counter of the number of pounds lost by their customers could be inspirational content, for example (figure 48).

fig. 48

An example of inspirational content

Convince

Content that convinces is the rational sales pitch portion of social content. Whereas content that inspires presents an ideal future state in emotional terms, content that convinces presents a concrete *why*. But it's important not to overdo it, on social media and elsewhere. An 80/20 rule of thumb is generally considered to be a best practice—aim for 80 percent content that entertains, inspires, or educates and only 20 percent content that convinces (figure 49).

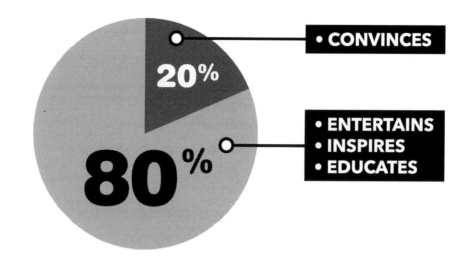

20%

• CONVINCES

• ENTERTAINS
• INSPIRES
• EDUCATES

80%

Ratio of content that convinces to content that entertains, inspires, or educates

Content that convinces consists of case studies, product summaries, feature spotlights, feature- and benefit-focused webinars or video presentations, and interactive or prerecorded demos. Given the current wealth of information regarding the success of their individual social posts, brands will ultimately grow into their own best practices based on what works, whom they are speaking to, and what platforms they interact on.

QUESTION

Q: Does all content fall into one of these groups?

Generally, yes. However, there is content that bleeds across the lines. Product comparisons, for example, are part educational and part content that convinces. E-books or blog posts can be some mix of inspirational, educational, and convincing—even entertaining. Whitepapers, reports, or case studies can be educational and convincing. A title such as "Case Study: How Our New Inventory Software Helped Nine Clients Save a Combined $160,000 in Reduced Shrinkage" easily illustrates this fact.

CAUTION

The matrix pictured in figure 47 is a guideline. The idea is to help marketers create a rounded strategy and to engage social audiences at the points that make the most sense relative to their customer journeys. It's also meant to encourage marketers to think about areas where their social and content strategies intersect. In other words, it's a good guide but is not meant to be used rigidly.

Converse

Content that "converses" with your audience is at the core of your social strategy. Brands on social media are best served when they are as human as possible, when they communicate and hold a dialogue with their audience, and when their audience seeks out their content. This is, of course, easier said than done. Content that converses with your audience is not in a category of its own but is rather a component of each content category shared by your brand on social platforms—whichever ones they happen to be.

Social media is, well, social. Don't forget that one of the main reasons you are on social media in the first place is because that's where your target market is spending their time.

Engage with your audience. Ask them to share their thoughts, and encourage them to provide feedback and tell their friends about your brand and the problem(s) you solve. In short, have a conversation with your target market. This conversation helps generate awareness among your audience, reminds your customers that you exist, and serves as a tool to increase your audience's temperature. Keep that in mind when deploying content on social media.

Associated Metrics

The success of a content marketing strategy and of individual content assets depends largely on the goals you had in mind when building the campaign. Are you trying to "warm up" a cold audience? Are you trying to convince "hot" audience members to make a purchase? These objectives will ultimately determine which metrics will be most helpful.

Content ROI

Contemporary content marketing isn't limited to blog posts. There is an entire range of media that can be utilized by savvy marketers. More important, there is an expectation from your audience that your brand will use different forms of media to reach them. After all, audiences seek out video for different reasons than a printed article. Podcasts can be listened to on the go or while doing other things. The list goes on. These forms of media cost money to produce, in some cases quite a lot of money.

In the pre-digital past, it was difficult to gauge which content assets contributed the most in generating revenue dollars and profit margin. But by combining your content strategy with your larger marketing strategy, using other tactics and techniques outlined in later chapters of this book, and leaning on digital marketing technology solutions, calculating the return on investment for your content assets is now much easier. Those calculations are essential to keeping costs down and understanding what kinds of content work best for your audience.

Medium-Specific Engagement Key Performance Indicators

Measuring the effectiveness of a podcast episode requires different tools than those for measuring the effectiveness of a blog post, but the objectives are generally the same. Social engagement, reach, bounce rate, watch time—these are all metrics specific to the medium in which they exist, and they all roughly measure how much time your audience spends interacting with your content.

Chapter Recap

» Search engine optimization (SEO) can be achieved through technical SEO, on-page SEO, and off-page SEO. All three are designed to drive traffic to a site and keep it there as long as possible.

» Creating websites that are, above all else, mobile friendly is important for convincing Google to place them at the top of search engine result pages (SERPs).

» Content comes in a wide variety of forms and has a wide variety of uses. It often forms the first rung of the value ladder, it can be a way to build trust, and it can be used to generate leads, increase SEO visibility, and refine your understanding of your customer avatar(s).

» Audience temperature refers to the level of awareness your audience has regarding your business, the products or services you offer, and how those products or services can benefit them.

» Content should be produced to speak to audiences of a specific temperature. It is not helpful to tell a very cold audience about a solution to their problem, since they are not yet problem-aware.

» Social content is a category of content all its own. The posts, images, and videos that make up social content are done in a calculated manner with clear goals and objectives.

» Social content falls into one of five main categories: entertain, educate, inspire, convince, and converse. Each type of content speaks to a specific blend of emotional and rational messaging and goals.

| 8 |
Directing Traffic

Chapter Overview
- » Directing traffic with paid search placement
- » Establishing a pay-per-click campaign
- » The basics of paid search
- » Understanding campaign metrics
- » Display advertising

Organic search marketing using content and SEO is an effective method of capturing a portion of search traffic. But focusing on SEO alone is insufficient—there is considerably more value to be gained from search engines and from the internet at large. Another part of the media mix (discussed in chapter 2) is paid media, and the most common form of paid media online, by far, is advertising. In this chapter we will look at a few areas where businesses both large and small advertise in digital spaces. Traditionally, advertising was inherently tied to the space it occupied. If you bought space in a paper or magazine, you knew when and where that ad would appear. It might be in the Sunday edition of the newspaper, for example, or in the August edition of a monthly fashion magazine.

These kinds of deals can still happen in digital spaces, but we're going to focus on much more modern and scalable systems of digital advertising in this chapter. Instead of one-off deals where ad buyers shop an inventory of places where their ads can appear, modern digital advertising networks rely on sophisticated algorithms to match ads to traffic based on targeting criteria. Known broadly as *programmatic advertising*, these algorithms define a plethora of parameters that determine exactly who sees which ads and when. This level of customization allows marketers to hone their messages with a high degree of precision and match their offer, as closely as possible, to the exact kinds of people they want to reach. For example, when purchasing ad space in a newspaper, instead of saying, "I would like the space on page A3 for the next three Sunday editions," digital marketers can say, in effect,

"I would like to buy a space in the cooking section but only if someone with the same characteristics as my ideal customer is going to turn to that page."

Behind the scenes, programmatic advertising is immensely complex, and the level of complexity is only going to increase as new technologies emerge. The good news is that all this complexity is kept under the hood and out of sight—advertising platforms make the interfaces and dashboards easy to use and intuitive for their customers (ad buyers). This extreme scale and power have made programmatic advertising the nearly uniform default for ad buying online today. Amazon, Facebook, Google, Twitter, Pinterest, Quora, you name it; if you are seeing an ad online, it was almost certainly purchased and delivered programmatically.

The specifics of a given programmatic advertising network may vary slightly, but the broad strokes are consistent across different platforms. Ad inventory—the places where ads can appear—is purchased by the advertiser via blind auction. Blind auctions are a fair way for advertisers to compete for ad inventory, but at the same time they are lucrative revenue streams for the platforms. Since competing advertisers have no way of knowing the bids of others, they can't collude to lowball the advertising platform. Likewise, brands with deep pockets can't simply bid one cent higher than all their competitors and win all the ad inventory. As Google puts it, "The auction is designed to ensure advertisers have an incentive to bid their true maximum value and to remove incentives for advertisers to bid lower than their true value."[7]

Q: If auctions are based on blind bids, how do advertisers know they're getting a good deal? How can they optimize their bids to save money?

To understand how to execute and optimize campaigns, we have to dig a little deeper into how the bidding process works. There are two main ways that platforms bill their advertisers: when a user is shown an ad and when a user clicks on an ad. Some social media platforms expand on this to include agreements to charge advertisers when a post is "liked" or some other engagement action is completed. Showing an ad to a user is known as *pay-per-impression* advertising. Generally, impressions are grouped by the thousand, so what is referred to as the CPI—the *cost per impression* that advertisers bid on—is actually a cost per thousand impressions. On the other hand, when advertisers are charged per click, this arrangement is referred to as *pay-per-click* (PPC) and advertisers are bidding on a cost per click (CPC). Let's take a look at a simplified bidding scenario.

Three advertisers are bidding on placement to appear for the same keyword. Advertiser 1, with the highest bid, wins and their ad is shown. They don't pay $1.40 in the event that a user clicks, however. Their bid is a *maximum* bid, and should a user click they will be charged ninety-two cents—the amount needed to beat the next-highest bidder.

GRAPHIC

fig. 50

	CPC BID	AD SHOWN?
ADVERTISER 1	$1.40	✓
ADVERTISER 2	$0.91	✗
ADVERTISER 3	$0.78	✗

It is, of course, in the best interests of the advertising platform—whether it's Google, YouTube, Facebook, or otherwise—to encourage their customers to spend more. Advertisers 2 and 3 from figure 50 will be able to see in the reporting associated with their advertising accounts that they are being outbid and that their ads are appearing less frequently as a result. It is then up to those advertisers to decide if they want to spend more or if an investment in that keyword isn't worth the money; this is all managed via a daily, weekly, or monthly budget setting. The decision to keep paying for ad placement next to relevant keywords isn't set in stone—part of an ongoing programmatic paid advertising strategy involves close monitoring of keyword performance: how much campaigns cost, how the landing pages associated with those campaigns are performing, and ultimately the degree to which advertising campaigns are contributing to marketing and business goals.

This last point is especially important. Programmatic advertising is a major cost, and because the purchasing and placement decisions are being made by a computer, those costs can get out of hand if not monitored. The price an advertiser pays per click or per impression is just half of the decision to determine whether or not programmatic advertising is "worth it." The thing that produces value for you as a marketer or business owner is how you generate revenue from the people who do interact with your ads. The work that you put into the landing pages where you direct traffic will make the difference between the success and failure of a campaign by justifying (or not justifying) the money spent on advertising. Think of it this way: if you're paying to send traffic to a landing page, make sure it's optimized for conversions.

While it is true that an advertiser's bid is the most important deciding factor in whether their ad is shown to traffic, the algorithms advertising platforms use take a variety of factors into consideration when they make the split-second decision to serve an ad. The targeting criteria an advertiser has selected, the interactions a given user has had with the advertiser in the past, and that advertiser's quality score—to name a few—are all considered as the ad is served. An advertiser's *quality score* is based on several factors, such as the quality and content of their landing page and their relevance to the searched keyword.

Now that we have a general understanding of how programmatic advertising works, let's take a deeper dive into the ad inventory at your disposal and how digital advertising campaigns help marketers meet their goals. For the following examples we'll be focusing on the Google Ads platform. At time of writing, Google Ads represents the gold standard of digital and programmatic advertising with regard to reach, targeting, and scalability. There are other players, however, and we'll touch on some of the most important names as we proceed. One form of digital advertising is conspicuously absent from this chapter: social advertising. We'll discuss paid social in the next chapter.

Paid Search

Ubiquitous, effective, and elegant in its simplicity, a SERP text ad is familiar to everyone. It appears at the top of the search engine results page (SERP) and, though clearly marked as an ad, is designed to look and feel like organic search results (figure 51). This is a form of native advertising also known as native design. By presenting sponsored search results in the same style and format as the surrounding content, advertisers encourage more clicks and conversions. In short, the less a piece of content looks like an ad, the more likely people are to interact with it. Like most programmatic advertising, these ads are served by a complex algorithm that takes a mind-boggling number of factors into account. Advertisers can use a wide variety of targeting criteria for these ads, ranging from location and time of day to browsing behavior, demographics, and retargeting (discussed later in this chapter)—to name only a few.

Paid search ads can be an effective solution for brands that are looking to get more leads, get more sales, or direct traffic to their website or landing page. They benefit from highly relevant targeting and can readily be shown to search traffic that is at any stage of the buying process. Another attractive aspect of paid search ads is that they are easy to set up and produce at scale.

Since they are a headline and a few sentences of copy at most, no special assets like images or video are necessary.

fig. 51

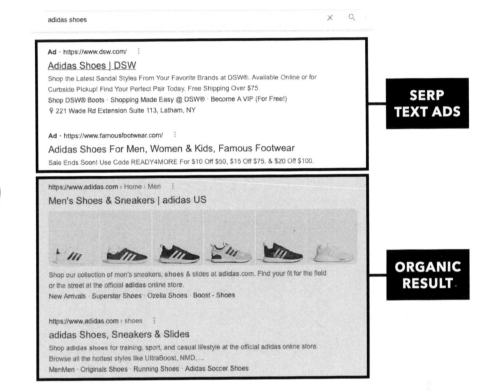

As we discussed in the previous chapter, the higher your brand appears on search engine results pages, the higher the share of clicks you will capture. Focusing on SEO will only get your brand so far, however. Search engines like Google rely on paid search ads for their revenue, so it's in their best interests to put as many ads into the SERPs as they can. But there is a limit. In the same way that allowing one brand to game the algorithm undermines the utility of using Google as a search engine, plastering the SERPs with sponsored results erodes the user experience. Over the years Google and other search engines have slowly introduced new ad formats and placements into SERPs. Search ads appear in the SERPs before the organic results, and display ads appear just about everywhere else. While the latest social media platform or other digital craze might be trendier or sexier than paid search, search engine PPC campaigns continue to deliver cost-effective results for brands of all sizes.

Executing a Paid Search Campaign

As with any ad platform, paid search advertising is broken down broadly into campaigns. Once you have established your goal and created a new campaign, you will be asked to define some basic targeting criteria such as geographic location, language, or an audience you define using demographic interests, online activity, or remarketing. After targeting parameters and goals are in place, you'll set your budget and bidding. Budgets are generally calculated daily with a defined budget for that day. Spending may fluctuate around this number, but over time the amount of money spent per day will average out to this amount. Google and other digital marketing platforms will offer bidding and daily budget guidance based on your targeting parameters and campaign goals. In fact, playing around in this portion of your ads dashboard is a great way to quickly get a good idea of how spending and targeting work.

Once you have defined your budget, it's time to create your ad groups. Ad groups are a way to keep ads organized within a campaign, not only for your own organizational purposes but also to help the advertising platform better understand which ads to show to which traffic. Ad groups match specific ads with specific keywords.

EXAMPLE

If you are an online shoe retailer, you might have one ad group associated with targeting customers who are seeking one name brand shoe and a separate ad group for a different name brand.

GRAPHIC

fig. 52

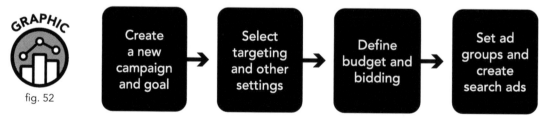

Create a new campaign and goal → Select targeting and other settings → Define budget and bidding → Set ad groups and create search ads

Paid search campaign creation process

Once your ad groups are defined with keywords or other targeting criteria, you can associate ads with each group. The ads you associate with each group will be shown to that group only, and the advertising platform will cycle through the ads you upload. Current best practices dictate at least three ads per ad group—an easy feat given that sponsored SERP results are text-only.

Display Advertising

Display advertising has developed a bit of a bad rap over the years. It's been with us since the early days of the internet, and though today's display advertising is a far cry from the crude iterations of the past, display advertising in general has retained its negative reputation as ugly, intrusive, and annoying in the eyes of some. Display ads are the image ads (sometimes motion-enabled) that appear around and throughout content. The most ubiquitous display ad is the banner ad; a long rectangular ad that appears at the top of content or as a vertical rectangle beside it.

fig. 53

An ad promoting AT&T Internet as it first appeared on HotWired.com on Oct. 27, 1994. Its design exemplifies the intrusive and annoying nature that has contributed to display advertising's reputation.

Again, Google is the uncontested master of modern internet display advertising. Over the years they have developed an extensive network of display ad inventory that spans nearly every corner of the internet. Think of display advertising, whether purchased through Google or another display ad network, as digital billboards. They can be good solutions for brand awareness and reach, but their true value comes through when they are employed as part of a retargeting campaign. Retargeting (or remarketing) is the practice of showing ads to traffic after they interact with an offer or visit a page on your site. Advertisers who use retargeting campaigns can "follow" site visitors as they travel around the web. A mix of display and social retargeting can be a powerful combo with which to capitalize on every site visitor.

For example, we have all had the experience of hearing about a product and searching for it online. After checking out the product's website and navigating away, we are suddenly seeing ads for the product on social media and seemingly everywhere online. That's the power of remarketing.

Q: Is there a way my site can make money with display advertising?

Yes, selling online display advertising can be a revenue source, but site owners should proceed with caution. Google can't sell display ads if they don't have access to spaces on websites where they can, uh, display them. To this end, Google's display ad business is made up of two parts: Google Ads and Google AdSense. AdSense is a program for *publishers*—sites that want to make money by displaying ads. AdSense participants place snippets of code on pages across their sites. These snippets communicate with Google's Ads program and serve ads from *advertisers* to site visitors. In return, Google pays AdSense participants a portion of the proceeds.

For large sites that publish content often, Google's AdSense (or similar programs) can be a way to cover editorial and hosting costs as well as produce steady revenue. However, the majority of business sites are better off sticking to their core business rather than trying to drive incremental revenue. Not only are the costs associated with adhering to a frequent publishing schedule onerous, but display ads can distract or even turn your audience away from your content, offers, or other site features. Unless your business is publishing content, your site is best used as a focused tool to support your business objectives and provide value to your customers.

fig. 54

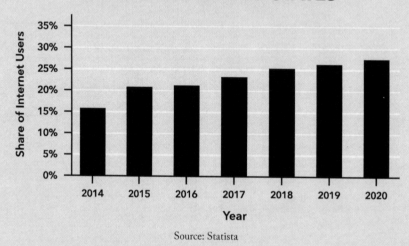

Source: Statista

The bombardment of internet display ads has caused a bit of a backlash among some users, who have taken to downloading ad blockers. Millions have installed ad blocker software. The most popular is AdBlock Plus, but dozens of other products are also available for this purpose. In

2020, Apple announced that its mobile operating system, which powers iPhones and iPads, would natively support ad blocking technology. Some advertisers are predicting that ad blockers will signal the end of online advertising, but others are more optimistic and believe the effect will not be monumental and that ad blockers could even signal some opportunities. We'll see.

Unlike search advertising, which uses keywords as its primary targeting option, display advertising provides unique targeting choices. ***Contextual targeting***, which is advertising on a website that relates to the page's content, is another layer of targeting available to marketers who use display advertising. An example of contextual targeting would be an ad for premium spices on pages with recipes containing relevant spices.

Demographic targeting enables advertisers to target their ads to consumers based on demographic information such as age, gender, race, education level, occupation, income, sexual preference, or geographic area. This can help to personalize your advertising, enabling potential customers to identify with your brand and establish customer loyalty. An ad for a high-end watch, for instance, would likely be targeted to web browsers whose incomes meet or exceed a certain level.

fig. 55

HOW TO MAKE CHOCOLATE CHIP COOKIES

Let's walk through how to make chocolate chip cookies step-by-step, and don't forget to watch the video.

A display ad featuring a tractor, placed in the middle of a blog about baking cookies. The ad doesn't relate to the content, it relates to you!

Another targeting choice, *behavioral targeting*, looks at internet browsing history and displays ads to people who seem to be likely matches for your product or service. You've probably looked online for running shoes or a patio heater, only to have ads for those products displayed on your screens for weeks or months afterward (figure 55).

Video

Generally speaking, video advertising is a format with high effectiveness—and potentially higher cost. Video content is everywhere, and that trend is showing no signs of stopping. Given the ubiquity of fast internet connections across a variety of connected devices, billions of hours of video content are just a few taps away. Video ads, regardless of the platform where they appear, are a good choice for marketers who are looking to increase sales, gather leads, increase traffic to their website, and increase brand or product awareness.

Video advertising is a big business, and video placements are more accessible to businesses of all sizes than ever before. Self-serve programmatic infrastructure on the largest video providers, like YouTube, Facebook, and Hulu, means that even small advertisers can appear on phones, tablets, and TVs alongside video content that commands millions of views. Like other forms of digital advertising at scale, ad placement is managed via the same bidding systems that digital marketers will already be familiar with. For platforms like Google Ads (including YouTube) and Facebook, video advertising is often integrated into the advertiser dashboard.

Video advertising can be broadly separated into in-stream and outstream placements. In-stream ads run in the same player or media window as the video content they accompany. We're all familiar with linear ads—in-stream ads that play before, during, or after video content (such as on YouTube or Facebook). You will see these placements referred to as pre-roll, mid-roll, or post-roll, based on whether they are displayed before, during, or after the video content.

| Q: Which "roll" is right for me?

Obviously, it benefits platforms to have as many advertising slots as possible for a piece of content, but not all in-stream placements are equally valuable for advertisers. Think about how you yourself engage with video content. If you are looking forward to watching a video, you will likely sit through an ad at the beginning. If you are enjoying the video, an ad in the middle probably won't make you click away. But an ad that runs at the end of the video doesn't necessarily have the same power to hold you—at this point you have finished the content you came to see, and you're ready to click away to find the next video rather than sit through an ad.

Outstream video ads play outside of a stream or video player. They overlay content on a page that might not otherwise be dedicated to video. Because outstream ads play independently of a video player and accompany content, they can be an effective way to grab your audience's attention. Additionally, outstream ads often can't be skipped and will stay on-screen as users read through the content they appear alongside. Outstream ads aren't immune to challenges. They are vulnerable to ad blockers, and they often have a lower quality of analytical reporting compared to in-stream ads. This means that it can be harder to assign a robust ROI number to justify continued investment in outstream ads. Because of this, outstream advertising is generally not recommended to new digital marketers or those with lower budgets, because without a big bankroll to test targeting or invest in quality outstream video ads, an outstream video campaign will likely fall flat.

Shopping

After it became obvious that e-commerce was going to be a huge market and moneymaker, Google launched Google Shopping in December of 2002. Google Shopping ads can be served using the same targeting criteria as SERP text ads and are measured in much the same way. Obviously, these ads are only for brands with a physical product to sell. As you can see in figure 56, New Balance has a large "above the fold"—visible without scrolling—presence for the search term "new balance sneakers." They are represented in a Shopping ads result, the first SERP text result, and the first organic result. Some of the other shopping ads we can see are for retailers that are selling New Balance shoes along with a result for a competitor, Allbirds.

Allbirds' marketing department may have data that people who are looking for New Balance shoes are also interested in Allbirds. They may also have historical data that indicates that Shopping ads for their products do well when shown to people who are searching for New Balance products. Compared to New Balance, Allbirds is a younger brand; another possible objective of their targeting of this key phrase is simply to increase exposure with shoppers who are familiar with established competing brands.

To appear in Google Shopping results and across Google's display network, your products must have an associated Google Shopping product listing. This is a small obstacle for many retailers, but keep in mind that Google strictly enforces minimum quality parameters for sellers on their e-commerce platform.

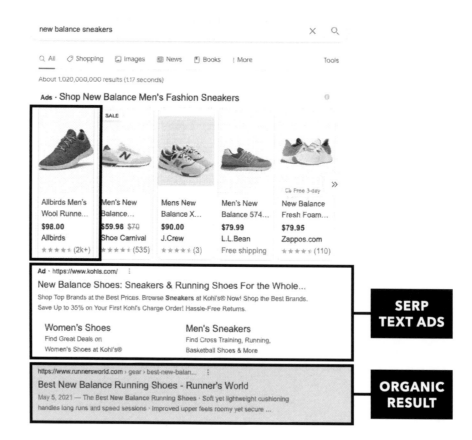

fig. 56

Selecting Keywords

We'll continue to use Google's advertising platform as our example. As with organic search, not all keywords are created equal. Google offers a Keyword Planner tool that makes it easy for advertisers to plan their campaigns. Using the tool, you can discover new keyword ideas based on keywords you provide, and you can identify the potential performance and cost of any keywords you have selected.

As a smaller brand or marketer, you may be starting out with a somewhat small number of keywords, though it is not uncommon for marketers to manage hundreds or even thousands of keywords as part of a sophisticated (and well-funded) PPC strategy. Campaigns at this scale are often the domain of major corporations that have the resources and staff needed to monitor, adjust, and service such a large keyword portfolio. For smaller brands, campaign management tools are available to automate tedious tasks and track keyword-level performance. These tools are invaluable and can act as an equalizer between large and small advertisers.

fig. 57

Keyword (by relevance)	Avg. monthly searches	Competition	Ad impression share	Top of page bid (low range)	Top of page bid (high range)
Keywords you provided					
new balance shoes	100K – 1M	High	–	$0.33	$6.05
Keyword ideas					
new balance	1M – 10M	High	–	$0.87	$16.15
new balance 327	10K – 100K	High	–	$0.36	$1.22
new balance 574	100K – 1M	High	–	$0.22	$13.00
new balance 530	10K – 100K	High	–	$0.43	$1.28
new balance 990	10K – 100K	High	–	$0.29	$1.25
new balance 550	10K – 100K	High	–	$0.41	$1.25

A sample of keyword suggestions based on the key phrase "new balance shoes."
Google recommends nearly 3,000 related keywords based on this seed phrase,
along with some bid range information.

The keyword selection process can be a daunting one. It is equal parts research, data collection, and experimentation. Once keywords have been selected, they are added to the campaign with a **match type** and ad copy. Match types determine how wide a net your campaign casts, and you'll read more about them in the next section.

In an effort to level the playing field, platforms like Google have introduced ad quality scores. Their systems score ads based on expected click-through rate, relevance to keywords, and landing page experience. Your final score, when paired with your bid, determines if your sponsored result will be the one shown on a given search results page. Ad quality systems ensure that not only are the ads that users see relevant to their interests, but they aren't spam or links to malicious pages. Most important for our purposes, ad quality scores ensure that marketers can't dominate the field simply by placing the highest bid. The ads or sponsored results shown are automatically selected based on both bid and quality score, and platforms will try to cycle through available relevant ads from as many advertisers as possible.

The science and sometimes art of selecting keywords could be the subject of a book all its own. Though the process can feel overwhelming, you don't have to go it alone. Google provides a free Keyword Planner tool, and there are similar offerings from Bing and Yahoo!. These software applications help you understand how popular specific keywords are, how you can discover new keywords, and, maybe most important, how much you can expect your campaigns to cost. In addition to the tools provided directly by the platforms, there is no shortage of third-party solutions to help you conduct keyword research, plan and execute your campaigns, and measure your results.

Of course, as with all endeavors, you can't spend all your time in the planning stage. At some point you have to commit and start running live campaigns. The good news is that this is one of the best ways to learn the intricacies of how programmatic advertising works. Planning tools can only tell you so much. The best testing and measurement are done with live campaigns using real traffic and a funded budget. This process is similar to scientific experimentation and should be treated as such. Keep a record of your successes and challenges with various key phrases and budgets. Treat each new campaign like a researcher would a hypothesis, and act according to the findings your tests produce.

Selecting keywords for paid search placement campaigns isn't much different from the process associated with organic search ranking. You are still focusing on search intent and the customer journey—both of which are discussed in detail in chapter 7. The big difference here is the cost factor.

Keyword Match Type

Keywords can be assigned one of three match types: ***broad match***, ***phrase match***, or ***exact match***. Broad match type assignments cast a wide net and will attempt to link your ad campaigns to searches that are even just slightly relevant to your keyword. Exact match types, on the other hand, will attempt to show your sponsored result only if the search is an exact match with the keyword you have indicated. Let's take a closer look at each of the match types.

fig. 58

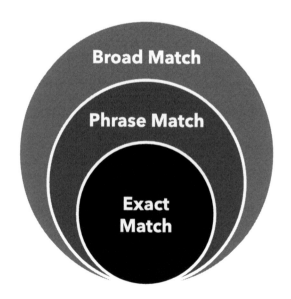

Broad Match

Using a broad match assignment, the platform will attempt to show your sponsored result to the most people for whom it could be even a little relevant. This is great for companies that are trying to get the word out about a new product or service and have cash to burn. Broad match types cover the widest demographic and can result in a whole lot of people seeing and clicking on your ad. That sounds fantastic, but it can be a double-edged sword. The more people who see your message, the more clicks your ad can garner. If your landing page isn't a perfect fit for what this traffic is looking for, they may leave without converting or spending any money. In this case, you will have incurred cost in the form of ad spend without generating revenue. Just a few broad match blunders like this in a keyword list can eat up a budget day after day; therefore, use broad match with care. As you can see from the example below, a broad match for "men's sunglasses" could display your sponsored results in response to a variety of obliquely related searches, including "men's accessories." If someone is searching for a wallet or a watch, he may click through your ad to see if you sell men's accessories in addition to sunglasses, but the chances of his suddenly deciding to buy sunglasses and completing a sale are much lower.

Broad Match Keyword: Men's Sunglasses

Also matches:

» Men's accessories
» Men's sun wear
» Men's beach wear
» Men's sunshades
» Men's sport sunglasses
» Men's aviator sunglasses

Phrase Match

Phrase matching refines the parameters even further to ensure that the keyword not only appears in the search query but isn't broken up by other words or search terms. In short, phrase matching keeps the keyword intact.

Phrase Match Keyword: "Men's Sunglasses"
Also matches:
- » Cheap men's sunglasses
- » Shop men's sunglasses
- » Durable men's sunglasses
- » Sporty men's sunglasses
- » Men's sunglasses sale

Exact Match

Exact matches mean only search traffic that enters your keyword exactly (or almost exactly) will potentially be shown your sponsored result. It is the most specific search type, and some marketers find it restrictive, even though Google has changed exact match specifications to allow matches for searches containing some variation of the keyword. Although it can reduce the number of people who see your ad, exact match is probably the safest spend approach, as it's likely that only people who are actively looking for exactly what you're selling will click on your ad.

Exact Match Keyword: [Men's Sunglasses]
Only matches:
- » Men's sunglasses (with some exceptions)

The match types you choose can have a big impact on your PPC and programmatic advertising campaigns.

Aligning Keywords with Customer Avatars

The better you understand your potential customers, the easier it will be to align your keywords with their searches and online activity. Employing a reliable customer avatar, or more than one if you offer numerous products or services, helps you make educated guesses about prospective customers' search queries and search intent. You need to have a solid understanding of their pain points and what they are hoping to accomplish.

Also called a "buyer persona," a customer avatar acts as a placeholder for your real customers and helps you segment your target market.

As you read in chapter 3, demographic factors such as age, gender, location, marital status, income, education, and occupation will be considered when developing a customer avatar. When you put together those factors with prospective buyers' pain points and goals, you should begin to get a very good picture of the person your PPC campaign is trying to reach and the search intent behind their queries. With that in mind, keyword selection becomes a lot easier. Always obey the results of testing with regard to customer habits and searches—double down on efforts that produce results, and don't be afraid to kill approaches that aren't delivering results.

Associated Metrics

Anyone who has ever managed a PPC account understands that there is a large amount of data available to track and analyze. While having access to that data can help you gauge the success of your PPC campaigns, it isn't always clear which metrics are the most important to track.

It's crucial that you monitor and analyze your ads so they can be adjusted as necessary. You might want to change your ad copy to make it more in sync with the content of your landing page, adjust bids and keywords, create new ad groups, or perform other tasks to optimize your ad results and get the most out of your ad budget.

Not everyone agrees on which metrics are most important. Check out ten marketing sites and you're likely to find ten different opinions regarding the metrics you should be regularly monitoring. As you get more involved with PPC advertising and your business expands, the relevance of metrics might change. Let's have a look at some metrics that are important to every PPC campaign and consider how they can work to help you gauge how well your campaign is going.

Cost Per Click (CPC)

The amount you pay per click is important because it is an indicator of the financial success of your campaign. Without clicks, you will have no customers, and without customers you will have no sales. Calculate your cost per click by dividing the cost of your clicks by the number of clicks. If you pay $100 and get 500 clicks, for instance, your average cost per click is $0.2, or twenty cents (this will be calculated for you by the ad platform).

Average cost per click is just what it says—the average that you spend for every ad click. Maximum cost per click is the highest amount you agree to pay per click. The average cost per click varies according to the competitiveness of your industry and other factors.

NOTE

It's interesting to note that the average cost per click varies tremendously depending on the country in which you live and do business. US businesses pay the highest CPC, followed by the United Arab Emirates. Rates in parts of South America and Australia average about 20 percent less than in the US, and in parts of Russia rates are 80 percent lower, according to WordStream, a search marketing company.

GRAPHIC

fig. 59

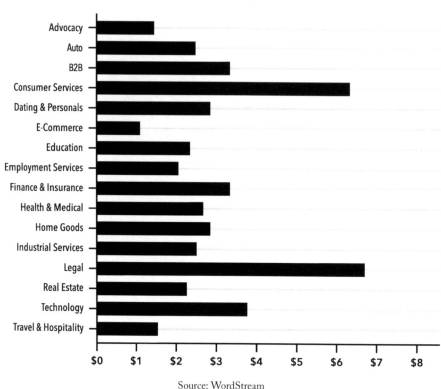

AVERAGE COST PER CLICK
BY INDUSTRY

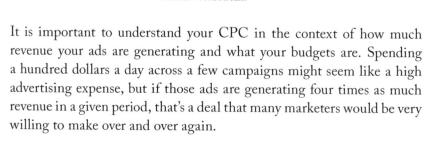

Source: WordStream

It is important to understand your CPC in the context of how much revenue your ads are generating and what your budgets are. Spending a hundred dollars a day across a few campaigns might seem like a high advertising expense, but if those ads are generating four times as much revenue in a given period, that's a deal that many marketers would be very willing to make over and over again.

Click-Through Rate (CTR)

The click-through rate, or CTR, is the rate at which people who see your ad end up clicking on it. If one hundred people saw your ad and seven clicked on it, you'd have a 7 percent CTR.

A high percentage of people clicking on your ad is a good thing, as it indicates that users are finding it to be applicable and relevant. You need these clicks to get potential customers to your website and ultimately purchase your product or service. Your CTR also affects your Google Quality Score, which, as you've read, can affect the cost of your ads and where they are placed.

fig. 60

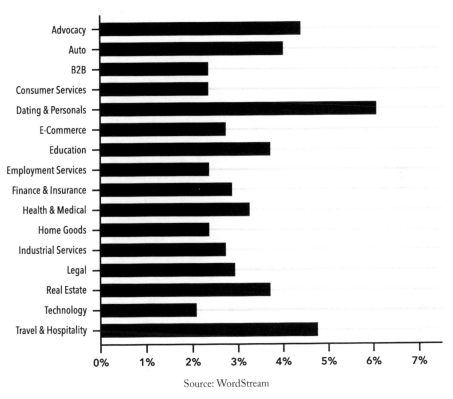

AVERAGE CLICK THROUGH RATE
BY INDUSTRY

Source: WordStream

While a high CTR is positive, it doesn't benefit you if it doesn't result in conversions, which is when the person who clicks through completes the desired goal, whether it be buying something, joining a mailing list, or completing a form. In fact, a high CTR without conversions is probably a signal that your keywords and ad text are not particularly relevant or useful. That's a problem that can end up costing you money, as you're paying for clicks without achieving results.

It's estimated as an average across industries that only 2.35 percent of visits to landing pages result in conversion. To address those who leave your site without converting, you can add *retargeting*—a form of online advertising that tracks this traffic and then re-engages it with targeted ads—to your toolbox.

You can find your CTR by using Google's free ad performance grader. What is considered a successful CTR varies by industry, type of business, your goals, and other factors, so take all those elements into account when gauging your success.

Quality Score

Your Google Quality Score, as you read earlier, is Google's rating of the relevance and value of your keywords and PPC ads. The score is based on CTR, relevance of ad text, quality of the landing page, keyword relevance, and past performance on Google Ads.

While your quality score isn't directly tied to revenue, it can impact how much you pay per click and where your ads appear. A low score means that Google believes your ad(s) or landing page(s) provides a less-than-ideal experience for their users, and therefore competitors will be given preference when bidding on key phrases. Underperforming campaigns and inflated bids are sure to follow.

To improve a declining quality score, review your keyword strategy. How do your conversions stack up against others in your industry? Does your ad copy speak to your customer avatar? Is your landing page—or the offer presented on it—compelling? A bad offer or a landing page that doesn't jibe with your ad copy or customer avatar is a fast way to tank your quality score.

Google's quality score system is one of many. Every platform that supports programmatic advertising has its own formula to police bad actors and identify ads that are spammy, low in quality, or simply ineffective.

Q: Why does Google (or any other platform) care if I am making money with my ads—they get paid either way, right?

Platforms need lots of advertisers competing for keywords to keep bids high. They also need advertisers to be willing to bid high—ad inventory isn't worth much if the people who click on it aren't spending money. If your ads don't convert, the platform is happy to give the placement to a different bidder.

Cost Per Acquisition (CPA)

Average *cost per acquisition*, or CPA, is arguably one of the most important metrics you should be tracking. Your CPA, sometimes referred to as *cost per action*, will help you understand how much it costs to obtain a new customer and whether that cost is effective. CPA measures the total cost of acquiring one paying customer during a campaign.

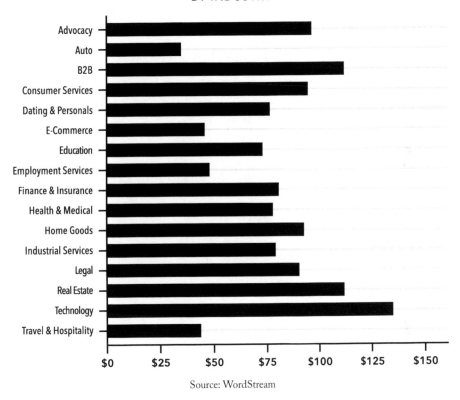

AVERAGE COST PER ACTION
BY INDUSTRY

Source: WordStream

fig. 61

The CPA metric is tied to the conversion rate, and those terms are often used interchangeably, but they are a little different. Conversions occur when someone clicks through your ad and completes a desired goal; the CPA is a financial metric. The conversion rate is an indicator of marketing success, and the CPA is used to measure the revenue impact of a marketing campaign. The CPA's single focus is on acquiring a new customer.

CPA is calculated by dividing the total cost of conversions in each period by the total number of conversions for that same period.

GRAPHIC

fig. 62

$$\text{COST PER ACQUISITION} = \frac{\text{TOTAL COST OF CONVERSIONS}}{\text{TOTAL NUMBER OF VISITORS}}$$

For example, if your ad produces three conversions costing $2.44, $3.25, and $2.86, your average cost per acquisition for that period would be $2.85.

Determining your CPA is a straightforward calculation, but understanding the meaning of the number you calculate can be more difficult, depending on the industry in which you operate or the lifetime value (LTV) of your customers. For example, an advertiser who sells a subscription-based product for $6.99 per month might balk at a $3.50 CPA—a cost of 50 percent of what they expect their customers to spend in their first month! But if that same subscription-based service knows that their customers stick around for an average of fourteen months, they realize that $3.50 is a manageable price to pay for nearly $100 in revenue.

Impression Rates and Impression Shares

Impression rates and impression shares report the total number of times an ad is displayed, with or without clicks. This helps advertisers gauge their auction performance and the visibility of their ads and are meant to provide a better indication of the positions in which their ads appear. The metrics are as follows:

- » **Top impression rate:** The percentage of total impressions that appear anywhere above the organic content on the SERP

- » **Absolute top impression rate:** The percentage of total impressions that come from the very top of the SERP

- » **Top impression share:** The rate at which impressions actually appear at the top of the SERP compared to the number of times the ads are eligible to appear there but do not

» **Absolute top impression share:** The rate at which impressions appear at the very top of the SERP compared to the number of times they are eligible to appear there but for some reason (usually technical in nature) do not

Top and absolute top metrics are *prominence metrics*, or metrics that estimate your ad's visibility on the SERP. While *impression rate* indicates position, *impression share* refers to the top or absolute top impressions you've received compared to the number of opportunities you had for top or absolute top impressions. These metrics let you know how often you missed the top or very top of the SERP due to a low budget or poor ad rank.

Underachieving impression rates and shares can be due to an insufficient budget, a poor quality score, or low target, bid, and conversion rates of your ad. Improving those aspects of your campaign can lead to greater engagement, impression rates, and shares.

Chapter Recap

» Programmatic advertising is administered through a blind auction in which several factors are considered, such as your bid, keyword relevance, and quality score.

» Paid search allows you to pay for ads that appear in the highly coveted top of SERPs before organic results. Paid search is part of a holistic digital marketing strategy and is an excellent companion to organic SEO efforts.

» Display advertising represents a variety of banner, pop-in, and other advertisement types that appear on sites around the internet.

» Video advertising allows even small marketers to purchase placement alongside video that garners millions of views. Video ads can be placed in-stream—in the same player window and in line with the content—or outstream, as videos that play over content or overlay on mobile screens.

| 9 |
Social

Chapter Overview
» The evolution of social media
» Social media and marketing
» Social advertising
» Damage control
» Measuring outcomes

Social aspects of the internet have been around practically since its inception. Broadly defined, social media is computer-based technology that enables users to share their thoughts, opinions, and experiences, or share information obtained from other sources, with a virtual community or network. Online social networks have been around for a while, but they have evolved so rapidly that early iterations would hardly be recognizable today.

One of these early iterations was Six Degrees, named for the "six degrees of separation" theory. In case you're not familiar, the theory espouses the idea that everyone on the planet is just six or fewer social connections apart. Introduced in 1997, Six Degrees was relatively short-lived, and at its peak, the number of users was only about 3.5 million (compare that to Facebook's 2.45 billion monthly active users in the second quarter of 2020).

Six Degrees was followed by services including AOL Chat Rooms, Meetup, Friendster, and Myspace, which from 2005 to 2008 was the largest social networking site in the world, with 100 million users a month. These and other early platforms, however, were hugely different from today's most popular social media sites in terms of size, intent of use, and the amount of money surrounding them.

The Evolving Nature of Social Media

Social media use exploded between 2009 and 2019, with the number of adults who used one or more social media sites more than tripling, from 21 percent to 79 percent.

But tremendous user growth isn't the only way social media has changed. The number and type of social media networks have also exploded, giving users a range of choices depending on their interests and the type of interface they prefer. From Twitter to Instagram to TikTok and beyond, potential customers have a variety of online spaces in which to pass their time.

Let's look at some of the factors that affect how social media platforms continue to change and evolve.

How to Think about Social

The popularity of specific social platforms ebbs and flows. The demographics they serve change, new platforms unseat older ones that can't keep up, and sometimes people just lose interest. As a marketer, it's important to be good at using the social platforms you commit to, but keep in mind that they may not be around forever. There is also a possibility that the people you need to reach will migrate from one platform to another, meaning you'll have to be ready and willing to pivot to another platform.

Market Share of Major Players

According to Statista, a company that specializes in marketing and consumer data, the three major social media players are, not surprisingly, Facebook, Pinterest, and Twitter. Facebook held a commanding 61 percent share of all social media site visits in the United States as of January 2021, with Pinterest next with a 20 percent share. Twitter followed with 14.5 percent of visits. YouTube, Instagram, Tumblr, and Reddit fall next in line, but their share of visits is minimal compared to the top platforms (figure 63).

Those numbers make these platforms intriguing to businesses looking to increase their visibility, promote their brands, and connect with their target audiences. A company can use Facebook pages to build a presence and connect with customers and potential customers, and can use ads, including video ads, to spread the word about its products or services. Businesses that market primarily to women might be drawn to Pinterest, as women represent more than two thirds of the platform's base, including eight out of every ten mothers in the United States. Those who use Pinterest go there for help in deciding what to buy, and a high percentage of users report having purchased something based on content from brands they saw there.

LEADING SOCIAL MEDIA WEBSITES IN THE UNITED STATES IN JAN. 2021

BASED ON SHARE OF VISITS TO EACH SITE

GRAPHIC

fig. 63

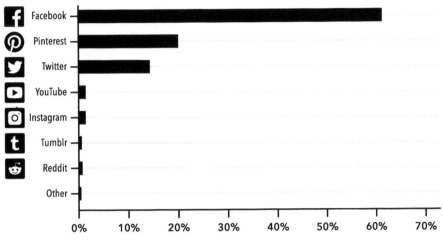

Source: Statista

Twitter urges companies to use its platform to build followings, launch new products, announce sales or other news, monitor their competition, and create customer service accounts. Businesses are encouraged to take advantage of Twitter Ads to increase attention, drive more traffic to their websites, and increase app downloads. Twitter stresses immediacy, meaning that fresh content is important.

While these "Big Three" platforms get a 96 percent share of all visits to social media sites, you don't necessarily need to jump on their bandwagons. They are very likely to be appropriate platforms for reaching your marketing goals—but not in every instance. If your best audience is not hanging out on Facebook, then there's not much point in spending time and money there. Analyze which platforms your audience trends toward and meet them where they are.

Social Media Marketing and Campaigns

Social media marketing, which includes tasks such as posting text, images, and videos to keep your followers informed and engaged, has become an increasingly important piece of the broader field of digital marketing. Social media marketing enables you to accomplish a variety of goals, such as generating leads and sales, listening to your followers and responding to their concerns or questions, and increasing the size of your contact list. Social media marketing enables you to get to know your customers and potential customers and permits them to get to know your business.

You can establish your company as an authority in your field by taking the lead and posting relevant and important content and building relationships with other social influencers. You can analyze results, run ads (more about that later in this chapter), and more.

Getting noticed on social media doesn't have to be elaborate or expensive. Gaming behemoth PlayStation got tons of attention a few years ago simply by posting congratulations to video game developer Naughty Dog on the phenomenal success of its game, Uncharted 4. Uncharted 4 was already a hot discussion topic, so by joining the conversation, PlayStation generated a lot of discussion and put both Naughty Dog and PlayStation in the spotlight.

Social media marketing is the bread and butter of your social presence and, over time, defines the culture of your business or organization. It is a process in which you engage on a regular basis. Recall that in chapter 7 you read about five categories of social content, each of which is important to your social media marketing. When your content entertains, educates, inspires, convinces, and converses, it serves every stage of the buying cycle.

Social media marketing is an ongoing process, whereas a *social media campaign* is a planned, coordinated series of actions intended to achieve a specific goal or goals. As with any type of digital campaign, your marketing goals will inform your methodology and tool selection; therefore, determining these goals is the all-important first step in any digital marketing undertaking.

Adding a campaign to your social media marketing is meant to accelerate your marketing process. Below are a few reasons you might initiate a social media campaign:

»   **Retargeting.** I'm sure you've had the experience of visiting a website, checking out some product, and leaving without buying anything, only to have banners for the website you visited start showing up everywhere you go on the web. That, as mentioned in chapter 8, is called retargeting, also known as remarketing.

»   **Creating a fundraiser that's tied to a hashtag.** This is a technique that allows social media users to follow an organization's story and donate to a cause that's important to them. Research has shown that using hashtags can produce positive results for a business or organization, but the hashtags should be well chosen and limited in number, because engagement actually decreases when a dozen or more hashtags are thrown up on a site.

» **Increasing your brand awareness and generating new leads.** Increasing the number of people who interact with your content can go a long way in increasing brand awareness. A campaign aimed at getting users to "share" and "like" content on your site can open it to a whole new network of potential customers who visit and become familiar with your products.

» **Improving customer satisfaction.** A campaign targeted at responding directly to customers who post comments on your pages can help to improve customer satisfaction by creating goodwill. A personalized response indicates that you're attentive to the needs of visitors and interested in their comments and concerns. Social media is just that—social—and this type of natural interaction humanizes your company and helps keep customers and potential customers happy.

Other goals of a social media campaign could be to improve brand loyalty, gain insight about your customers, enhance marketplace insights, position yourself as a thought leader, achieve higher conversion rates, create more inbound traffic, generate more leads and sales, increase profits, launch a new product, enter new markets, or target new customers.

A fundraiser tied to a hashtag was initiated in 2014 by FEED, a nonprofit that works with its giving partner, Feeding America, to provide food for American families. FEED asked supporters to raise funds by hosting dinner parties and collecting donations from guests, then posting pictures of the dinners at #FEEDsupper. The dinner party phenomenon quickly took off, and soon thousands of people were hosting, posting, and raising money for FEED. By the end of the campaign, enough funds had been raised to provide more than two million meals for those who needed them.

Choosing Appropriate Goals for Your Social Campaign

There are a great many goals to choose from when preparing to launch a social campaign, and prioritizing them can be difficult. Do not, however, be tempted to proceed with a campaign without first identifying clearly defined goals. Regardless of the type of business you have, the duration of your social campaign, or what social networks you'll be focusing on, having goals in place before launching is imperative.

The goals you establish will help you understand what kind of budget you'll need. They will encourage you to monitor your campaign and will hold you accountable for the results. When choosing goals, start by identifying the reasons your business has a social media presence in the first place. Are you there to increase recognition of your company, product, and/or brand? Are you looking to increase your social media following, build your customer base, or enhance customer loyalty? Examining your larger objectives can help you whittle them down into specific goals that will direct your campaign.

The most often cited primary goals of social marketers (which won't necessarily be your social campaign goals) include increasing brand awareness, generating more sales/leads, increasing community engagement, expanding their brand's audience, and increasing web traffic.

Remember the SMART goal framework you read about in chapter 5? That same framework, which helps you break down those larger objectives into manageable and actionable steps, applies to social marketing and can be your best friend when you're getting ready to launch a campaign.

SMART is an acronym for Specific, Measurable, Actionable, Relevant, and Time-bound. The SMART framework will define what you are attempting to achieve, how you'll know when you've achieved it, whether it's something you can achieve, whether achieving the goal will solve the problem you're facing, and a reasonable time frame for achieving the stated goal.

Using the SMART framework to identify and express your goals will help you focus and direct your efforts toward the business outcomes you're looking for. It enables you to transform vague, unhelpful goals into actionable steps and makes your objectives easier to communicate.

How the Media Mix Changes on Social Media

If you think back to chapter 2, you may recall an explanation of the media mix, which, in both traditional and digital media, consists of paid media, earned media, and owned media. While a social media campaign can employ paid, earned, and owned media, those three components tend to blur and overlap. You can buy an ad on Facebook, for instance, which is paid media. If five hundred people like or share it, your paid media takes on the characteristics of earned media and can drive traffic to media you own, such as your website, a blog site, or a social media channel.

Your primary objective should be to get traffic to your owned media. Your social media campaign will be effective when you post on Facebook that you've just released a new T-shirt, and within the first six hours you get one thousand visits to your website from people who want to check out the new shirt. That's the power of social media, and you'd be smart to take advantage of it.

When considering what combination of media to use on social, consider your budget and your objectives. If you have a limited budget, use the paid media you can afford to drive earned media and direct traffic to the media you own. Using retargeting, PPC, and display ads can result in increased traffic to your website or other owned media and, as a result, increased sales.

Putting in the Work

Getting ready to launch a successful social campaign requires a lot of work. You'll need to choose your goals, research your target audience, check out your competition, identify your most important metrics, devise a workable timeline, create your content, and make sure everyone on your team is on the same page. And that's before the campaign is even launched!

Once the campaign is up and running, you'll need to keep tabs on how it's progressing, using your identified metrics to measure results. Without ongoing analysis, you won't know how one social campaign stacks up to another or whether your message or placement needs to be tweaked. Monitoring the metrics enables you to identify small changes that need to be made, which can save you the angst of later needing to make large, time-consuming changes.

Social campaigns are becoming increasingly important in an overall marketing strategy. The careful planning and execution of a social campaign must be followed by continual monitoring and tinkering, with a willingness to change course if necessary.

Advertising on Social Media

Anyone who spends time on social media is aware of the prevalence of advertising there. Statista reports that in 2018 nearly $27 billion US dollars were spent on social media advertising, and almost $40 billion by 2020. Advertising for the 2020 presidential election alone generated more than $200 million for social media sites, with Donald Trump spending $107 million between the beginning of the year and October 24 and Joe Biden spending $94.2 million. Although Biden was declared the winner, perhaps the real winner was Facebook, which took in the lion's share of that spending.

Social advertising has become mainstream, and for good reason. It allows you to engage with viewers, building a two-way relationship. That form of advertising is far more effective than, say, a billboard, which viewers merely glance at as they drive by, or a newspaper ad, which may or may not even be seen. Social advertising ensures an audience and enables you to build rapport as you communicate directly with viewers.

Businesses collectively spend billions to advertise on social media, but it's typically much less expensive than traditional advertising. According to LinkedIn, it costs about fifty-seven dollars to produce a direct mail ad that will reach one thousand people, and the cost to reach the same number of people on social media would be less than three dollars.

A downside, however, is the clutter. Advertising on social media is certainly more competitive than a direct mail ad, which recipients are pretty sure to notice. It's also more competitive than email advertising, because the many ads on social tend to run together. After spending twenty minutes on Facebook or a similar site, it's often difficult to remember what you've looked at. To combat clutter, your ads need to stand out.

Choosing a Platform or Platforms

While niche social media networks do have the potential to connect an advertiser with likely customers, remember that, as mentioned earlier in this chapter, the great majority of social network users frequent the big sites like Facebook, YouTube, and Instagram. We've also mentioned that different networks—even the biggest ones—appeal to different audiences. You might have to experiment to figure out which sites are best for you, perhaps establishing a presence on each of the major platforms and then shifting efforts as you learn more about which are most effective. Let's look at five of the largest and most popular sites; the number of monthly active users, or MAUs; and some features of each site to help you develop an idea of which might be a good fit for your advertising plan.

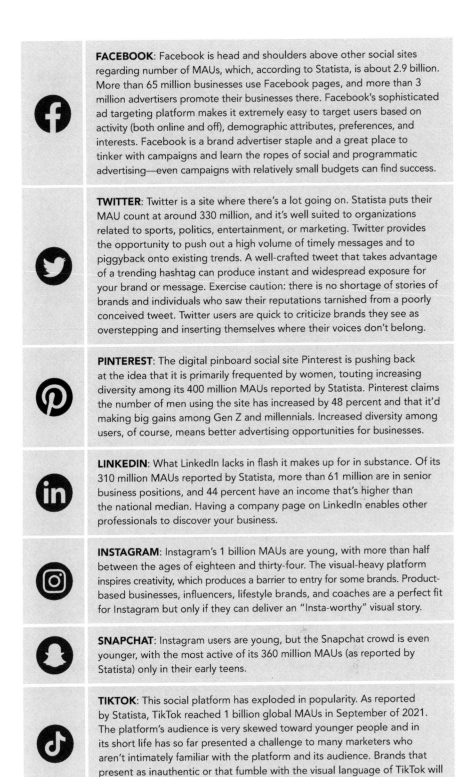

FACEBOOK: Facebook is head and shoulders above other social sites regarding number of MAUs, which, according to Statista, is about 2.9 billion. More than 65 million businesses use Facebook pages, and more than 3 million advertisers promote their businesses there. Facebook's sophisticated ad targeting platform makes it extremely easy to target users based on activity (both online and off), demographic attributes, preferences, and interests. Facebook is a brand advertiser staple and a great place to tinker with campaigns and learn the ropes of social and programmatic advertising—even campaigns with relatively small budgets can find success.

TWITTER: Twitter is a site where there's a lot going on. Statista puts their MAU count at around 330 million, and it's well suited to organizations related to sports, politics, entertainment, or marketing. Twitter provides the opportunity to push out a high volume of timely messages and to piggyback onto existing trends. A well-crafted tweet that takes advantage of a trending hashtag can produce instant and widespread exposure for your brand or message. Exercise caution: there is no shortage of stories of brands and individuals who saw their reputations tarnished from a poorly conceived tweet. Twitter users are quick to criticize brands they see as overstepping and inserting themselves where their voices don't belong.

PINTEREST: The digital pinboard social site Pinterest is pushing back at the idea that it is primarily frequented by women, touting increasing diversity among its 400 million MAUs reported by Statista. Pinterest claims the number of men using the site has increased by 48 percent and that it'd making big gains among Gen Z and millennials. Increased diversity among users, of course, means better advertising opportunities for businesses.

LINKEDIN: What LinkedIn lacks in flash it makes up for in substance. Of its 310 million MAUs reported by Statista, more than 61 million are in senior business positions, and 44 percent have an income that's higher than the national median. Having a company page on LinkedIn enables other professionals to discover your business.

INSTAGRAM: Instagram's 1 billion MAUs are young, with more than half between the ages of eighteen and thirty-four. The visual-heavy platform inspires creativity, which produces a barrier to entry for some brands. Product-based businesses, influencers, lifestyle brands, and coaches are a perfect fit for Instagram but only if they can deliver an "Insta-worthy" visual story.

SNAPCHAT: Instagram users are young, but the Snapchat crowd is even younger, with the most active of its 360 million MAUs (as reported by Statista) only in their early teens.

TIKTOK: This social platform has exploded in popularity. As reported by Statista, TikTok reached 1 billion global MAUs in September of 2021. The platform's audience is very skewed toward younger people and in its short life has so far presented a challenge to many marketers who aren't intimately familiar with the platform and its audience. Brands that present as inauthentic or that fumble with the visual language of TikTok will struggle to gain a foothold with the platform's audience.

GRAPHIC

fig. 64

While the social media platforms mentioned above are some of the biggest players, there are plenty of other options. So how do you go about choosing sites on which to advertise?

The first step is getting a good handle on who it is you're trying to reach. Next, you must clearly define your goals, whether they're to attract new customers, develop relationships, get repeat customers to buy more from you, provide customer support, or other efforts.

Finally, you'll need to match the advertising site to your audience. If you're marketing to teens, for instance, LinkedIn is not where you want to be. But if B2B is your thing, you'll want to consider that network. You may be able to gauge where your target audience is spending its time based on where your competitors are advertising. Or you can go straight to the source and survey your customers regarding their social media habits. Ultimately, the data will be your best friend. Measure the performance of your campaigns and review your progress regularly.

Start on a platform you are comfortable with. It's better to master an advertising and growth strategy on one platform than to struggle on every platform you come across.

Audience Targeting and Building

You read about identifying your target market and ideal customer in chapter 3, and a lot of that information also applies to reaching people on social media. With any sort of marketing, it's important to identify the group of people you want to appeal to, because they will be those most interested in your product or service.

With billions of people on social media every day, targeting the audience you want to reach is crucial. Most social sites offer predefined audiences, or you can use tools they offer to help you define your targeted audience and get the best advertising results. If you are setting up an ad to run on Facebook, for instance, its Ad Center will help you create your target audience using not only general demographics such as gender, age, and location, but more specific demographics including income, employment, interests, behaviors, travel habits, and so forth.

The trick is to target an audience that is large enough to justify your advertising costs but small enough to reach only the people who would be interested in your product or service. It can seem counterintuitive to aim for a relatively small audience. Let's face it, the more people who see your ad, the better, right?

The size of your audience, however, depends on your objectives. If you simply want everyone to know you have a new product available, a very large target audience is appropriate. Generally, though, a smaller target audience is more helpful because it means you won't waste precious dollars reaching people who have absolutely no interest in what you're selling.

Also, it's much easier to test your targeting criteria and gauge the success of your ad with a smaller audience. If your audience is six million people and your advertising is not resulting in many click-throughs, it will be very difficult to gauge why, because you have so many people and so many different demographics contained within the audience. A smaller audience is easier to analyze, tweak, and adjust.

When you've narrowed down the audience you want to reach, you will have created your customer avatar, which, as you read earlier, is the template for your ideal customer. Having a good knowledge of that avatar will help you develop your brand guidelines and enable you to communicate with and engage your audience. If your company sells more than one product or offers more than one service, you may have more than one avatar.

Once you've got a good idea of who your target customers are, you need to discover where on social media they are most active. Do your homework to learn where they're spending their time, so you know where you have the best chance of reaching them. Test the waters, and if you find you get a good response on one site but not another, adjust your social media advertising plan.

Once you're satisfied you've got your target audience in place, work on building that audience to maximize the number of people who see and respond to your advertising. You can increase the frequency of your advertising or create ads targeting a broader audience than you've reached before. As you increase your reach, pay attention to how many people you are reaching and engaging. If you're reaching more people but your sales are not increasing, you may have strayed away from your best target audience and will need to refine it or change your ads.

Testing and Data Collection

Testing and data collection are indispensable tools for gauging the success of your social advertising because they help you achieve a better understanding of who you are reaching and who else you might need to reach.

When you pay for advertising on social media, you get significant information about who is seeing and interacting with your ads. You can use that information to increase your knowledge about your target audience and potentially expand it. For instance, if your target audience is males between eighteen and thirty-four years of age who like hunting and fishing, Facebook might tell you that, according to your recent ad campaign, your audience also likes auto repair and camping. Having that information helps you to better understand your customers, know what they like, and discern how you can best connect with them.

It's important to remain flexible, be receptive to data, and use it to inform your decisions. If the data tells you that your ideal customer likes camping in addition to hunting and fishing and you don't add camping gear to your product line, it's likely that you're missing out on sales opportunities. Data is not always foolproof, but it is informative, and you should pay attention to it.

The data you collect will provide information about how effective your advertising efforts are and what you should be testing. If the data reveals that your target audience likes camping, you could test how members respond to an ad for a camp stove or a sleeping bag you're offering at a discounted price for a limited time. Compare the response you get on that ad to the response for previous ads, and use the information to inform your next wave of advertising. You won't always get it right, but if you understand your customers and consider the data, your best-informed guess should be pretty solid.

Don't be afraid to tweak your ads to see what is most effective. Maybe you need to change a headline or state an offer differently in order to see what customers respond to. It might be something as simple as saying a product is on sale for 40 percent below its original price instead of saying the product is on sale for twelve dollars less than its original price, even though the final price paid by the customer is ultimately the same.

If you discover that a particular ad or sale or offer doesn't work, consider that to be valuable information to be used in the future, and move on. Being willing to admit defeat will prevent you from getting bogged down in a campaign that isn't working.

Messaging and Creatives

We've already discussed the various social sites that are attractive to advertisers and different models of paid advertising, such as search ads and display ads. Within those ad categories, however, are a variety of ad types, such as text, image, and video ads.

There are many types of ads you can display on social media, with some typically achieving better results than others. Generally, social media ads fall into two categories: static image ads and video ads. Within those categories there are many different flavors.

The type of ad you use should depend on your objectives, your goals, and, as always, your budget. Let's have a look at some of the most often used types of social media ad formats and consider what might make sense for your social campaign.

»   **Static image ads**. These ads, also called photo ads, are appropriate for showing users a product, making an announcement, or calling attention to a promotion. Image ads tend to be affordable, they send a clear message, their size can be adjusted, and they tend to display well, even on older web browsers. They're generally accepted by all platforms and are easy to produce. The thing about image ads is that they've got to command attention. If you've heard the phrase "attention interrupter," it likely applied to an image ad.

»   **Video ads**. As you read earlier, video ads often are considered the gold standard of social advertising, but they can be expensive to produce and run. However, because video works well with short-form content, it may fit into your budget. That could be advantageous, as video consumption is rapidly growing and has been shown to increase email open rates.

»   **Carousel ads**. This format lets you show up to ten images within a single ad. It's an interactive form of advertising because each image has its own link, giving viewers a chance to explore. These ads are a great way to showcase a product by demonstrating different ways it can be used or by letting viewers see it from different angles.

» **Story ads**. Instagram story ads were launched in 2017, with Facebook and Messenger launching them shortly after. They can be either static images or video—video is more engaging—and are displayed on a full screen and are technically placed outside of the news feed to be viewed separately. The popularity of story ads, with both advertisers and consumers, has increased dramatically in past years.

If you're not feeling like a strong creative, check out services like Canva, which is a sophisticated and simplified image and video creator designed specifically for digital marketers. Additionally, social platforms will offer guidance on what works best for their audiences. Spend some time thinking about who you want your ad to reach, how the ad can best represent your brand, the tone you want to convey, and what you hope your ad will accomplish.

One of the best sources of inspiration for social advertising comes in the form of other social advertisers. When you are browsing social media on your own time, pay special attention to the ads you are shown and the posts that you see. Take screenshots of the posts and ads that do something you like, and create a swipe file. Add notes or brainstorm the ways in which you would use the same techniques or visuals to convey your message or offer. A social media swipe file can be an invaluable reference tool when producing your own creatives or can be a source of inspiration for a designer you hire.

Chat and Messenger

Short Message Service (SMS), or text messaging, has been around for decades. A team of German and French engineers invented it in the mid-1980s. The very first text message, according to an article in the *New York Times*, was sent in 1992 by a twenty-two-year-old engineer named Neil Papworth. The technology for sending messages from a cell phone was not yet available, so Papworth used a personal computer to send a two-word text message to his colleague Richard Jarvis. The message? "Merry Christmas."

SMS has advanced tremendously since then, of course, changing not only the way individuals communicate with each other, but also the way customers and potential customers communicate with businesses. Today it's a vital tool for digital marketers, as it enables personalized, immediate connections with followers. It's also an asset for customer service—another important aspect of your business.

Facebook's Chat and Messenger enable you to pull users out of their news feeds and grab their attention. You could, for instance, message a group of followers to announce a new product being offered at 30 percent off for the next twenty-four hours. Hopefully, a significant number of those followers would stop what they were doing and click over to your website to check out and order the product.

According to Facebook, 83 percent of consumers use live chat to be in touch with businesses and learn more about products and services, and 75 percent end up buying something. Live chat, as the name implies, is real-time online conversation between someone visiting your site and a representative of your business.

Along with live chat, chatbots have become a popular marketing technology, enabling businesses to save time and money while maintaining contact with customers and potential customers. Sometimes called "conversational agents," chatbots are apps that imitate written or spoken speech to facilitate customer service conversations. They employ natural language processing, the same technology used by virtual assistants such as Siri or Alexa.

Customers use chatbots to get quick answers to questions, report and resolve complaints, obtain more information, and get connected to a human. Businesses use them to automate conversations, eliminating the need for an employee. They can gather information about customers and potential customers that can generate leads and revenue and provide support to customers outside of regular business hours.

Damage Control at the Speed of Social

We live in a highly charged social environment, in which hypersensitivity seems to be the norm. This makes it difficult to gauge what may be considered offensive to someone and leaves the door open to missteps. While this can happen in any setting, social media has exacerbated the opportunity for offense and for that offense to be shared—widely and quickly.

A statement on social media that seems innocuous to the person posting it can set off a firestorm if misinterpreted or considered offensive by another individual or group. If this happens in your business, it can damage your reputation and brand. The same tools that make it easy to spread your message can also highlight a mistake or a problem. Negative social media, regardless of whether it's a result of backlash against something you post, the rants of an angry customer, or the work of a hacker, can wreak havoc on trust in your brand.

Maybe you remember the spectacularly bad decision Pepsi made in early 2017 when it launched a commercial in which celebrity Kendall Jenner sought to defuse a tense situation during some sort of demonstration by offering an armored police officer a can of Pepsi. Reaction on the internet was swift and universally negative, forcing the company to quickly pull the ad and issue an apology for what was viewed as gross insensitivity. If mistakes of questionable judgment can occur with a company like Pepsi, which surely employs a robust approval process, it's not out of the realm of possibility that it could happen to you.

If a gaffe in your business finds you facing a public relations ordeal, don't panic. There are steps you can take to minimize the damage. Regardless of the size of your company, you should have a plan in place so that you're not left trying to figure out what to do during a crisis or forced to hire a consultant to fix the problem for you.

After thoroughly assessing the situation to find out where and how the problem occurred and who has been affected, you'll want to publicly acknowledge and address the situation. If an apology is warranted, issue one. However, do not apologize again and again, as that only feeds the fire.

Let customers know what you plan to do to make the situation right, and follow through on your intentions, keeping customers informed of your actions. Doing so will help restore their trust and confidence. Remember that while the controversy is difficult and will require work to resolve, the attention spans of most social media users is fairly short, and another issue is bound to pop up elsewhere to redirect them from your problem.

Whatever you do, avoid responding to criticism in an angry or defensive manner. That only encourages more criticism and makes a bad situation worse. Keep your responses professional and courteous.

Associated Metrics

Social media metrics are important because they help you measure how well your campaigns and strategies are doing so you can share that information with others. If applicable metrics reveal you are not meeting the goals you've set for your business and your social campaign, then you can tweak your plan to improve it. If the metrics show you've exceeded your goals, then you've earned some bragging rights. Either way, you should be aware of how things are going, and important metrics can help you do just that.

Social media platforms include dashboards that let you see all the information you'll need to measure results related to your account. In addition, there are social media monitoring tools like Hootsuite, Semrush, and HubSpot that can track conversations related to your brand, let you see what your competitors are doing on social, track specific keywords, compare hashtag performance, manage and track social reach through campaigns, and much more.

Engagement

Social media engagement is good, but it is not an end in itself. The rate of engagement is a metric that indicates how actively your followers are involved with your content. Your overall engagement metric includes things like clicks, likes, shares, comments, and mentions. A high engagement rate is good, as it indicates your audience is responsive and paying attention to your material.

Some marketers feel engagement is a vanity metric that, when favorable, makes a business feel good about itself but doesn't go very far in advancing business goals. You can have thousands of clicks and likes, for instance, but if users aren't hanging around to check out your product or learn more about your company, they aren't worth very much.

Engagement such as comments and shares, however, which help to connect your current audience with others and can raise awareness of your brand, are very useful, as they link your social media with your real business objectives. Engagement metrics generally pertain to the awareness part of your social media funnel.

Follower Count

Follower count, or the number of followers you have on social media, is another metric that some people consider to be very important and others, not so much. Let's look at it this way. Having lots of followers does give you the opportunity to capitalize on those numbers and use them to get word about your brand out to a great number of people. On the other hand, it could be that your customer and potential customer bases are small and you are already reaching all the people you need to without having a huge follower count. Or you could have a small follower count on one social media platform and a really big one on another platform, depending on where your audience spends its time.

Having presented that argument, I will say that follower count is important because the message you put out on social media won't do any good if it's only getting to a few people. A brand that has a large number of followers tends to command respect, and more followers jump on board. So, while follower count can be considered a vanity metric, there is value in adding followers to your social media account. Follower count falls in the awareness part of the social media marketing funnel.

Reach

Reach metrics focus on the size of your audience and your potential audience, and how much and how quickly they have grown. Reach also indicates the frequency with which your messages are reaching your audience and how well those messages are being received. In paid social, reach also applies to CPM, or cost per thousand ad impressions. Reach is simply the number of people exposed to your social media presence.

NOTE

Social media reach is often confused with number of impressions, but they are two different metrics. Reach is the number of people your message gets in front of, and impressions are the number of times a message is viewed. If you are scrolling through a social media feed and see the same message three times, that is three impressions. But it's only one reach, because you are one person who has seen the message three times.

You can track your reach metrics by monitoring individual post reach, overall campaign reach, the increase in number of followers, and the rate at which your audience has grown. Reach is a top-of-the-funnel metric but an important one to monitor, as it is an indicator of the strength or weakness of brand awareness.

ROI

ROI, or return on investment, is a critical metric because it measures how well your marketing efforts are doing and whether they are resulting in growth for the company. However, measuring ROI can be cumbersome. The temptation is to try to gauge ROI using metrics such as "likes" and "tweets," but a business needs to be more concerned with numbers that indicate real success, like conversions and email subscribers.

Google Analytics is a helpful tool for gauging the ROI of social media. Its social reports indicate on which social networks you're experiencing the best level of success, which of your content is the most popular, the impact of social actions such as texting and image posting, and how social can produce conversions.

Measuring ROI in social media can remain elusive. What social does best is build relationships, as exemplified by the social funnel. But building relationships takes time, and there is not always a clear cause-and-effect factor. Nevertheless, ROI is certainly important and a metric to be carefully considered.

Conversions

Your business is largely dependent on conversions for its success, so conversion metrics, which fit within the action section of the funnel, are clearly important. These metrics demonstrate how effective your social engagement is for your marketing campaign, and they should be a priority for your business.

A high conversion rate indicates that your social content is valuable to members of your audience, and a low conversion rate is a wake-up call telling you that content needs to be improved.

You can track the number of conversions that result from your social media campaign by using UTM parameters in the link you're promoting. In case "UTM parameters" isn't ringing any bells for you, they are just short text codes you add to a URL. When the link is clicked on, the codes are relayed back to your social media site's analytics platform and can be tracked.

Chapter Recap

» Social media changes quickly but has become increasingly important for business marketing.

» Social *marketing* is ongoing, but a social media *campaign* occurs within a defined timeline and includes specific, stated goals.

» Advertising on social media enables you to reach customers and potential customers where they are while facilitating interaction.

» Chat, chatbots, and Messenger are becoming increasingly important as business marketing and customer service tools.

» Damage can occur quickly on social media, meaning you need to have a plan in place to counteract it.

| 10 |

Following Up with Email

Chapter Overview

- » The value of email
- » Building a list
- » Using lead magnets
- » The parts of an email
- » Making it personal

Despite some speculation that email marketing is old-fashioned or even obsolete, the fact is that according to Statista, 4.03 billion people around the world use email, and in the United States more than nine out of every ten people receive and send email messages from phones, computers, and tablets. Email is ubiquitous. It's a communication workhorse.

In fact, email generates the highest ROI for marketers, beating out social, display, TV, and other forms of advertising. For every dollar spent, a well-planned and well-executed email marketing campaign can generate forty-four dollars in ROI, according to Campaign Monitor.

Messages in a person's inbox are much more personal and exist in a (relatively) less competitive environment than those on social or other locations. Plus, email has a huge reach. It delivers the message you choose to put out, drives conversions, and, for many people, is still the preferred method of communicating. Of course, other tactics that we've discussed, like paid search, social, and display ads, are valuable, too—and they can work well together with email. Let's take a look at why achieving a strong email list is so important to your business.

The Money Is in the List

As a digital marketer, your primary goal is to ascend your customers up the value ladder, making sure the offerings you present to them increase in price, frequency, and value. While digital marketers have an incredible number of marketing tools to choose from, email is still the most prevalent means of achieving the goal of ascending customers. To reach and ascend customers using emails, however, you need to build your list. Generally speaking, a robust email list leads to more subscribers, which leads to increased reach, which leads to more conversions. That's a winning combination, and it's why a great list is one of your business's most valuable assets.

All email lists are not the same in value, however. It doesn't matter how many contacts you have if you're sending out emails to people who aren't interested in your content. Ideally, those on your email list will be looking to build a relationship with your business and will be happy to hear from you.

NOTE

To ensure that the email addresses of those who sign up are properly collected and stored and that your subscribers receive the emails you send, you'll want to choose an email service provider to help you build your lists and send emails. Options like Keap, GetResponse, Mailchimp, and Constant Contact are popular offerings but there is an entire world of email service providers out there for new marketers to explore. When shopping for an email service provider, look for a service that scales with your business needs in both functionality and capacity.

Let's look at how to build your email list by attracting subscribers.

Getting Subscribers

Subscribers are indispensable to growing your business. An obstacle to this growth, however, comes in the form of subscriber hesitancy. Many people exercise caution when it comes to giving out their email address. They've been burned by spammers and are understandably not eager for it to happen again. To convince them your company is worth taking a chance on, you need to provide an offer that's too good to pass up.

Leaning on Your Lead Magnets

As you know, a lead magnet is something you give away in exchange for an email address or other information. Lead magnets are nothing new, but they continue to be an effective means of generating email subscribers. It doesn't have to be overly complicated to convince a visitor to your website or someone reading your blog to take the bait and give up an email address. But you must be able to offer something that's valuable to the person you're looking to gain as a subscriber. It's got to be an enticing offer that is exciting to your potential customer and speaks to solving a problem they face.

fig. 65

An example of an opt-in form using lead magnets to attract potential customers

Remember that a lead magnet shouldn't appeal to everyone, only those who have the potential to become loyal, valuable customers. If you offer a free ice cream cone to every person who enters an email, you're likely to get a lot of email addresses, but all you know about those who sign up is that they like ice cream. Your offer should be something that clearly leads to your product or service and that segments your audience.

If you offer more than one product or service, you're likely to need more than one lead magnet, because you want to attract the audience that's most likely to buy what you're offering. A very specific lead magnet makes it easier to understand who is subscribing to your emails, which makes it easier to build a targeted sales funnel.

Making Sure Your Lead Magnet Gets Noticed

Once you've come up with a lead magnet that will appeal to potential customers, you've got to make sure they see it. You can promote the magnet on your website by making it the first thing a user sees when arriving. Or you can place a banner at the top of all the pages of your website reminding people of your offer.

There are a lot of ways to promote a lead magnet on social media, such as posting status updates with an image and a link to your landing page or running an ad promoting the lead magnet on a platform that's applicable to your audience.

You could advertise your offer on a content hub, which is simply a site on which content is organized around a specific topic, or anywhere else where content is viewed. Be creative in order to get your lead magnet in front of as many people as possible.

Testing Different Offers

You'll know that a lead magnet is working when you see your email subscriber list growing, but how do you know it's working better than another magnet might? Just as you can do with the ads you run on social media, you can use an A/B test to help determine which lead magnets are getting you the most email addresses.

An A/B test presents two versions of a page of your website. The versions are exactly the same except for one thing: the lead magnet. So some visitors are directed, for instance, to a landing page advertising a free webinar, and others are directed to a landing page touting a free consultation.

If, over time, twice as many people give you their email addresses in exchange for the free consultation as for the webinar, you know that the consult offer is more attractive to visitors to your site.

You can get online tools to help you with A/B tests (they are quite cumbersome to execute manually). You can repeat the tests as you come up with new lead magnets, eventually amassing a collection of successful ones.

The Anatomy of an Email

An email has several parts, all of which are important. You can write killer email copy, but if the subject line doesn't inspire people to open the email, the copy doesn't matter. Let's face it. People get and send a lot of emails, and many struggle with the amount of time required to manage their inboxes. Keeping your emails succinct, interesting, and engaging can go a long way toward keeping subscribers happy. Let's take a look at the various parts of an email.

The "From" Label

The "from" label tells subscribers who is the sender of the email. It's the first thing many people look at, so make sure your business name is recognizable and professional in order to avoid having your email sent to a spam or trash folder.

The Subject Line

The subject line of an email is extremely important because it's what makes people decide whether to read its contents. A subject line should be short, no more than five or six words, and should provide a clear explanation of the email's content.

Shorter subject lines are a good place to start; however, some marketers have seen success with other lengths, including ultra-short (just one or two words) and longer subject lines. Try experimenting with a variety of configurations—numbers, capitalization styles, use of emojis at the beginning, middle, or end of the line, and so on.

Think of the subject line as a title or headline. It needs to let subscribers know what to expect, in a clear and interesting manner. Opinion regarding subject lines (as with most everything else) varies. Some people favor using humor, insults, or shocking text to get readers' attention, while others feel those things can be off-putting and discourage users from opening the email. If you know your audience well, there's probably more room for a subject line that is funny or in-your-face. Just remember that they may not appeal to everyone. Here are some pro tips regarding copy for subject lines:

» **Personalize it.** Though some people feel that including a name in a subject line has become overused, referencing something that the user knows can be attention-grabbing. Example: *Hey Sara, we've reserved a spot for you!*

» **Use action words.** Words that suggest action or evoke emotion or curiosity typically work well in a subject line. Verbs such as "discover," "become," "improve," or "try" have proven to be engaging. Example: *Transform your living space on a budget.*

» **Avoid sounding like spam**. A subject line that sounds needy, pushy, cheap, manipulative, or just "out there" will turn off a significant portion of your audience and run the risk of being intercepted by spam filters. Example: *Reply now or you'll regret it tomorrow.*

» **Numbers**, especially when they indicate a list, can be attention-getters. Example: *The 8 worst plays in Sunday's Super Bowl.*

» **A little mystery**, such as indicating that something exciting is about to happen. Example: *You did not see this coming!*

» **FOMO**. Everybody wants in on a deal or opportunity. Subject lines suggesting you'll miss out if you don't act fast tend to perform well. Example: *This vacation deal is almost gone.*

These tips will help your subject lines get noticed, but don't be tempted to use every tactic on every email. Focus on one approach—using a numbered list or tapping into FOMO, for example—and change it often.

Many email service providers will help by warning you if your subject line is too long, too short, or likely to be flagged as spam.

While honing your email skills, make it a habit to collect emails with subject lines that appealed to you, convinced you to open, or otherwise seem like a good fit for your own brand to draw inspiration from. And always subscribe to your competition's lists! Being a subscriber to the competition is a good way to glean important information, not only about how often they send email and the kinds of subject lines they use, but other helpful business intelligence like how often they run sales and release new products, and the kinds of features and benefits they focus on.

Attempting to trick subscribers into opening your message by misrepresenting its contents is not only a good way to drive unsubscribes and tick off subscribers, but in egregious cases may result in fines or other penalties from the FTC.

Email Copy

Once an email is opened, it becomes all about the copy. Generally speaking, shorter emails have proven to be better received than long ones, although brands that have mastered long emails might argue with that. The copy should be organized, easy to scan, and easy to read on a variety of devices. If your message contains a lot of copy or text, like in a newsletter, use bullet points to call out important information, and break down large blocks of text with headings and frequent line breaks.

Organize copy with headlines, and don't be afraid to include photos and/or links to video. Email generally makes a poor environment for a video player, and attaching a video file can cause the email's file size to balloon. A best practice for video in email is to include a still frame from the video with a play button symbol superimposed on the image. Link this image to the video hosted elsewhere, such as on YouTube, Vimeo, or your own site, to keep email file size small and load time fast.

fig. 66

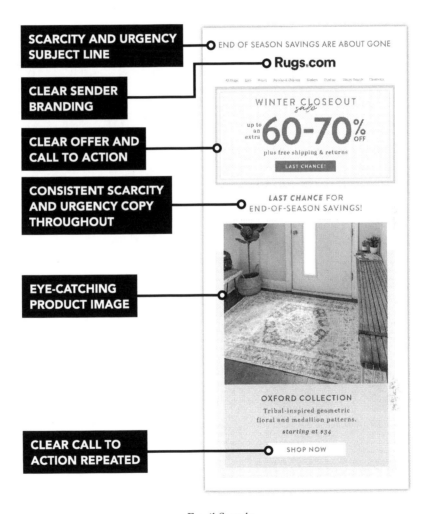

Email Sample

Source: www.reallygoodemails.com

Call To Action

Don't forget to include a call to action, which is typically the reason for the email. A good call to action will instruct readers in what they must do to take the next step and will encourage them to do so. The call could direct your audience to your company website, an article, a social site, or elsewhere.

Keep your message consistent across the subject line, body copy, and CTA. You will always see better results focusing an email on a single ask or call to action rather than making your subscribers choose between multiple calls to action. As a rule of thumb, if you want your subscribers to take two actions, send them two emails.

Compliance Information

By law, every bulk commercial email is required to include an unsubscribe link and the physical address of the sender. These are typically inserted at the bottom of every message and are generally handled by the email service provider (you don't have to remember to include them yourself). In addition to being required, the unsubscribe link improves the user experience because it gives subscribers who no longer want to receive your emails a quick and easy way to discontinue them.

CAN-SPAM

The CAN-SPAM Act, which stands for Controlling the Assault of Non-Solicited Pornography and Marketing, was enacted in 2003 in response to consumer complaints about unsolicited emails.

It's important to understand the rules of the CAN-SPAM Act, because the Federal Trade Commission is authorized to levy hefty fines (as much as $43,280 per email) against violators. Don't be overly alarmed, though. Making sure every email you send complies with the CAN-SPAM Act may seem daunting, but once you get a template that has all the requirements embedded, you can use it for all the emails you send. What's more, the FTC offers tips for marketers on how they can remain compliant with the CAN-SPAM Act. Here are the most important points:

» **Keep your header honest**. You are required to clearly identify the business that's sending the email in the "from," "reply to," and "routing information" sections.

» **Keep your subject line honest.** You cannot state something that's not true, such as "You've just won a ten-day vacation in Italy!!!" to cajole someone into opening an email.

» **Admit the email is an ad.** It doesn't have to be in the subject line, but if your email contains an advertisement, you've got to state that somewhere within it.

» **Share your location.** If your business has a physical location, it must be included in every email you send. If you don't have a business address, you can use a P.O. box number.

» **Include an easy opt-out option.** You can't hide this or make it cumbersome for someone to indicate they no longer want to receive your emails. The opt-out option has to be accessible and simple.

» **When someone opts out, they opt out.** A person who opts out must be removed from your mailing list within ten days, and you are not permitted to use, transfer, or sell that person's email address from that point on.

» **Maintain oversight.** Remember, you are on the hook for CAN-SPAM violations. If you have a third party creating and managing your emails, be sure they understand and adhere to the rules of the act.

Staying within these guidelines ensures not only that you'll stay within the law, but that your relationship with your customers will be transparent and truthful. It also will make your email a lot less likely to be categorized as spam.

Converting Subscribers

One of the simple truths about maintaining and leveraging an email list is that it takes work, and that work is never done. On the front end, acquiring subscribers can be a grind. Success means using a mix of paid, earned, and owned media to direct traffic to your lead magnet offer. As we have covered, once this process is established it operates largely on autopilot. That being said, a sophisticated and well-designed comprehensive digital marketing strategy includes monitoring and anticipating *subscriber churn*. Subscriber churn is the natural gain and loss of subscribers that all email lists experience.

There are a number of reasons why people unsubscribe from email lists. It's no secret that the rigors of modern communication produce increasingly competing demands on our time, and our email inboxes are no exception. Another top reason that people abandon email lists is that they don't find the messages valuable, relevant, or helpful. After all, they are expending time and focus to open and read the messages they're sent; it's only fair that they should expect to get something out of that time.

DETOUR

As you move through this book, I'm sure you're realizing there are a lot of pieces to digital marketing, and there will be some days when you feel like you've hit a brick wall. Hang in there, though, because in time all the pieces will start to come together, and the concepts you're learning about will fall into place. And remember, if there's an area of digital marketing that you find particularly difficult, like writing killer email messages, for instance, there are plenty of talented freelance copywriters standing by to help you accomplish your marketing goals.

When courting your subscribers, keep the following guidelines in mind.

Start at the Subject Line

As you read earlier, the subject line of an email is your chance to connect with your audience. If you've been able to get a good sense of your subscribers—their preferences, what they need and what they want—you should be able to connect with them in an email. The better the sense you have of your audience, the easier it will be to find a voice that fits for correspondence. Should it sound formal or informal? Funny or serious? Relaxed or right to the point?

Understanding the habits, wants, and needs of your audience will provide prompts for your copy, enabling you to write subject lines that resonate.

Establish a Contact Cadence

Email marketing is subject to an interesting dilemma. Send too many emails in too short a period and you will inundate your subscribers. Four or five emails a day will understandably push *anyone* to unsubscribe no matter how useful or relevant the content may be. On the other hand, if emails are few and far between you run the risk of fading into obscurity. Wait too long to send your next follow-up message and a subscriber could have forgotten why they signed up in the first place. Think about how often it's important for you to reach your subscribers, and time your emails accordingly. And don't be shy about reminding them of the value you provide!

The 80/20 Rule

Also known as the *Pareto principle*, the 80/20 rule makes an appearance in many aspects of the business world. When applied to the world of business generally, the 80/20 rule states that "80 percent of your revenue will come from 20 percent of your customers." It may seem anecdotal, but this line of thinking has proven true time and time again for business owners in a wide variety of sectors.

In the world of email marketing, the 80/20 rule translates into a rough prescription for the content of your email marketing efforts. Generally speaking, 80 percent of your email messages should provide pure value to your audience, and no more than 20 percent should push a product, advertise a sale, or otherwise be "salesy." Even in today's landscape of ad fatigue and skepticism of paid messaging, your audience understands that as a brand you will market to them at some point. In fact, your audience *expects* some level of "salesy" messaging. Of course, they also expect that you will deliver value to their inboxes.

Intimacy Equals Extreme Personalization

To date, and for the foreseeable future, email is one of the most intimate forms of digital communication. As we have discussed, your audience's inboxes are a less competitive environment (as compared to social media and the internet at large), and they are very personal. Short of phoning your prospects, email is the closest you can get to a one-on-one conversation that is persistent, ubiquitous, and personalized. We refer to the sum of these characteristics as "intimate," and as far as digital marketing is concerned, intimate means extremely personalized.

Considering the technology available today, we can see that audiences expect personalization that runs deeper than merely including their name in the subject line. Today's personalization speaks to the needs of your audience; it speaks to their familiarity with your products; it speaks to their specific, unique problems; and it speaks to their values and experience. In short, today's communication technology means that the market/media/message mix is more important than ever.

DETOUR

The mention of any direct messaging technology outside of email runs the very real risk of dating this text. Two decades ago, a book similar to this one would have included AOL Instant Messenger as an intimate, personalized, and low-competition communication method. Today we know the fate of AOL IM. It is the intent of the author to focus on concepts and practices that transcend today's tech and speak more closely to the lasting human aspects of digital communication. There is no shortage of communication platforms today that are trying to kill email as we know it and replace it with a more efficient system. Congratulations to the platform (or platforms) that is ultimately successful, but the point here is that the communication system that email represents—personal, intimate, and low in competition—will always be a facet of digital communications no matter the name it bears or the technology it's served on.

Using Tech-Enabled Personalization Methods

Contemporary email service providers have spent a considerable amount of money learning what drives opens, clicks, and subscriber retention. To this end, email service providers have labeled the most relevant information mail merge fields, which are placeholders that correspond to personal information that is tagged in a database. It works like this: if I want to send a message to a thousand of my contacts about their recent order, the message might say something like "Hello <first name>, thank you for your recent order <order number> for <order value>." When sending, the appropriately tagged information will be filled into the merge fields so that each person receives a message that is specific to their name, order number, and order value. Let's take a look at some of the creative ways in which these fields (and other customer information) can be used to produce favorable results.

Instead of Sending Generic Coupons

Send specific, relevant coupons. It is the rare (and inadequate) e-commerce store that does not collect customer behavior information. Using this information to send category-specific messages to your audience will result in better open rates, better click rates, and potentially more revenue per customer. The exact method by which this strategy is carried out varies from platform to platform, but generally speaking, the CRM (customer relationship management) aspect of your e-commerce vendor combined with the customer tagging rules of your email service provider are used. You could send a customer a special birthday coupon, or a coupon timed to coincide with her finishing her sixty-day supply of face cream.

A basic example is an online clothing retailer that sells clothing for men, women, and kids. Instead of sending a generic "Save 20 percent on your order before midnight tonight" coupon, digital marketers find better results by sending category-specific coupons. Shoppers who have a history of purchasing women's clothes are much more interested in a coupon like "More of what you love—20 percent off women's styles for spring." The same goes for men's clothing, children's clothing, etc. As with any recommendations or best practices, the data you collect should be your guide.

Instead of Dictating a Narrative

Put your audience at the center of the story and keep them engaged in what is happening. Don't make it about the product or service itself, but about the benefit it will provide to the customer. Lush, an upscale cosmetics company that features package-free products, does a great job of making customers feel special by telling them they are part of the solution to saving the environment by buying its "naked" soaps and shampoos.

Instead of Letting Items in Shopping Carts Go Unpurchased

Use software that reminds customers they haven't completed their purchase. We've probably all received abandoned-cart messages, which are gentle nudges (sometimes with an incentive like free shipping) to get customers who have completed all the purchase steps to go ahead and make it final.

Instead of Just Signing Your Name

Add a signature that directs your audience to highly relevant content that will delight them. Every part of an email message can be leveraged to convey trust and a personal touch. You can also make your email more personal by telling customers something about yourself along with your signature. For instance, you could point readers toward your latest blog post or invite their feedback regarding your role in a campaign or other event.

Instead of Messages Without a CTA

Use every email to convey a message or plant a seed. If you plan to launch a new product two weeks down the road, for example, your email could contain an implicit CTA urging readers to keep an eye on their inbox because there's something coming. Once the product is launched, then you'll send another email with an explicit CTA to check it out and, hopefully, purchase it.

Instead of Ignoring Life Events

Use them to connect with subscribers. Birthdays, anniversaries, and other milestones are a great excuse to reach out to your subscribers and help them celebrate. Special birthday discounts let your subscribers know you are paying attention and care about them. Anniversaries or other milestones, such as one year since a customer's first purchase, are a great way to cement your brand in the lives of your subscribers.

Don't Forget about Mobile

With more and more people opening their emails on phones, make sure your content holds up there. Also consider how it appears on different browsers, as the appearance can vary. The last thing you want is to waste your time and money generating a great email but dropping the ball by not checking to see what it will look like when someone clicks it open from a mobile device. Always check to make sure it renders properly, the display is good, and the color is what you're expecting.

An Email Sequence Crash Course

As you've read, emails have the capacity to help you build relationships with your subscribers. You get to know them as they advance through the marketing funnel, moving from awareness to consideration, on to action, then engagement, and finally reaching advocacy. And, while landing pages, email opt-in forms, and lead magnets are excellent means of generating new subscribers, employing an email sequence can help to build and maintain those relationships.

So what exactly is an email sequence? Basically, it's a series of emails sent automatically to groups of subscribers depending on where they fall within the marketing funnel. These scheduled emails meet subscribers where they are and contain the information they need to move forward to the next stage. Different types of email sequences apply to various situations. If someone signs up for the weekly email tips you offer, for instance, you could send a sequence of welcome emails to establish a relationship and generate trust.

After the welcome sequence, you could follow up with a series of onboarding emails with the goal of moving your subscriber to the action or engagement part of the marketing funnel. These emails would contain information about your product or service that subscribers need, engaging content to keep them interested, and social proof that others have benefited from what your business has to offer. Social proof can be presented through customer stories, testimonials, or product reviews that establish value and encourage recent subscribers to buy.

Once a subscriber is established as a customer, and particularly as a repeat customer, an email sequence can continue to move the relationship forward by letting them know that their business is appreciated. If someone has purchased a product, an email should be timed to arrive two or three days after the expected delivery date. It might ask for feedback regarding the product and the purchase experience, while letting the customer know you are grateful for their business.

Another email several days later might contain information about other products, along with an offer for 20 percent off one item or free shipping.

Another form of email sequencing involves following up with former customers to try to get them back. This is called a reengagement email sequence. Statistics show it's easier to reengage a former customer than to acquire a new one, meaning a reengagement sequence can be well worth the effort.

A reengagement sequence is usually short, since former customers already have information about your business and are familiar with your products or services. The point of the sequence is to remind them that you welcome their business and to perhaps provide a little incentive for them to come back.

While the email sequences just discussed are among the most common, they are not an exhaustive representation. Sequences are also used to remind subscribers about an upcoming event, such as an in-person seminar or conference or an online semiannual sale. And they have proven helpful in getting almost-buyers who abandon their shopping carts to come back for another look at your products.

You can create your own email sequences, tailoring each of them to a different segment of subscribers. The content of each sequence is important, of course, so you'll want to put some time into it and think about what's important for customers at every stage of the funnel. There also are pre-built automation files and email templates you can use if you're not overly confident about your writing skills. Consider what you hope to accomplish by using an email sequence and what you'll need to give customers to accomplish your goal.

Associated Metrics

Many of the most important metrics that are used to measure the success of email marketing campaigns will by now be familiar to you. Conversion-based goals and measurements are par for the course, but there are some email-specific metrics that are unique to reporting the effectiveness of email campaigns. General industry benchmarks can be used for each of these metrics to help determine which results are "good" and which are "bad." Ultimately, the best indicator of a campaign's performance is based on comparing it to historical data for similar offers to the same or similar lists.

Open Rate

The open rate is a basic indicator of a campaign's success. This metric shows the percentage of messages that were opened compared to the total number of messages sent. High open rates are good—an email that is not opened means an unseen message and unclicked links. When open rates are high, it means that your subject line was a good fit for your audience. It piqued their interest and stood out in their mailbox. A declining open rate can be a fluke. If it becomes a trend, it could be a symptom of a variety of underlying issues.

If open rates plummet, consider what you're doing differently. Did you change the days on which you send out messages? The general rule of thumb for email marketing is that midweek, midday is the best time to send messages, but don't be afraid to test different timing parameters. Other causes for declining open rates are low-quality or irrelevant subject lines, poor sender reputation leading to messages being marked as spam, or an old, outdated list.

Click-Through Rate (CTR)

As with just about every other form of digital marketing, the conversion is in the click. When we discuss the CTR of an email campaign, we are looking at the number of people who, after opening the message, clicked on a link (either in text or an image).

Conversion Rate

Conversions count in any type of marketing campaign, because your business depends on them for much of its success. It's great to get a high click-through rate, but even better is a high conversion rate, which indicates that subscribers completed a specific action. A high conversion rate reveals that your audience is engaging with the email, reading it, and heeding the CTA it contains. A low conversion rate means you are not getting or keeping readers' attention or generating enough interest for them to complete the CTA.

You can track the number of conversions your email campaign generates by creating UTM codes for your email links and tracking them in your web analytics dashboard. These simple codes get added to the end of a URL and let you track where website traffic comes from. This enables you to identify the sources of clicks that result in a conversion and calculate the conversion rate. UTM codes and other tracking links are generally created by your email service provider.

Bounce Rate

Email bounces pertaining to the world of email marketing are different from the type of website bounces discussed in chapter 6. As a website performance metric, bounces measure the number of people who visit a website but leave before completing a desired action. When an email bounces, it means that the message could not be delivered successfully, for one of any number of reasons.

fig. 67

$$\text{BOUNCE RATE} = \frac{\text{BOUNCED EMAILS}}{\text{SENT EMAILS}} \times 100$$

Bounces can be classified into one of two groups: hard bounces and soft bounces. A hard bounce occurs when a message is undeliverable because the recipient's address or domain no longer exists. A hard bounce means the intended recipient is permanently unreachable; most email service providers automatically cull hard bounce addresses as they crop up in your lists. A soft bounce, on the other hand, is usually a temporary delivery error. If the recipient's inbox is full, for example, this will trigger a soft bounce. Soft bounces are a nuisance, but they usually don't mean that the intended recipient is permanently unreachable. Different email service providers handle soft bounces differently, but after a recipient triggers enough soft bounces, that address is usually considered a hard bounce and unreachable. Bounce rates—the number of bounces compared to the total number of messages sent—are higher on older or outdated lists.

Unsubscribe Rate

The unsubscribe rate for a particular message is the number of recipients who unsubscribe as a direct result of the message in question compared to the total number of messages sent.

fig. 68

$$\text{UNSUBSCRIBE RATE} = \frac{\text{UNSUBSCRIBERS}}{\text{DELIVERED EMAILS}} \times 100$$

People unsubscribe from lists every day, for a variety of reasons. The best email service providers populate the unsubscribe page with a short survey that must be filled out before the unsubscribe action is complete. This gives you some insight into why the person left your list and can help you spot trends or potential issues. Here are some of the most common reasons people unsubscribe from email lists.

» I get too many emails in general.
» These messages are not relevant to me.
» I no longer want to continue receiving these messages.
» I am no longer interested in this kind of content.
» These emails come too frequently.

As you can see, not all of those reasons are directly tied to your actions—a certain number of unsubscribes will happen no matter what efforts you make. Nonetheless, if you fail to deliver on your promises, send irrelevant or low-quality content, or spam your subscribers, then *all* of the unsubscribes will be your fault! Unsubscribes are generally bad news. As a diligent digital marketer, you will be spending considerable time and resources growing your list to include as many people as possible. The money is in the list, and the larger the list, the more money there is to be made. But there is a silver lining to unsubscribes.

A healthy list is an active list, regardless of size. When someone unsubscribes from your list, they are effectively self-identifying as someone who is not interested in opening your messages, clicking through, or spending money on your products. Therefore, they are doing you a favor by opting out and cleaning up your list at the same time.

Don't spend too much time worrying about unsubscribes. If a message generates an especially high number of unsubscribes, take a look at what might have rubbed people the wrong way. Learn from the experience and move on. It's true that if you never send any emails, you will keep 100 percent of your subscribers—but then how will you get any clicks?

Growth Rate

A list's growth rate is the number of new subscribers that are added to the list within a given period. The period could be daily, weekly, or monthly—whatever measurement period seems most helpful to you. Growth rate is a good lagging indicator; that is to say that it provides feedback about the success of other efforts, such as new content or lead magnets. Of course, growth rate has to be higher than unsubscribe rate or it is only a matter of time before your subscriber list is depleted.

GRAPHIC
fig. 69

$$\text{GROWTH RATE} = \frac{\text{\# OF NEW SIGN-UPS}}{\text{UNSUBSCRIBERS}} \times 100$$

Growth rate is most helpful when it's tied to discrete efforts. It is helpful to know, for example, that your list is growing by about 250 new subscribers per month. It is significantly more helpful to know that about 100 of those new subscribers come from blog content and the rest from paid search ads. Armed with this knowledge, you can very easily make the case (to yourself or your team) that paid search spending should be increased.

Spam Complaints and Sender Reputation

Spam messages are annoying, irrelevant, and unsolicited messages that often don't seem to have much of a point other than wasting the recipient's time. The most sinister of these messages are outright scams, attempts to steal personal information, or delivery systems for computer viruses or other malware. It should be quite obvious by this point that spamming subscribers is not a viable digital marketing strategy. One of the aspects of spam messages that make them such nuisances is that they only provide value to the sender (buy my product, send me money, download my file, etc.) and have complete disregard for providing any value to the recipient—the absolute opposite of sound digital marketing principles.

When users of an email platform mark an email as spam, they are not only pushing the message in question out of their inbox, but they are also telling their email provider to scrutinize that message and its sender. The tactics that spammers use are always evolving. This puts email platforms into an arms race of sorts to stay one step ahead and protect the inboxes of their users with filters that catch unwanted messages. If someone marks a message of yours as spam, the email service provider will count that as a mark against your domain. If you get too many marks against your domain, all your messages could be intercepted by spam filters and never reach the inboxes of your audience.

This system of training spam filters is referred to as *sender reputation*. As a small business owner already balancing a range of concerns, how much should you worry about your sender reputation? Is it something to lose sleep over? Not really. The occasional message may be marked as spam, but as long as you follow value-forward principles in your email campaigns, you should be fine. Oh, and don't spam people.

Q: Can I see my sender reputation?

Yes, more or less. The specific formula used by individual email providers is not shared with the general public. In the same way that sharing the specifics of search algorithms would allow eagle-eyed marketers to game the system, revealing the exact methods by which spam messages are identified and intercepted would help spammers cheat the system.

Chapter Recap

» Email has been around for a long time, but statistics show it generates the highest ROI for marketers.

» A robust email list is important because it lets you reach large numbers of people who have been identified as likely customers and advocates.

» Lead magnets, which are simply incentives for people to sign up for your emails, are valuable in helping you attract subscribers and build your list.

» Each part of an email—the "from" label, subject line, copy, and unsubscribe link—is important and should be carefully constructed.

» Email provides opportunities to personalize your messages and connect with subscribers.

» Email sequencing can target groups of subscribers depending on where they fall within the marketing funnel.

PART III

EXECUTION

| 11 |
Building a Sound Marketing Strategy

Chapter Overview
» The phases of a sales funnel
» Funnels as proven marketing tools
» A sales funnel is a work in progress
» Metrics to gauge success
» Outside of funnels and ladders—employing a strategic mindset

Part II of this book offered insights on some of the marketing tools that are available and how to use them effectively. On your website you can use landing pages, sales pages, opt-in pages, and other tools to engage potential customers and lead them toward your products and services.

You can also create great content as part of an SEO strategy to organically rank higher on search engine results pages and capture search traffic to your site. Using paid search results, display ads, and social ads, you can direct traffic to key landing pages based on a robust keyword strategy. Social media can also be used to communicate and engage with your audience and prospective customers. Finally, we discussed the importance of building an email list that allows you to follow up with customers and keep the conversation going while providing additional value and generating new sales.

All these strategies are tools to help you acquire new customers and ascend them along your value ladder, which, as you read earlier, is the framework for a series of offers that increase in price and value. So far, we've spent a lot of time talking about the value ladder and the suite of tools and strategies you will use to attract and convert customers. Now it's time to dive into the ways that savvy marketers bring all these pieces together—and how you can develop your own digital marketing strategy to grow your business and improve your bottom line.

The Digital Marketing Funnel
If you have spent any time in sales or marketing circles, you have probably

heard of the concept of a funnel. In the sales and marketing sense, a funnel is a series of steps your audience will take toward achieving a desired goal, such as making a purchase. Think of these steps, or phases, as corresponding to the top, middle, and bottom of the funnel. From your perspective, the top is generally dedicated to marketing, the middle to sales, and the bottom to customers who have taken action. The phases of the funnel loosely translate into the journey your buyers will take as they go from the coldest temperatures (problem/product unaware) to the warmest (paying customers).

FOUR PHASES OF A SALES FUNNEL

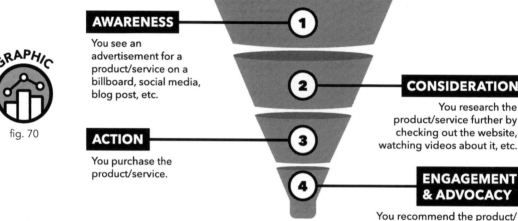

AWARENESS
You see an advertisement for a product/service on a billboard, social media, blog post, etc.

CONSIDERATION
You research the product/service further by checking out the website, watching videos about it, etc.

ACTION
You purchase the product/service.

ENGAGEMENT & ADVOCACY
You recommend the product/ service to others via word of mouth, online review, etc.

fig. 70

» **At the Awareness phase**
Your audience is product-unaware or even problem-unaware—cold traffic. The objective of your marketing at this level should be to increase awareness in your traffic and cast a wide net. Marketing at this stage is sometimes called "feeding the funnel."

» **At the Consideration phase**
The awareness-level marketing has connected with people, and at this phase of the funnel your marketing efforts are built around encouraging your audience to take action and make a purchase. Your audience is considering your product—along with similar products from your competitors.

> » **At the Action phase**
> Your audience makes a decision and commits to making a purchase. This purchase is often the result of product comparison or research.

> » **At the Engagement and Advocacy phase**
> Members of your audience have become customers and received value from your brand. It is incumbent on you to stimulate repeat purchases, encourage your customers to share your brand with others, and ascend them along the value ladder.

Q: Will the funnel for my products follow this same pattern?

The exact steps in a buyer's journey will vary based on the product or service being sold, but building your digital marketing and sales strategy around the concept of a funnel with these broad phases of the customer journey will yield the best results. The most important thing to understand about the digital marketing funnel is that because each stage of the buyer journey is distinct, different tactics and tools apply at each stage of the funnel. Which makes sense—the market/message/media mix that speaks to someone who isn't familiar with your product or service won't be a good match for someone who is already a loyal customer, and vice versa.

The Top of the Funnel

The top of the funnel represents the broadest segment of traffic you will be interacting with, as part of your awareness phase. These are people at the first stage in the buying journey. From a marketer's perspective, top-of-the-funnel marketing generally consists of brand awareness tactics and lead generation strategies. The shape of a funnel is particularly apt here, because you want your digital marketing efforts to be wide enough to accommodate a large group of potential customers. This is done with the understanding that not everyone you reach at this stage will advance to the next stage, and fewer still will make a purchase at the narrowest point of the funnel—hence the shape.

This means that salesy marketing won't bear the same fruit at this funnel stage as it will later on. Instead, content marketing, SEO, and SEM (search engine marketing) tactics targeting keywords that reflect problem-aware (or even problem-unaware) search intent are great tools for top-of-the-funnel marketing. Especially helpful in this regard are "how-to" queries—how to alleviate foot pain, how to lose weight, how to get more sales. These kinds of keywords demonstrate the search intent your top-of-the-funnel marketing should be designed to speak to. Your chief objectives here are increasing awareness and generating interest. Before executing a top-of-the-funnel campaign, ensure that you can answer the following questions:

> » What challenges do your ideal customers face? What goals do they want to achieve?
> » Where do your ideal customers go to find information? Where do they spend time in digital spaces?
> » How does your ideal customer organize and prioritize their goals? What would change this priority and produce urgency to solve the problem your product or service addresses?

The Middle of the Funnel

The middle of the funnel is for people who are on the hook—possible customers who are in the consideration phase, as well as those have moved into the action phase. Your objectives at this stage revolve around driving home the benefits of your product or service and converting a solution-aware, brand-aware audience into paying customers. Traffic that has made it to this stage of the funnel needs to be shown in crystal-clear terms how your product or service will solve the problem(s) they are facing and how you are a better fit for their needs than the competition. As opposed to the awareness-centric marketing that is more appropriate for traffic at the top of the funnel, here customers are being steered more directly toward sales.

As mentioned above, and as you can see in figure 70, the middle of the funnel includes both the consideration and action phases. Digital marketing tools that specifically target the consideration phase include free webinars, SEO and SEM efforts, and video and social advertising that speaks to the features and benefits of your product or service. When selecting keywords and phrases for a middle-of-the-funnel campaign— the consideration phase—focus on search intent related to comparison shopping. For example, a company that sells organic soaps might use some of the following key phrases to target traffic in the consideration phase:

> » Difference between organic and nonorganic soap
> » Mass-produced soap alternatives
> » Organic soap comparison
> » (Your soap company) vs. (competitor)

» (Your soap company) alternatives
» (Competitor) alternatives

At all phases of the buyer journey, it is advantageous to collect contact information from your audience, but the consideration phase of the buyer journey is your first and best opportunity to collect this information. A well-placed lead magnet that speaks specifically to a person who is at this stage of the buyer journey can supercharge a middle-of-the-funnel marketing campaign. It is important to remember, however, that simply because someone opted in, that doesn't mean it's time to inundate them with sales messages. People who opt in at this stage are still in the consideration phase of the buyer journey, so you will find the most success using direct communication channels like email, SMS, or Messenger to steer them toward middle-of-the-funnel content that educates them and directs them toward the features of your product or service that solve their problem.

Before executing a middle-of-the-funnel campaign that targets traffic in the consideration phase of the funnel, ensure that you can answer the following questions:

» How does your ideal customer settle on a solution to the problem they are facing?
» What level of understanding does your ideal customer have of the pros and cons of every alternative before they make a decision?
» What criteria do buyers use to make the decision to purchase?

The middle of the funnel also includes the action phase—the all-important conversion event. Traffic that has made it to this point should be ready to buy a solution to their problem. It's your job now to close the sale and convince them that *your* solution is the best fit for their needs. Closer to the top of the funnel, the emphasis should be on language of education and comparison, rather than sales. But once customers have gone this far, the focus shifts to promotion. The tactics that work best here are a blend of marketing and sales efforts. Free trials, demos, free samples, coupons, exclusive discounts, and other sales-forward marketing tools are the best fit here. If applicable to the product or service you sell, a free consultation, free quote, or free evaluation can also be a powerful tool at this stage in the buyer journey.

SEM, video and social advertising, effective landing pages, sales landing pages, and most forms of paid and owned media are still effective at this stage. Additionally, any contact information you have collected will be of particular use here. A dedicated email that contains a promotional code, exclusive discount, or other sales enticement can produce real results when it comes to tilting the balance in your favor for a conversion.

Before executing a middle-of-the-funnel campaign that targets traffic in the action stage of the funnel, ensure that you can answer the following questions:

» What do your customers appreciate about what you have to offer?
» How is this information present in your middle-of-the-funnel marketing?
» Are there words, offer specifics, or messaging regarding your product or services that could cause you to lose the sale?
» What, if any, steps remain for your prospects to complete before becoming customers?

Bottom of the Funnel

The bottom of the funnel represents all the post-purchase and loyalty-building activities that help you get the most value out of each and every one of your customers. It's where the engagement and advocacy phase kicks in, and it's here that the majority of your value ladder ascension will occur. After all, it's easier to sell products and services to customers who have already received value from your brand! The specific bottom-of-the-funnel activities will differ from brand to brand based on each brand's sales cycle. In fact, the entire digital marketing funnel will look different depending on these brand-to-brand differences.

The *sales cycle* is a map of the specific steps a buyer goes through when making a purchase. For example, the sales cycle for purchase of a car includes a considerable amount of research, test driving, possibly several trips to the dealership and multiple interactions with salespeople before settling on a make, model, and features package, and then negotiating financing and finalizing the sale. The sales cycle for a new cell phone would follow the same general pattern but would be compressed in time and effort. Likewise, purchase of a new coffeemaker would follow the same basic pattern but would likely be further compressed in duration and effort—considerably less research is needed to decide on a coffee maker, and many customers would simply purchase based on price and little else (something that would likely be just one factor among many for a car buyer).

The specifics of the sales cycle dictate many of the broader features of the digital marketing funnel, represented by the answers to some of the questions posed in the earlier sections of this chapter. How much research does your ideal customer do before making a decision? How much support will they need post purchase? Your objective at this stage of the funnel is to develop your one-time customers into repeat customers and ascend them as far along the value ladder as possible. You also want the market/media/message mix at this stage of the buyer journey to deepen the connection your customers have to your brand and the unique way in which your product or service solves their problem. Encouragement to produce positive earned media is another goal of bottom-of-the-funnel marketing. Whether by simply asking or by using incentives, coaxing your loyal customers to evangelize others about your brand will be another marketing objective at this stage.

As we discussed earlier, earned media is exactly that—earned. There is no better time to ask for a review, ask your customers to share your brand on social media, or collect other user-generated content after your customers have had a chance to experience the value your brand has to offer. Don't wait to ask; your customers will be most responsive when the value they have received from you is fresh in their minds.

Remarketing campaigns work well at this stage, along with direct communication channels like email, SMS, and Messenger. It's also important to remember that the salesy content shouldn't just be used to reach customers in the consideration and action stages. In addition to regular sales, coupons, and other promotions, think about your sales cycle. SaaS (software as a service) companies rely on their customers to continue using their products and often have a sales cycle that includes a demo or free trial. Once a customer has been converted and makes a purchase, the bottom-of-the-funnel marketing revolves around encouraging them to keep re-upping their account and exploring new features that include an upcharge, as well as bringing team members or colleagues to the platform.

DIGITAL MARKETING TOOLS
FOR EACH STAGE OF THE FUNNEL

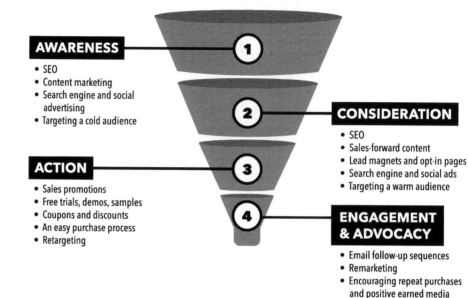

fig. 71

AWARENESS
- SEO
- Content marketing
- Search engine and social advertising
- Targeting a cold audience

CONSIDERATION
- SEO
- Sales-forward content
- Lead magnets and opt-in pages
- Search engine and social ads
- Targeting a warm audience

ACTION
- Sales promotions
- Free trials, demos, samples
- Coupons and discounts
- An easy purchase process
- Retargeting

ENGAGEMENT & ADVOCACY
- Email follow-up sequences
- Remarketing
- Encouraging repeat purchases and positive earned media

Q: How much of my marketing strategy and budget should be devoted to each funnel segment?

The diverse nature of business models, product margins, and customer expectations means that it is impossible to be prescriptive with dollar values for each stage of the funnel. But here are some aspects to consider when thinking about how much money to spend on your marketing funnel. First, consider your gross margin and your customer lifetime value. Are your offerings priced to accommodate marketing costs, or do you have razor-thin margins? It isn't uncommon for a newer business to spend 20 percent of gross revenue—or more—on marketing with a focus on the top and middle of the funnel. This eye-popping cost can sometimes be justified when compared to the lifetime value of each customer, for example, or the need for a newer company to quickly establish market share and ensure a favorable position in the future. All businesses are looking for new customers, but established companies can lean on existing customers and brand recognition to replace the more aggressive marketing strategies relied on by newer companies.

Some other factors to keep in mind when setting your funnel marketing budget: What are my goals for next year? The next two years? The next five? If your goals include business expansion, you may want to consider a proportionally higher marketing budget with a focus on the top and middle of the funnel. Trying to grow revenue with your existing customer base? A focus on bottom-of-the-funnel tactics will likely take center stage.

Tying It All Together – Lifecycle Marketing

Lifecycle marketing is the term for a series of steps and techniques that modern digital marketers use to move members of their target market through the digital marketing funnel. Put simply, it consists of providing the communications and experiences that members of your target audience want and need to become brand-loyal customers. By following the steps outlined in the lifecycle marketing process, digital marketers have a repeatable blueprint for attracting, converting, and retaining customers. Critically for our purposes, the lifecycle marketing approach ties together all the digital marketing elements we have covered so far in this text.

The lifecycle marketing process consists of three stages, each broken down into three specific activities. At a high level, lifecycle marketers use the three C's: collect, convert, and create. They start by collecting leads, then they convert those leads into customers, and finally they create fans. These stages correspond to the top, middle, and bottom of the digital marketing funnel. Within each stage, digital marketers undertake further actions, as shown in figure 72, to develop their audience into customers.

GRAPHIC

fig. 72

THE LIFECYCLE MARKETING PROCESS		
Collect Leads	**Convert Customers**	**Create Fans**
• Target • Attract • Capture	• Engage • Offer • Close	• Deliver • Impress • Multiply

NOTE

Filling in the lifecycle marketing process with your own products, digital tools, and customer avatar(s) is the easiest and simplest way to build your own effective digital marketing strategy from scratch.

Collect

The "collect leads" lifecycle marketing phase is dedicated to feeding the top of the digital marketing funnel. All the parts of your digital marketing strategy are important—the individual pieces work together to contribute to a continuous stream of revenue from converted customers—but getting the top-of-the-funnel portion correct can be the deciding factor between thrilling and lackluster marketing results. There are three main activities within the "collect" phase: target, attract, and capture.

» **Target**

The targeting activities of your strategy consist largely of the groundwork that was laid by your earlier efforts to define your customer avatar. Using your robust customer avatar, it's time to make some decisions. What's the best way to reach these people? What segmentation methods make the most sense for an audience based on your customer avatar? The results of these decisions will inform the channels your strategy focuses on.

» **Attract**

Now that you know who you're targeting, how are you going to attract traffic to your brand's online footprint? A well-rounded strategy often includes some of the tactics and tools we've covered so far in this text. Content that speaks to top-of-the-funnel search intent is an excellent first step for nearly any industry, product, or service. In addition to content marketing and organic SEO tactics, paid search and display or social advertising are also good methods to drive traffic to your website and landing pages.

» **Capture**

You know who you're targeting and how you will attract them. The capture portion of the "collect" lifecycle marketing phase addresses how you will capture contact information from the traffic you have directed to your site. What lead magnet will you offer on your landing page? Why is this lead magnet a perfect fit for the traffic you have attracted to your landing page? Email address collection is a must, and phone number collection for SMS messaging is also of high value. Exactly what you ask for depends on your audience and the nature of your business. Some businesses thrive on traditional phone calls; others encourage traffic to join their Discord server or a semipublic Slack channel. The point is, you need to be able to follow up with the people who convert on the landing page, or you won't be able to advance them through the funnel.

Convert

In the "collect" phase of the lifecycle, we figured out who we want to target, how we are going to attract them to our brand, and how we'll capture their contact information so that we can increase their temperature and entice them to make a purchase. Next, the "convert" lifecycle phase is dedicated to doing just that: enticing them to make a purchase. Like the "collect" phase, it consists of three main activities: engage, offer, and close.

» **Engage**

Now that you have collected contact information from your audience, you can initiate a dialogue in earnest. Email is an excellent medium for this. Marketing automation can schedule and pace messages so that they run on autopilot. They should always provide value and should have the ultimate goal of helping the recipients better understand how your product or service will solve the problem(s) they are facing. Because you have already done the work of targeting and attracting these customers, you can send them these messages with the confidence that you are speaking to their pain points.

This is the time to pull out all your value-forward big guns. Purpose-built content created for the middle of the funnel is put to good use here: webinars, how-to videos, and any content or messaging that agitates the problems your email contacts face while positioning your products and brand as the ideal solution.

» **Offer**

Now that your email contacts have received a huge amount of value from your brand and have had a chance to get to know you and your products, it's time to make a sale. The temperature of someone reaching this stage should be hot—not only are they problem-aware, but they should be well-versed in the solutions to their problem. Furthermore, it should be obvious that your solution is the best one available.

Remember, at this point your audience has been on the hook for a while and you have spent time increasing their temperature to prime them; now is not the time to drop the ball or get greedy. Your offer should be hyper-compelling and provide a wealth of clearly defined value with an absolute minimum amount of friction. Free demos, steep discounts, and free bonuses that speak directly to the pain points your customers are experiencing can tip the scales in your favor and consistently convert email contacts.

Q: How do I know when it's the right time to switch from engagement to making an offer?

There is no one-size-fits-all answer to this question. The exact details of your sales cycle determine when it's appropriate to pivot to an offer from messages that engage. Ultimately, no one knows your customers better than you. Does your sales cycle include a long decision period in which prospects comparison shop or examine the alternatives? If so, match the length of your engagement period to your buyer journey. If your customers make decisions quickly, the length of your engagement sequence can be shorter, and the messaging in those emails should reflect that. Not getting the results you're looking for, or starting from scratch? That's okay—test your best guess and see how the results stack up before attempting to optimize the activities in the "convert" stage of your marketing strategy.

» **Close**

You've presented a hyper-compelling offer to someone in your marketing funnel. Now what? Closing the sale goes beyond the transaction alone, but the transaction itself is a good place to start. Ensure that your checkout process is as easy and straightforward as possible. We have all experienced an unpleasant or clunky checkout that left a negative impression on us as customers. A fast checkout in as few steps as possible goes a long way toward maximizing conversions at the point when customers are actually handing over money. This is also true for transactions that take place in physical places. A confusing, lengthy, or otherwise ungainly checkout process frustrates customers and results in negative brand perception.

Outside of the transaction itself, there are some other considerations marketers should keep in mind when carrying out closing activities in the "convert" phase of their digital marketing strategy. Trust and transparency are big at this stage, especially when customers are checking out online. Most e-commerce and point-of-sale (POS) systems come with industry-standard transactional security features. It's your role to communicate this to customers as yet another way to reinforce that completing the purchase is the right path.

Create

The "create" lifecycle marketing phase is all about the bottom of the funnel. By this point, someone has gone through your digital marketing funnel and has converted into a customer. Now it's time to maximize the value of that customer by reinforcing the value your brand delivers, continuing the relationship, and amplifying the benefit a happy customer can have with your brand. This will create not just one-time customers, but loyal fans. There are—you guessed it—three main activities in the "create" lifecycle phase: deliver, impress, and multiply.

» **Deliver**

You've closed the sale, and now it's time to deliver the value you have been promising to your customer. This could be as simple as bagging their purchase and handing it to them, but for products or services in digital spaces there might be a little more to it. Order fulfillment, providing accurate tracking information, and communicating to set expectations may not be the first activities that come to mind when people think about marketing, but they are an essential part of developing one-off customers into raving fans. For example, if a product takes two weeks to arrive, it's imperative that this information be relayed to the customer. Online shoppers have the expectation that their purchases will be shipped on time and arrive promptly. Setting appropriate expectations before they become a customer service issue means more happy customers and more money in your pocket.

Delivering value isn't only about setting expectations, however. The more you can do as a marketer or business owner to anticipate customer needs and/or pain points and specifically address them, the happier your customers will be. Are your customers conscientious about their carbon footprint? Make it clear that your packaging uses recycled material. Do your customers expect a premium experience when they purchase or use your product? Incorporate the feeling of exclusivity into your product or user experience. Delivering value doesn't have to be hard—just packing your products with care and including small bonuses in the package like stickers or other little perks can result in a great positive experience for customers.

» **Impress**

Marketers learn to see customers as worth much more than just a single transaction. As we discussed in chapter 2, activities undertaken by marketers to impress their customers are an essential part of maximizing customer lifetime value (CLV). How are you working to ascend your customers along the value ladder? What other products or services do you have to offer?

It's worth reiterating that developing repeat customers and maximizing CLV is a two-way value street. Thinking of your customers only in terms of dollar signs is a sure way to lose them. When ascending customers along your value ladder, make sure that the higher-ticket products, bundles, or services you are offering provide a proportionally increased amount of value—value that solves a burning problem faced by those customers.

Periodic sales, loyalty programs, and personalizing your customers' experience are all great ways to impress them and differentiate yourself from the competition.

» **Multiply**
This is the stage of your customer's journey where you capitalize on the goodwill you have been generating through delivering value. Here your goal is not only to multiply sales, but to multiply customers. This is the best time in the customer journey to ask for reviews, referrals, or other forms of earned media or social proof— while the value you have provided them is fresh in their mind. But remember that simply asking will only get you so far. Even if you are consistently delivering world-class value, your customers will rightfully say, What's in it for me? It's a best practice to incentivize customers to take action.

MY TAKE

The first step in asking for earned media from your customers is to, well, ask. If you feel uncomfortable soliciting a review, ask yourself where that feeling comes from. If you have delivered serious value to your customers, if you have an excellent product, if you are running a great customer-centric business, then asking for an endorsement from your thrilled customers is a logical next step. Have confidence in your business and the value it provides!

We've all received emails or texts offering a coupon code as an incentive to review a product, fill out a post-purchase survey, or share our experience on social media. These incentives not only encourage reviews or social shares, but they can also produce return shoppers. Now that you have a customer who loves your brand, it's time to strike while the iron is hot!

Building a Funnel

In this chapter so far, we have discussed the relationship between a digital marketing funnel and the lifecycle marketing approach to advancing traffic through that funnel. Now let's put these ideas into action. We'll take a look at a sample digital marketing funnel and how a marketer would use a lifecycle marketing approach to move traffic through that funnel and measure success at every stage. Meet the fictional meal replacement brand Restore. Restore offers meal replacement powders, bars, prepackaged meals, and shakes. In this example we're going to follow along as Restore builds their digital marketing strategy from the ground up using a lifecycle marketing approach.

Target

As with any marketing undertaking, Restore has to determine exactly who they will be targeting. Focusing on the benefits of convenience, healthy dietary balance, and performance, Restore needs to determine the kind of people who have the pain points that its products addresses. After some research and brainstorming, the Restore team decides on the following customer avatars:

»   **Fitness Enthusiast**
    Stacy is a fitness enthusiast who visits the gym early in the morning before heading to work. She keeps careful track of her diet and owns products like fitness trackers and free weights. She is already familiar with the concept of a meal replacement product and already uses fitness supplements such as protein powders.

»   **Athlete**
    Mark is a marathon runner and cyclist. He competes frequently and carefully tracks both his diet and his fitness regimen. Mark's demanding and competitive lifestyle means that he is very familiar with meal replacement products. He scrutinizes new products and considers the pros and cons of changing his routine before making a purchase.

» **Busy Professional**
Brandon works at a video game development company where he keeps long hours. He's not as diet and fitness conscious as Stacy or Mark, but he generally wants to eat healthily and feel good about the food he eats. He is familiar with convenience products such as frozen or easy-reheat meals, but he's new to the concept of meal replacement products such as bars, shakes, and powders.

In the future, Restore may decide to test a new customer avatar—maybe dieters with a focus on weight loss or college students in need of quick meals. But for now, they are prioritizing the three customer segments represented by the aforementioned avatars. Every customer segment Restore decides to add to their marketing strategy will come with increased costs, so starting with the segments they believe have the most potential is a smart business decision.

Attract

Now that they have some customer avatars nailed down, the marketing team at Restore can determine the best way to reach and attract traffic represented by those avatars. Like many brands, Restore decides to go with SEO-supported content and search engine marketing. There's just one hitch; you'll note that audience temperature across the avatars is not the same. Busy professionals might resonate with the pain point that Restore's products solve in the form of convenience, but they may not articulate this need, and they aren't solution-aware (that is to say, they aren't familiar with meal replacement products). Fitness enthusiasts and athletes will certainly be aware of meal replacement products (solution-aware), but they may not be product-aware. This is especially true if Restore is a new brand.

This means a one-size solution won't fit all the customer avatars Restore wants to target with respect to their search intent or the features and benefits that their market/media/message mix communicates. Aware of this fact, the Restore team identifies search terms that reflect the search intent of each audience separately. For example, an athlete very familiar with meal replacement products might search for "meal replacement shake with over 15 grams of protein." Someone more closely aligned with the busy professional customer avatar who has a much colder audience temperature might search for something like "fast and healthy lunch." Figure 73 shows a summary of the search intent and key phrases that Restore might come up with.

	FITNESS ENTHUSIASTS	ATHLETES	BUSY PROFESSIONALS
SPECIFIC BENEFIT	Health and balance	Performance	Convenience
SEARCH INTENT	Getting more out of my workouts	Meal replacement shakes with over 15 grams of protein	Fast and cheap lunches
	Workout-friendly meals	Best meal replacement for runners	Easy office lunches
	Easy-prep workout meals	High-performance meal replacement	Healthy takeout alternatives
CONTENT	Get more out of your workouts with these workout-friendly meals	Maximize your healthy protein intake with these high-performance meal replacements	Optimize your office lunch—these healthy meals are ready in minutes

GRAPHIC

fig. 73

QUESTION

Q: Should I start my own digital marketing strategy with as many customer avatars as possible?

It's not a bad idea to explore your SAM—your serviceable available market (think back to chapter 3)—and see how many customer avatars make sense for the problems your product or service solves. A deep understanding of potentially untapped markets is never a bad thing. This information can be used to justify marketing expenses to your boss or other stakeholders. If you are the boss, this information can be useful when pitching to investors, suppliers, or other external stakeholders. That being said, the more people you are trying to reach, the higher your overall marketing cost will be. Cost is the driving factor behind the creation of a customer avatar and customer segmentation activities in the first place. Even the wealthiest megacorporations with cash to burn can't afford to reach *everyone*. Segmentation and the customer avatar creation process help companies of all sizes refine their market/media/message mix so their advertising and marketing dollars will go farther. What does this mean for you? Start with the customer avatar—or avatars—that have the most revenue potential and go from there. Successfully marketing to a single segment can fund an expanded scope that reaches other segments.

With a keyword list in hand, Restore's marketing team can start producing the content that will speak to the search intent they have identified for each customer avatar. If cost is a factor—and it almost always is—the Restore team should start with the customer avatar with the highest revenue potential or the highest temperature. This keyword list can also serve as the foundation for Restore's search engine marketing campaigns, which will come into play in the next stage of the funnel-building process.

Capture

With a plan to attract traffic and the content to execute that plan in place, Restore's marketing team can move on to capturing customers. In the same way that each customer avatar requires its own content based on temperature and search intent, each customer avatar will require a lead magnet that provides them with value. For example, when targeting a customer avatar that is health-conscious, offering them a calorie tracker or calculator in the form of an online form and accompanying fillable PDF in exchange for their contact information might be a good fit. The Restore marketing team inserts opt-in forms for this lead magnet into the content created for their health and fitness enthusiast customer avatar as a way to collect contact information and send follow-up messages in the next stage of the digital marketing funnel.

Q: This seems like an awful lot of work to make a single sale. What about simply presenting traffic with a sales offer?

That can work. And if you think it will, it's worth experimenting with. Part of the reason digital marketers build funnels is to create a scalable process that can be replicated time and time again. The idea is that, as marketers, it's our job to usher internet traffic through the sales process—traffic that may be totally cold to our products and the problems they solve. But if we can isolate a warmer segment of traffic using keyword intent, advertising, email sequences, or other tools, then presenting those people with an offer that speaks directly to their needs or temperature is a good choice.

Engage

Now that the Restore team has captured someone's contact information, they can engage with that person and increase their temperature relative to the brand. This is most commonly done with an email sequence designed to appeal to the customer avatar and reinforce the brand's value proposition. In the case of Restore, this could consist of explaining how to use the lead magnets that were provided, sharing more content, or encouraging the recipient to otherwise participate in the Restore community. A straightforward email sequence could feature information about how environmentally sustainable meal replacement products are, social proof from satisfied customers or influencers, calorie or other health comparisons, or information about how cost-effective and convenient these products are.

When considering how to engage with your own contacts, return to your customer avatar and the ways in which your product or service solves a problem for that person. This sequence doesn't have to be long—even just one or two emails can do the job. The right number of messages varies from business to business and industry to industry. Also think about the next step: the offer. Is the offer a big ask? If so, more emails might be called for to warm up the contacts. On the other hand, if the offer is going to be something like a free sample where you are asking very little of your contacts, a minimal engagement sequence is required.

Offer

The communication marketers and brands have with their audiences revolves around asking people to take action. Nowhere is that truer than in the offer portion of a digital marketing funnel. At this point you have selected people who are likely to buy from you and have attracted them to your brand using SEO and advertising. You've captured their contact information and provided them with value—in short, there has never been a better time to ask them to spend money on your brand.

Earlier in this book, we touched on what makes a hyper-compelling offer—such an abundance of value that no one could walk away from it. The importance of getting your offer right can't be overstated. You have spent time and money to bring your contacts along the digital marketing funnel, and this is the make-or-break moment that makes it all worth it. Tactics like discounts, free bonuses, urgency, scarcity, guarantees, social proof, and just about anything else at your disposal should be put to use and tested. The offer you present here should be the next logical step for your audience after the groundwork you have laid with the engagement sequence.

For our example health-and-wellness company, Restore, a marketer might test with a sample pack of their most popular products at a discount. To sweeten the deal and make it irresistible, the offer could include a free shaker bottle or sports towel. They aren't asking for their prospect to start a total meal replacement plan that costs hundreds of dollars a month. The discounted sample pack with the free gift is a small ask and something that a person who is interested in making dietary changes in their life can take advantage of without a huge commitment.

Of course, the sample pack is the first of many offers that this person will be presented with by Restore. In fact, a savvy marketer knows to strike when the iron is hot. If a prospect has said yes to the discounted sample pack, whatever obstacle was keeping them from making a purchase has been overcome and they are ready to get out their wallet. Here is a good place to build an upsell into the offer—why not double the sample pack for a few more bucks? Whatever Restore's marketers choose to offer as an upsell, the value it provides needs to be crystal clear. The same goes for upsells you add to the offers in your digital marketing funnel.

Close/Deliver

When making a sale face-to-face, a salesperson walks their prospect through the buying process. Movies, TV shows, and sales gurus have created a narrative in which this process ends with a charismatic salesperson saying the exact magic words that entice their prospect to buy. Say the wrong words at this crucial moment, this narrative tells us, and your potential customer will walk away—you've blown the sale. The reality is that all the work to get prospects to buy has already been done by this point in the conversation. A well-crafted offer, clearly communicated value, and a targeted audience are what set up successful sales, no matter how much sales gurus might want to take all the credit.

In digital spaces, closing the sale is about reducing friction and overcoming those final nagging objections that your audience might have. Providing a secure, easy checkout experience allays fears of being scammed. Money-back or quality guarantees reduce the perceived risk surrounding the decision to go ahead with the purchase. Setting clear expectations regarding what items are in stock and when they will be shipped makes the process more user-friendly. If your customers are booking appointments on your site or scheduling service calls, making it clear when they can expect status updates or reminders eases the experience, too. More broadly and perhaps most importantly, you need to regularly reinforce the idea that the decision to make a purchase was a good one. Taken together, these small aspects are greater than the sum of their parts and can go a long way toward closing sales and encouraging repeat buyers.

Impress

It has never been easier to start your own business, and this is especially true in digital environments. This means that no matter how unique or valuable your product or service is, there will be competitors nipping at your heels. Not only will your business have to stand out in a sea of competitors, but you are also vying for the attention of your audience. As your relationship with your customers deepens, use what you learn about them to anticipate their needs and delight them with service.

Many aspects of the digital marketing funnel require close cooperation between sometimes disparate parts of a business. Sales and marketing need to work together, for example, to craft compelling offers. Web design and marketing have to work together to ensure that the checkout process is easy and frictionless. For large corporations with siloed departments, this can be a challenge—solopreneurs and small teams have a much easier time coordinating the necessary cohesion between marketing and other aspects of the business. The "impress" stage of the digital marketing funnel similarly requires this type of close cooperation.

Impressing your customers means anticipating their needs and delighting them with solutions. This can consist of simple gestures, such as throwing a few stickers in each box, or more complex efforts, like attractive packaging, high-quality printed box inserts, courtesy calls if appropriate, or emails that track life milestones—anything that helps your customers get more value out of your products or makes their lives easier.

EXAMPLE

E-commerce behemoth and "everything store" Amazon has made impressing customers a central tenet of their business philosophy. In an April 2018 letter to shareholders, founder and then-CEO Jeff Bezos referred to Amazon's customers as "divinely discontent." Citing the changing expectations of Amazon's customers as the driving force behind the company's breakneck pace of innovation and growth, Bezos said, "People have a voracious appetite for a better way, and yesterday's 'wow' quickly becomes today's 'ordinary'. I see that cycle of improvement happening at a faster rate than ever before. You cannot rest on your laurels in this world. Customers won't have it." While it is true that business activities like changing product packaging or box inserts aren't strictly the purview of digital marketers, a holistic view of customer expectations and a constant drive to surprise and delight them in new and innovative ways is a must in the contemporary business landscape.

Multiply

Early on in this text we discussed the concept of thinking about your customers in terms of their lifetime value rather than the value of a single transaction. From this perspective, our work as digital marketers is never done. There is always more value we can provide for—and extract from—our audience and customers. The "multiply" stage of the digital marketing funnel isn't just about multiplying the number of times your customers spend money with you but multiplying the number of customers who shop with your brand. Let's look at the former first.

Businesses that have subscription services or automatically rebill their customers have a pretty good idea of when those customers will pay them. Everyone else has to work to keep their customers coming back. Yet another example of why it is so crucial to capture contact information from your customers is seen in the "multiply" lifecycle marketing stage. Being able to maintain a line of communication with your customers once their initial purchase is complete is the main way you will influence them to return and spend more money. Bounce-back coupons—coupons giving customers a discount on a future sale—are a simple incentive that can be deployed quickly and automated at scale. Regular sales, loyalty programs, promotional events, and more are all components of the "multiply" lifecycle phase that rely on a marketer's ability to contact customers and encourage them to return.

On the multiplying the number of customers side of things, deputize your customers as brand evangelists and incentivize them to spread the good word. Discounts for referring friends, incentives for customers who post about their experiences on social media, and other creative methods of getting the word out are worth their weight in gold. As you have seen, getting to this point in the customer relationship has taken numerous steps and significant communication. In many cases, marketers pay to direct customers into their digital marketing funnels via advertising. Customers who can be converted from referrals or word of mouth are much more cost-effective and potentially much more primed to spend—after all, who wouldn't trust a recommendation from a friend?

fig. 74

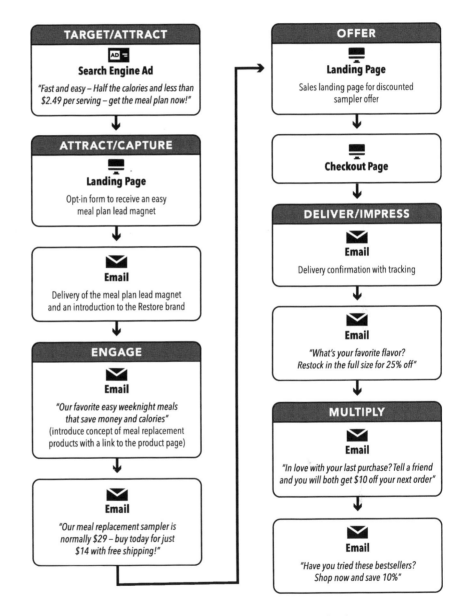

A functional example lifecycle marketing process for the fictional health-and-wellness brand Restore

A Final Thought on Digital Marketing Funnels

The process of creating and executing an effective digital marketing funnel using lifecycle marketing tactics might seem daunting if this is the first time the concept is being presented to you. The truth is, once you roll up your sleeves and get started, the steps laid out here start to feel natural. In fact, if you have begun any digital marketing efforts, you may already be doing some of these steps. It may seem like a confusing spider web of messages, landing pages, and process steps, but digital marketing funnels don't have to be complex. Most contemporary digital marketing tools are already set up to follow this general pattern, with templates, suggestions, and resources. It's often a question of using these tools in a coherent and consistent way, rather than reinventing the wheel every time out.

Let's return to our fictional health-and-wellness example brand, Restore, for a look at a digital marketing funnel in action, and see how few assets it really needs to be up and running effectively.

In figure 74, we can see that Restore is using seven emails, two landing pages, a search engine ad, and the checkout page already present on their website to pull contacts through their digital marketing funnel. Contemporary digital marketing tools have functionality not only to automate all these emails, but in most cases to build the necessary landing pages as well. In short, building a basic lifecycle marketing campaign isn't as challenging as it might at first appear.

In the next chapter we'll look at ways digital marketers can harness the power of automation, optimize campaigns and performance, and troubleshoot solutions for lackluster results.

Chapter Recap

» A sound digital marketing strategy starts with an understanding of the digital marketing funnel and the journey your audience will take before considering a purchase. The digital marketing funnel can be broken into four general phases: awareness, consideration, action, and engagement and advocacy.

» Think about your digital marketing efforts in terms of which part of the funnel they target. The top of the funnel is the broadest segment of people you will be attempting to connect with. Here your focus will be on increasing awareness of the value you provide. At the middle of the funnel your efforts will focus on increasing the temperature of the traffic in your funnel. At the bottom of the funnel your efforts will focus on generating repeat purchases, encouraging word of mouth, and delighting customers in order to get the most out of the lifetime value they represent for your brand.

» Lifecycle marketing is a structured, scalable approach to moving traffic through the various funnel stages and converting customers. Collecting leads, converting customers, and creating fans are steps in the lifecycle marketing process, which is designed to produce repeatable results in digital environments.

» Digital marketers employing lifecycle marketing "feed their funnel" by targeting their ideal customers, attracting those people with lead magnets or other offers, and capturing their contact information.

» After marketers have captured contact information from their target audience, they can convert those customers by engaging them, presenting them with a compelling offer, and closing the sale.

» To create fans, digital marketers deliver the value they promise, continually work to delight and impress their customers, and multiply both sales and new customers as a result—all activities that are only made possible by capturing customer contact information in the first place.

| 12 |

Digital Marketing Efficiency

Chapter Overview

- » Using marketing automation to move traffic through your funnel
- » Optimizing campaigns
- » Troubleshooting poor performance

When working to build a business, you can use all the help you can get. Time is at a premium, you need to carefully monitor your spending, and your to-do list never seems to get any shorter. Fortunately, when it comes to digital marketing, you can turn to automated solutions to help with critical processes.

Marketing automation refers to any tool, platform, or solution that limits the need for human interaction and helps you simplify and measure the tasks associated with your marketing efforts. Marketing automation can help you manage emails and social media, promote blog posts, manage leads, test your website, identify which campaigns are producing the best ROI, and easily complete other tasks. Automating these tasks can save time and money for your company while increasing the effectiveness of your marketing efforts. Every aspect of your digital marketing funnel can be automated, meaning your customer acquisition and conversion efforts can be scaled nearly effortlessly. Let's look at some of the ways marketing automation is used and how it might help you better reach customers and prospective customers.

Behavior-Based Automation

Behavior-based automation is based on user activity. For example, when someone opts in to your contact list for the first time, your marketing software triggers a series of communications to welcome them. Another common automation handles the reactivation of customers. Say a customer hasn't opened any of your emails for six months; a message can be sent asking what you can do to re-engage them. At the risk of beating a dead horse, let me remind you that it's only possible to leverage the power of marketing automation if you have captured contact information from your audience.

Employing marketing automation enables you to set up workflows that perform certain appropriate actions in response to specific behaviors relevant to business objectives. The behaviors prompt the actions automatically, allowing you to "set and forget" your emails and giving you more time to work on your to-do list.

Most email service providers have automation services baked into their service offerings, and if not, there are plug-and-play services available. Often your email service provider will offer templates and prompts to help you customize them for your business, based on actions of your customers—simply select the templates or behaviors most relevant to your business and you're already more than halfway to your goal of maintaining a meaningful dialogue with your audience.

Let's have a look at some situations in which behavior-based automation can work for you.

Welcome Sequences

A sequence of emails, SMS, or other direct messages that welcome new subscribers to your list(s) is an absolute must for any digital marketing strategy. It gives you a chance to introduce potential customers to your company and tell the story of your brand. Potential customers who sign up for your email list obviously are interested in what you have to offer. A well-crafted welcome email acknowledges their presence and lets you begin to communicate how your product or service can solve their problem, even if the visitor does not yet recognize that they have a problem (a cold audience).

Welcome emails generally have higher open rates than other marketing emails. They give you a way to convince visitors to stay with you, which reduces your list churn (the rate at which subscribers unsubscribe). The number of welcome emails included in a sequence varies but usually ranges between one and three messages. By mapping this automation to your digital marketing funnel, you can clearly see how easy it is to warm up the temperature of your contacts. Let's take a quick look at the type of content each email might contain, using a sample contact we'll call Matt.

» **First email**: This email should be sent right away after Matt signs up for your email list. Thank him for placing his trust in your brand and affirm that he's made a good decision in joining your list—specific examples of the advantages of joining the list are a great asset here. If applicable, deliver the lead magnet that enticed Matt to give you his email or other contact info, and briefly communicate what he can expect to see in future emails.

» **Second email**: Set the automation to send the second message a day or two later. Use this email to start engaging with Matt by sharing something of value, like an offer, a coupon, or a compelling piece of content. Keep the copy in your messages specific to Matt's customer avatar and his temperature as a member of your audience. Short and to-the-point messages are standard for welcome messages, but some brands have found success with longer ones.

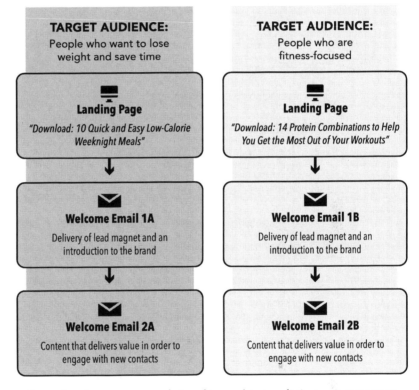

fig. 75

Example welcome sequences designed to speak to two distinct customer avatars

Q: How do welcome sequences fit into the concept of a digital marketing funnel?

Welcome sequences are generally associated with the top of the funnel. They are triggered when members of your audience opt in and are used to deliver lead magnets, engage with customers, and generally warm the temperature of traffic in your funnel. What about traffic that is already warm? Then you'll want to strike while the iron is hot. Members of your audience enter your digital marketing funnel from a variety of entry points; a best practice is to create welcome sequences tailored to the audience coming in at each of those entry points.

As an example, let's say Restore has two lead magnets: 10 Quick and Easy Low-Calorie Weeknight Meals and 14 Protein Combinations to Help You Get the Most Out of Your Workouts. As we discussed in the last chapter and earlier in this text, it is important to tailor your lead magnets to the segment you are targeting. In this case, Restore is using the first lead magnet to target people who are looking to lose weight and save time, and the second to target people who are fitness-focused. Restore's marketing team will create a welcome sequence associated with each lead magnet, not only to ensure that the correct lead magnet is delivered to customers after they opt in, but also to keep communication with contacts consistent with their customer avatar (figure 75).

Lead-Nurturing Sequences

Welcome sequences feed into lead-nurturing sequences, the messages you will use to engage with your customers.

Sales Sequences

Sales sequences follow welcome or lead-nurturing sequences with the intent of turning leads into customers. If your product is face cream, for example, you could send an automated email commiserating with potential customers about the discomforts of dry, chapped skin, along with an explanation of how and why dry skin occurs.

The next email might contain information on how your face cream fixes the problem of dry skin by repairing small cracks and smoothing out dry patches. After that, you'd send an email offering a free product sample or discount.

Abandoned Cart Sequences

After all the work you have put into getting your audience to the point where they are ready to pay, the last thing you want is for them to leave without completing the transaction. Unfortunately, it happens all the time. In fact, a compilation of forty-four studies on e-commerce shopping cart abandonment showed a nearly 70 percent abandonment rate.

Shoppers abandon carts for all sorts of reasons, often because they're just browsing or comparing prices or looking for a possible gift. Others, however, abandon carts because of issues you need to know about. The following are some common reasons for cart abandonment:

» High additional costs like shipping and tax
» Didn't trust the site with payment information
» Didn't like the return policy
» Unwilling to create an account as requested by the site
» Website errors made the transaction too difficult
» Checkout process took too long or was too complicated
» Delivery time was too slow

An automated email sequence that reminds shoppers about the contents of their cart and offers them discounts or other perks to push them to complete the transaction is an essential tool for closing the cart abandonment gap. Abandoned cart email sequences should incentivize purchases and create a sense of urgency, but endlessly pestering your customers will do more harm than good. A sequence of two or three emails is sufficient.

In this sequence, the first email should simply remind them that items were left in the cart unpurchased. These messages often have a subject line like "Hey, it looks like you forgot something!" and arrive within a few hours, at most, of cart abandonment. The next message should present the offer designed to incentivize the completion of the sale and create urgency where possible. Add free shipping to the order, a coupon for a modest discount, a free item, or other incentives. The second message can be sent after twenty-four to forty-eight hours. You want it to arrive at a time when the customer's shopping activity will still be fresh in their mind, but not so soon that they become "trained" to wait for the abandoned cart offer. A third message can reinforce the offer or warn that the items saved in the customer's card will be removed. This last point is a bit of a gamble—it contains a strong urgency factor to encourage completion of the sale, but it could rub some prospective customers the wrong way.

Re-engagement Sequences

A re-engagement email sequence, also known as a win-back sequence, serves the purpose of reminding someone who has been out of touch that your brand has value to offer. We generally think of behavior-based automation as being triggered by the actions taken by a contact or customer—opting in, abandoning a cart, etc. Win-back sequences are set up to be triggered when a customer doesn't act within a predetermined period, usually thirty to forty-five days. This window of inactivity isn't set in stone, however. Pick a time frame that makes sense for your business and the frequency of communication you have with your customers. A win-back sequence can be as simple as a single email that includes a coupon, a link to value-added content, or anything else that will get your contact back on your site.

List Hygiene

Keeping a list "clean" is an important maintenance task for any marketer. It is always true that the money is in the list, but a list that is cluttered with contacts who don't want to hear from you, aren't interested in making a purchase, or are simply dormant can result in less-than-optimal results. Most email service providers offer basic automatic list hygiene tools. They will unsubscribe contacts who mark your emails as spam, remove contacts who have full or unreachable inboxes, and purge lists of contacts who entered their email incorrectly. Pruning the deadwood out of your email list not only improves the accuracy of your metric reporting but can have a positive impact on your sender score, and the bare minimum is already taken care of for you.

Email providers on the recipient end—services like Gmail, Yahoo!, and Outlook—work tirelessly to protect their customers from bad actors and spammers. The more emails you send that are marked as spam or go to dead-end addresses, the lower your sender score in the eyes of these email providers. That's why it's important to go above and beyond the bare minimum they contribute and keep your lists free of dormant contacts.

List-hygiene tactics range from aggressive to nearly nonexistent. On the aggressive side, a marketer might be very zealous about cleaning their list and setting up automation that removes contacts after just a few weeks if they haven't made a purchase or interacted with any emails. Why keep people who aren't going to buy, the thinking goes, and if you can replace the unreceptive contacts, you will keep open rates and click rates high. On the other end of the spectrum, a marketer might wait until a contact hasn't clicked on two consecutive win-back sequences or simply hasn't opened any messages in several months. A lazy marketer might leave dormant contacts on the list for years, muddying their metrics and potentially harming their sender score.

MY TAKE

It can be difficult to part with hard-won contacts, especially if you are paying to direct traffic to an opt-in page or if your list isn't growing as fast as you would like. After all, deleting contacts means flushing down the drain the potential lifetime value those people may have provided for your business. It may feel that way, but the simple truth is that, for whatever reason, these people aren't engaging with your messages and they aren't resonating with your brand. Your time, money, and effort will always be better spent focusing on the people with whom you have a strong connection rather than trying to win back a contact who hasn't opened a message in over a year.

Optimizing Campaigns

You have a clean list, a compelling lead magnet, a long list of keywords, and some PPC ads sending traffic your way. How do you improve your performance and keep costs low? If you're just starting out, it can be hard to even understand when a campaign isn't doing well. That's because the biggest asset you have in determining how well your campaigns are doing is historical data. Digital marketing leaders are at the head of the pack because they are always monitoring results and they are always testing. The platforms where you purchase advertising rely on historical data as well, although the exact ways in which that data is collected and used is not made available to us as marketers. As the aphorism goes, no plan survives contact with the enemy. In this context, there is only so much preparation and best practices you can employ; the true test of your campaigns comes when they are live and funded, and this is the first point where novice marketers have the potential to hurt the success of their campaigns.

As we have discussed, programmatic advertising is governed by algorithms, and these algorithms need time to "learn" how traffic interacts with different ads. A common mistake in the world of programmatic advertising is to prematurely end a campaign before the algorithms in play have had time to understand exactly whom the ads should be served to. Furthermore, prematurely ending an advertising campaign means that the data available to assess the campaign's success or failure will be inconclusive. Fifty respondents in a survey of whether or not people like ketchup on hot dogs isn't a big enough sample size to determine the ketchup preferences of the entire United States; in the same way, a few days of ad data isn't enough to determine if a campaign is doing well or poorly.

How Long Should My Campaign Run?

As with many aspects of digital marketing, the answer is: It depends. First, ask yourself what you want to accomplish with this campaign. If you're looking to drive traffic to a time-sensitive offer, you already have a firm end date for when that campaign will come to a close. For more evergreen offers—those that are ongoing and don't have a firm end date—this question becomes a little trickier to answer. In short, if you are running an evergreen campaign that is staying within budget and delivering results, let it run as long as it continues to be successful and profitable. Even effective campaigns will plateau in performance, however, and an important aspect of efficient digital marketing is monitoring and adjusting them as needed.

When discussing campaigns, we are broadly discussing all the marketing surrounding a specific offer within a discrete period. A campaign could be isolated to one social media channel or just one platform, like Facebook. It could also include a multi-channel approach, such as search engine marketing coupled with social media advertising. Basically, we're taking a view of your marketing efforts from 50,000 feet up—not going down into the nitty-gritty unless otherwise specified.

Next, look to the market/media/message mix that makes up your marketing formula. What you are offering, who you are selling it to, how you are communicating with them, and what you are saying all contribute not only to the overall success of a campaign but to how long the campaign will need to run to gain traction and deliver results. An old marketing adage called the Rule of Seven states that a prospect needs to see or hear your marketing message at least seven times before they take action. This isn't a hard-and-fast rule; in fact, in our ad-saturated and highly targeted modern media landscape it may not be true at all anymore. But what's important to understand about the Rule of Seven is that it should be in the back of your mind when assessing the success of a campaign. Remember that people need to see your message more than just once, and it might take some time for your advertising to produce conversions. If results aren't looking great, ask yourself the following questions:

» Has this campaign been running long enough for members of my target audience to see, hear, or interact with it more than just once or twice?

» Is there an opportunity for members of my audience to see, hear, or interact with my campaign on more than one marketing channel?

» What is the deeper story that my campaign metrics are telling me?

While it may not be literally true that members of your target audience will have to see your ad exactly seven times, the fact remains that seeing an ad once won't cut it. Complex products or services, products with a long sales cycle, or products that are new or novel need lots of touchpoints with their target audience to push them to take action. Additionally, if you are restricting your campaign to a single platform or channel—why? It's unlikely that your target audience is spending time in just one small corner of the internet. Unless your customer avatar dictates otherwise, the more places you can expose your audience to your advertising or content, the better.

Finally, ask yourself what the story is that your campaign metrics are telling you. Are clicks and conversions trending down? Are people clicking on ads but not converting once they reach your landing pages? Are impressions high but clicks low? And if you have historical data, how does performance in this period compare to previous periods? The answers to these questions can help you diagnose what might be going awry in your campaigns, where to focus your efforts to produce corrective action, and how to rectify poor performance.

Troubleshooting Poor Performance

In a world where we are constantly bombarded by advertising and marketing messages, a lot of things can go wrong with marketing campaigns. By using metrics—and the deeper story they can tell—we can better understand exactly how our campaigns are doing, and we can get a hint of what's not doing well. Let's take a look at some of the elements of contemporary digital marketing campaigns and how we can attempt to diagnose and troubleshoot poor marketing performance (these are in no particular order).

Content and Organic Search

It's no secret that there's a lot of information on the internet. When the content you have created to organically rank—that is, rank for search terms relevant to your customer avatar—isn't getting viewed as often as you would like, a number of issues might be the culprit. As we discussed in chapter 7, in order for a web page to show up in a search, that page must first be indexed by the search engine. This is the first thing to check if your content isn't appearing anywhere in the search results at all. Google and other popular search engines provide tools to diagnose this issue; the URL inspection tool in the Google Search Console is designed expressly for this purpose. After linking your Search Console account to your website, use the URL inspection tool to understand vital statistics about your pages, particularly underperforming pages. From this screen you can request indexing if your page isn't in Google's search index, and you can see how Google rates your pages in terms of being mobile-friendly.

Google Search Console is really powerful and totally free. It has a wealth of information to be discovered regarding how Google sees your site and is a good way to detect issues early. The first time you access the dashboard it can take a second to get your bearings, but once you do, I'm sure you'll agree with me that it's an essential tool for monitoring search performance and catching issues on your site. It isn't an afterthought from the Google team either—Search Console is really robust and regularly updated.

Okay, Google has confirmed that they have crawled the page that doesn't appear to be ranking. What's next? It takes time for pages to rank. A number of factors go into Google's decision to serve a specific page as a result, and two of the biggest factors are page age and domain authority. A comprehensive study from SEO services provider Ahrefs found that the fastest a new page could rocket into the top 10 search results was sixty-one days. High SERP placement is like Rome in that it isn't built in a day. The more high-authority backlinks you can get pointing to the page, the better your overall site structure, and all the on-page and technical SEO tactics we discussed in chapter 7 can help expedite this process.

Finally, it's time to take a look at your keywords. All the aspects of troubleshooting poorly performing search engine optimization are important, but they are generally boxes to be checked—clear problems with clear solutions. The tougher problem comes from the keywords you are attempting to rank for in the first place. As the monthly search volume of a key phrase increases, so too does competition. If your content is consistently being beat in rankings by other larger sites with the same keywords, it's time to try to find (and create content for) keywords with a longer tail (see chapter 7). It's a good practice to check traffic volume for keywords, both for those you are planning on targeting and for those you are already targeting. Interest in a given topic waxes and wanes over time. If search traffic has dropped off for the key phrase you're targeting, that could partially explain why content isn't ranking.

On the topic of the content itself, look for the deeper story the data is telling you. Are people landing on your content and bouncing off? How long are they spending on the page? Using a combination of the audience behavior metrics from Google Analytics and the search results information from Google Search Console, you can start to build a picture of how people are interacting with your pages and your site as a whole. Using this data, you can determine if the content on your site truly resonates with people who are landing there, what terms they searched to get there, and how long they spent looking at the content.

Search Console is free and easy to set up, with basically no technical expertise needed. Google Analytics is a little more involved on the setup end. Google provides you with a segment of code that needs to be added to the head of all the pages you want to track behavior on (usually just about all your pages). This isn't challenging, but it does require a small amount of technical know-how or the know-how of a freelancer who will do the job for you. The crème de la crème of user behavior tracking comes in the form of Google's Tag Manager program. Tag Manager adds another layer of tracking over your site's existing content and can return powerful insights, like exactly how far down the page a reader scrolled before navigating away, how much of a form they filled out, which links were clicked on and when, and some other really helpful insights. Here's the catch: Tag Manager massively simplifies a lot of coding activities that developers would otherwise have to do by hand, but it is still pretty complex. It can totally overwhelm the uninitiated and, when implemented incorrectly, can drag down page load times. Implementation and use of Google Tag Manager is outside the scope of this book, but keep it in the back of your mind as your site grows.

Social Media

As platforms like Facebook took off in popularity, the role played by paid advertising in their revenue growth became more and more prominent. This has resulted in two chief outcomes relevant to digital marketers:

there is more content than ever on social media, and social media platforms have to work harder than ever to show their users only content that's relevant to them. This, coupled with the platforms' need to capture ad revenue, means that it is much harder to grow organic reach than it was in the past. This isn't to say that brands can't cultivate dedicated and engaged followers on social media, but paid advertising plays a much larger role than before.

First, what do you do when your organic reach—the number of people who see and have the potential to interact with your posts—is declining? Or worse, isn't even getting off the ground? Everyone has to earn their place in the news feed on platforms like Facebook and Instagram. Post content that no one engages with, and the algorithm won't increase the prominence of your content. When crafting content for social media to boost your organic reach, think about the kinds of content you engage with when you're scrolling through social media on your own time. Does your brand's content genuinely speak to topics that might engage, inspire, entertain, convert, or converse with (chapter 7) your target audience? Focus on the value your content provides to your audience first, and make sure that you are putting out the kind of content they will respond to.

A strong social media presence starts with good content, but the best content in the world won't get in front of too many people if the platform you're on actively works to restrict it. Skirting terms of service or other platform policies—purchasing followers, spamming hashtags, or sharing inappropriate, prohibited, or otherwise low-quality content, for example—can result in your reach being throttled by the platform itself. In some cases you will receive notice from the platform, and in others you may not realize your posts are being restricted until you see declining metrics. Do some investigating if you're seeing a drop-off in reach or engagement, but it's not something that most brands need to actively worry about. Those that follow the rules and engage with social media users in good faith rarely face content restriction.

Many brands find success with organic reach on social media, but the truth in today's competitive social media landscape is that social success is a pay-to-play undertaking. There are a multitude of reasons for social ads not performing as well as a marketer would like. Often, problems stem from decisions the marketer made when starting the campaign. If your ads aren't performing well, look at your targeting criteria and your campaign objectives. The platform's advertising service will do its best to show your ads to users who are likeliest to convert, but if your ads aren't relevant for the audience you have indicated, performance will suffer. Most platforms will provide a measure of ad relevancy, and this can be an early indicator of a mismatch between targeting criteria and ad content.

A good way to test different audiences and ensure that your relevancy is as high as possible is to assign different targeting criteria to different ad sets within a campaign. Programmatic advertising on social media is generally organized in the same way as programmatic advertising found elsewhere. Facebook, for example, starts with campaign-level objectives. Then ad sets are assigned to the campaign, and each set is made up of individual ads.

GRAPHIC
fig. 76

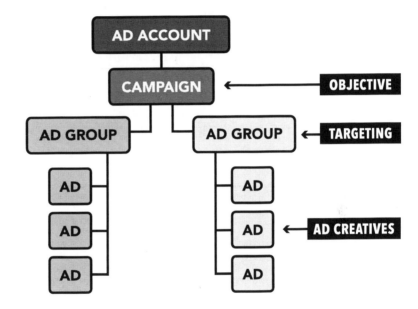

Campaign objectives are defined at the campaign level. Each ad group can have its own targeting assigned to increase the relevancy of ads to platform users.

If you are experiencing low performance with ads that don't have the right level of relevance, include another ad group with updated ads, and adjust targeting as needed. To minimize ad fatigue, each ad group should have a minimum of three or four creatives, and the ads in each group should be as personalized to the target audience as possible. This is also a great way to test new audiences and new ad creatives. For example, instead of using one ad group to target men and women who are interested in tennis, a tennis retailer might create an ad group targeting only men, with ads featuring male athletes, and another ad group targeting only women and featuring female athletes.

The Importance of Split Testing

Split testing, sometimes referred to as A/B testing, is a method of marketing experimentation. Using the split testing technique, you present multiple versions of the same general message, creative, or offer and see which gets the best results. Thus you can undertake campaigns with confidence that you have done your due diligence and have set yourself up for success. Split testing can be used to measure small things, like whether to place a button at the left-hand or right-hand side of a page, or big things, like whether a landing page should feature images of a product being used by actors or images only of the product itself.

A split test, like any other experiment, starts with a hypothesis.

» "I want to test the effectiveness of adding an emoji to the subject line of a promotional email."

» "I want to test the effectiveness of changing the position of the opt-in form on my home page. Should it hug the top of the screen instead of the bottom?"

» "I want to test the effectiveness of a two-step checkout form versus a single compact form."

Split testing should be done whenever possible, and many modern marketing tools provide the ability. It's particularly well-suited to presenting two versions of a web page, an email body, an email subject line, a landing page, or an ad creative.

The Larger Role of Digital Marketing

Marketing has traditionally been considered a stand-alone department of a company, but businesses are learning that marketing—digital marketing in particular—is an integral part of many functions within an organization.

When you think about it, the role of digital marketers is to get to know a lot about customers and prospective customers. Marketers work hard to understand who their customers are, what they enjoy doing, where they live and work, how much money they make, how they spend their free time, what their families look like, and other aspects of their lives.

That means marketers hold valuable insights and information about customers that should inform other departments. A product designer trying to match features to best meet the needs of a target audience, for instance, can save a lot of time and gain a lot of insight from information the marketing department has already gathered. As they say, there is no point in reinventing the wheel.

The tools you've learned about, those you will use as a marketer, can be applied to and benefit nearly all aspects of an organization. Let's look at a few areas in which marketing can be integrated.

Digital Marketing and Customer Service

It makes sense that as businesses become increasingly digital, their customer service efforts must move into the digital space as well. This concept of serving customers online (e-care) has become vastly more commonplace in recent years, as evidenced by the increase in live chat, social media support, and other services that were once relatively niche (or unreliable). Customer service and digital marketing go hand in hand, as both require a sound understanding of products and services offered, who can benefit from them, and how to convince potential customers that those products and services are needed.

Incorporating the types of tools we've mentioned can enhance your customer service while reducing costs. It also lets you track the service needs of customers so you can better understand and anticipate what they want. A study from McKinsey & Company, a global management consulting firm, concluded that by digitizing customer service, companies can increase customer satisfaction by 33 percent and cut costs by 25 to 35 percent.

Today's customers are savvy and used to getting quick results when looking for a product or service. Companies that are not ready to respond on demand or can't keep up will be left behind. Customers with questions about a product who can't get immediate answers are likely to look elsewhere. The following tips can help you anticipate their needs:

» **Make sure information is available where customers look for it**. If most are engaging through your website, make sure they can find what they need there. Learn your customers' and prospective customers' preferred communication channels and make sure everything they need is available there.

» **Present information in a way that is intuitive so users can find it and engage quickly.** No one wants to spend more than a minute or two looking for information they need. Anticipate customers' needs and let them know you sympathize with them. Make sure your virtual tone is understanding and matches your brand.

» **Make sure customers get prompt replies to their questions and concerns.** Automated customer service ensures that customers' questions and concerns can be addressed quickly and professionally. Non-prompt response is a common complaint among customers—and one that can be avoided.

» **Make every member of your team a customer service representative.** Having everyone on board will ensure that customer service—and customers—are at the forefront of your efforts.

Just as metrics can be employed to measure digital marketing efforts, they can also help you gauge the success of your customer service efforts. Some metrics to consider using are customer satisfaction score, customer retention rate, customer churn, first response time, first call resolution rate, and net promoter score. As customers continue to demand faster, more personalized service, customer service and digital marketing can work together to increase satisfaction.

Digital Marketing and Product Design

Design is the silent ambassador of your brand.

– PAUL RAND

Digital marketing and product design may not at first seem to go hand in hand, but marketing is actually a huge piece of the design process.

Product designers and digital marketers should work together to introduce products that will meet customers' needs on every level, including the practical, financial, and emotional levels.

Any product or service your company offers should mesh with the needs and wants of customers, based on the information used to create your customer avatars. Product design requires a keen understanding of end-user customers, with products devised to address their habits, behaviors, preferences, and frustrations. Designers and marketers should work seamlessly to anticipate, understand, and meet customers' needs.

Also, marketers and designers can team up from the beginning of the design process to make potential customers aware that a new product is on the horizon and to build anticipation as the product launch becomes imminent.

Digital Marketing and Process Design

Simply stated, process design is the way workflow occurs within your business. It's the way your invoicing is done, how payments are collected, documents are approved, new employees are onboarded, and so forth.

None of those process steps, especially those being newly implemented or changed, should be designed independently of your digital marketing team. All the goals and many of the tools that apply to marketing will also apply to process design. If there's a problem with your billing process, for instance, marketing strategies can be applied to address that problem and turn it into sales opportunities.

Process design requires a broad view of the organization and should be geared toward delivering the greatest possible customer value. Your marketing team, with its knowledge of customer needs and preferences, can be an integral part of your company's process design.

Digital Marketing and Strategic Pricing

If anyone tries to tell you that strategic pricing and marketing are unrelated, ignore them. Determining prices for your product or service has marketing written all over it, because pricing involves implication of value, emotional impact on customers, gaining advantage over competitors, and establishing your brand. I'd argue, in fact, that pricing strategy is central to your business's marketing efforts.

Determining a price for your product or service isn't just about coming up with a number. You need to consider the profit you wish to achieve, all the costs that go into preparing the product or service, how much customers will be willing to pay based on their needs and perception of the product, and many other factors. You run two risks: charging more than customers believe the product or service is worth, and undercharging, which can throw doubt on the value of what you're selling.

The trick, of course, is finding just the right price, and drawing on the knowledge and tools of digital marketers can help by providing valuable insight into customer preferences.

Digital Marketing and Recruitment and Human Resources

Marketing and human resources departments can work together in a couple of ways. Human resources recruitment involves advertising, a field in which digital marketers have acquired extensive knowledge. They understand where to place ads, whom the ads should target, how to get people to see and respond to them, and other finer points of advertising. Human resources should develop their recruitment ads with digital marketers and use marketing tactics to place and follow up on advertising.

Help-wanted ads can be valuable marketing tools in themselves. Simply by letting viewers know you offer fair, competitive wages and benefits in a pleasant work environment, you're portraying a positive image of your company. The ads also provide an opportunity to present other types of information—your production processes are environmentally sustainable, for instance, or part of your profits support a particular charity.

Chapter Recap

» Leveraging the power of marketing automation means you can work to move traffic through your digital marketing funnel at scale.

» Behavior-based automation enables you to send messages to contacts in response to specific triggers.

» Welcome messages deliver lead magnets, coupons, or other incentives and increase the temperature of your audience.

» Lead-nurturing sequences are used to engage with contacts and warm their temperature in anticipation of presenting them with an offer.

» Sales sequences consist of one or two emails that present an offer and attempt to convert your contacts.

» Abandoned cart sequences are triggered when a customer puts items in their cart but fails to complete the purchase. These sequences are essential for e-commerce brands attempting to recover revenue from what would otherwise be a lost sale.

» Re-engagement or win-back sequences are used to reactivate customers who have been inactive for a long time. These sequences usually consist of just one or two messages and usually offer a coupon or some other enticement.

» Campaigns need to be monitored and optimized to keep performance high.

» Listening to the story that campaign metrics are telling you is the best first step in diagnosing issues.

» Digital marketing efforts can play a larger strategic role in how an organization functions.

Conclusion

The marketers of today must wear many hats and pay attention to many trends and platforms, often coming at a breakneck pace, if they want to become the marketing leaders of tomorrow. If you are feeling overwhelmed or discouraged, remember that although the tools and tactics may change to match emerging technology, there is one constant in the marketing world—the people. The core tenets of the market/media/message mix and the drive to always be providing value to your audience will stand the test of time even when platforms and channels rise and fall in popularity.

It has always been true that no business can survive without a marketing investment. That was true thirty, fifty, a hundred years ago when there were significantly fewer demands on our attention, and it is even more true now. Monitoring your marketing spend, focusing on appearing in places where your target audience spends time online, and always testing and monitoring will result in keeping your audience engaged and ready to convert.

Writing a book about digital marketing comes with some of the same challenges that digital marketers themselves face. There is simply so much ground to cover, in an industry that changes constantly and quickly. In fact, during the writing of this book, Facebook announced a parent-company name change to Meta, which it says will better reflect its emerging bet on the metaverse—a kind of virtual reality space that is still taking shape. What do digital marketers need to know about the metaverse, or about any emerging digital marketing space, for that matter?

I hope by this point you can see that the answers are in this book. Concentrating on delivering value and warming the temperature of your audience by focusing on the customer's journey and their lifetime value will always be the right first step, whether you are marketing in our world or the virtual one. On that note, what does the future of digital marketing look like? I'll use this space as a place to make some speculative predictions.

Privacy Concerns Will Continue to Grow

After years of consumers not really paying much attention to how their data is collected and used, the tide is turning. Apple in particular is emerging as a privacy-first digital services ecosystem. When a tech behemoth like

Apple makes moves, the rest of the industry is sure to follow suit. Privacy-forward changes are only a concern for unscrupulous marketers or those who are set in their ways. Changes in the ways platforms and people collect personal data might cause short-term disruptions to digital marketing as it has always been done, but in the long term, industry participants will always settle into whatever the new normal looks like. If you want to stay ahead of the curve, find marketers who are on the cutting edge and who are thinking ahead, and listen to what they have to say. Ultimately, an internet where we are all protected as consumers is a good thing, even if it does mean some short-term headaches for marketers.

Consumer Expectations Will Be More Stringent

For better or worse, we want it all. As savvy marketers get better at anticipating the needs of their audiences, they raise the bar for everyone else. There was a time when online shoppers would grudgingly accept shipping charges without too much fuss. Now, so many companies offer fast free shipping that the customer expectation is that they won't have to ever pay shipping fees again. The same goes for providing tracking information for shipments—at a minimum, customers expect to be able to track their orders. The online experience has become so saturated with marketing and advertising messages that today's consumer expects to be marketed to when they go online. Both the internet and internet advertising have become so ubiquitous that we have accepted that's just how it is. And since a proliferation of marketing messages online is the norm, we also have an expectation that those messages will be professional and compelling and will offer personalized value. If you want to keep your brand in the forefront of your audience's minds, be sure to keep an eye on trends and keep all your marketing collateral attractive and professional. There are many things that can harm a brand, but failing to put your best foot forward is among the worst of them.

Gen Z Is Coming, and They Grew Up on Social

If you were a digital marketer in the late aughts and the twenty-teens, you doubtless read some of the mountains of breathless industry reporting about the newest and fastest-growing consumer demographic: millennials. Initially, millennials—generally anyone born between the years 1985 and 1996—created problems for legacy marketers. Having grown up with the internet, millennials were digitally savvy, often more so than the marketers who were targeting them. They were also discerning shoppers, and they were critical of marketing campaigns that didn't reflect their values. This was a problem for legacy brands that were slow to react to demographic changes and had marketing teams made up of people from a different generation. There is no shortage of articles in internet archives exclaiming that millennials were immune to marketing. The truth, of course, is that there is nothing special or unique about millennials. Once marketers took the time to understand their needs and preferences as a cohort, the hubbub surrounding millennial consumers died down.

We're at the beginning of the cycle again with Gen Z—people born between 1997 and 2012. The oldest members of this cohort are entering the workforce and building up disposable income, meaning they are entering the sights of marketers. Don't make the mistake that legacy brands did when confronted with young millennials. Members of Gen Z have grown up in a world defined by online access and the "always on" nature of social media, but the same basic principles of providing personalized value and meeting their customer expectations are as true for this segment as for any other. Listen to what they have to say and meet them where they spend time online, as you would with any other segment.

If there is one thing I want to leave you with, it's a reminder to stay excited. It takes work to put all the pieces of your digital marketing strategy into place. Setting up automation, writing email copy, putting together ad creatives—these tasks can sap the excitement you have for connecting with customers and growing your business. Here's the thing: once you get the formula right and you can see your efforts paying off, it's an awesome feeling. Marketers get the same satisfaction as a mechanic watching a well-oiled machine running smoothly.

Don't lose sight of that excitement, whether you are on your first campaign or your fiftieth.

REMEMBER TO DOWNLOAD YOUR FREE DIGITAL ASSETS!

 Strategic Planning Worksheet

 SEO Fundamentals Checklist

 Digital Marketing Toolkit

 Customer Avatar Worksheet

TWO WAYS TO ACCESS YOUR FREE DIGITAL ASSETS

Use the camera app on your mobile phone to scan the QR code or visit the link below and instantly access your Digital Assets.

or www.clydebankmedia.com/digitalmarketing-assets

 SCAN ME

📺 VISIT URL

Appendix

Recommended Reading

The digital marketing elite know that the best way to hone their craft is to rely on a diversity of perspectives. There are a number of other books on the market that explore the topic of digital marketing from the unique perspectives of their authors or dive into a specific corner of the digital marketing world. It is often said that change is the only constant in the business world, and marketing is no exception. That means the best way you can set yourself up for success is to stay current, try new things, and never stop learning.

To start, let's look at some books that dive into some more advanced digital marketing concepts. Bring the insight provided in the pages of this book to your reading experience with the following titles:

> » *Digital Marketing Strategy: An Integrated Approach to Online Marketing.* By Simon Kingsnorth, published April 3, 2019

> » *Digital Marketing That Actually Works, the Ultimate Guide: Discover Everything You Need to Build and Implement a Digital Marketing Strategy That Gets Results.* By Krista Neher, et al., published Feb. 21, 2019

> » *Digital Marketing: Strategy and Tactics – 2 ed.* By Jeremy Kagan, published Aug. 10, 2020

> » *Change. Adapt. Rock.: The Ultimate Digital Marketing Book for Your Online Business.* By WildRock Public Relations and Marketing, published Feb. 8, 2021

> » *Digital Marketing: Strategic Planning & Integration.* By Annmarie Hanlon, published Feb. 22, 2019

> » *Digital Marketing.* By Dave Chaffey and Fiona Ellis-Chadwick, published Oct. 11, 2018

» *How to Get to the Top of Google in 2021: The Plain English Guide to SEO (Digital Marketing by Exposure Ninja).* By Tim Cameron-Kitchen, Dale Davies, and Andrew Tuxford, published Jan. 7, 2020

» *Building a StoryBrand: Clarify Your Message So Customers Will Listen.* By Donald Miller, published Oct. 10, 2017

There is a lot to say about digital marketing, and plenty of bloggers who spend their time generating discussion relating to it. Blogs can be incredibly valuable in helping you keep up with changing regulations and offering valuable insights and strategies. Some worth checking out include the following, in no particular order:

» **Search Engine Journal**
An excellent resource that focuses on search engine optimization and paid search breaking news (it happens more than you might think), general reporting, and insights. Reporting ranges from beginner-friendly to quite sophisticated, so there is something here for everyone.

» **Hootsuite Blog**
This varied blog is heavy on social updates but also offers profound digital strategy insights and advice. Hootsuite is used by some of the most successful brands on social media and as a result they have a wealth of information for digital marketers who are trying to get the most out of their social presence.

» **Content Marketing Institute**
A multi-author, daily blog that lives up to its strong reputation in the content marketing industry. With topics ranging from beginner-focused to expert level, there is something here for marketers of all stripes.

» **Moz Blog**
An inbound marketing and SEO blog with frequent input from industry experts, Moz provides tips for improving your search, social, and inbound marketing. Moz is a household name in the world of search engine optimization and they have the tools and resources to run the kinds of tests and digital marketing case studies that digital marketers and entrepreneurs rely on.

» **Copyblogger**

This classic has been around since the beginning of 2006 and continues to provide a wealth of information for marketers and content creators. As the name implies, this outlet focuses on copywriting and content marketing. If you're planning on handling all of your own copy and content creation, checking this site out is a must.

» **Neil Patel's Blog**

One of the top marketers in the industry, Patel offers strategic resources and practical solutions for marketers, along with insights into content marketing, email marketing, social marketing and more. Pay special attention to the tools and tactics Patel uses to sell his own products and services. Marketers who market to other marketers—what a mouthful—need to really know their stuff.

» **Duct Tape Marketing**

Written with small businesses in mind, this blog covers a wide swath of topics in a practical, down-to-earth manner. Starting from the first principle that marketing is the most important small business function, the Duct Tape Marketing author, blogger, and podcast host John Jantsch focuses on practicality and efficiency for small business owners in both digital and traditional spaces.

» **Digiday**

Probably the most professional resource on this list, Digiday provides the gold standard in contemporary digital marketing reporting. Produced with agency and enterprise marketers in mind, this paywalled publication assumes that its readers are already intimately familiar with the current state of affairs in the world of digital marketing at scale. Recommended for new marketers who want to learn a lot very quickly and have some disposable income in their business (Digiday is a trade publication and is priced accordingly).

» **HubSpot Academy**

HubSpot is an enterprise-level customer relationship management (CRM) service with an excellent free learning hub called HubSpot Academy. From content marketing to social, email, and sales, HubSpot Academy is an excellent resource for both new and experienced marketers.

About
the Author

BENJAMIN SWEENEY

Benjamin Sweeney is a digital marketer and author. He has accumulated over a decade of digital marketing experience, most recently as the marketing manager for ClydeBank Media. He maintains a focus on the business sphere that draws from scholarly research and practical experience from time spent as an entrepreneur and consultant.

With well over a million written words under his belt and a marketing role that has him sending more than a million emails a year, Ben knows what it takes to get more customers for a small business, no matter what industry they're in.

About ClydeBank Media

We create simplified educational tools that allow our customers to successfully learn new skills in order to navigate this constantly changing world.

The success of ClydeBank Media's value-driven approach starts with beginner-friendly high-quality information. We work with subject matter experts who are leaders in their fields. These experts are supported by our team of professional researchers, writers, and educators.

Our team at ClydeBank Media works with these industry leaders to break down their wealth of knowledge, their wisdom, and their years of experience into small and concise building blocks. We piece together these building blocks to create a clearly defined learning path that a beginner can follow for successful mastery.

At ClydeBank Media, we see a new world of possibility. Simplified learning doesn't have to be bound by four walls; instead, it's driven by you.

Glossary

4 C's of marketing

An alternate customer-centric interpretation of the marketing mix that replaces the 4 P's of marketing with four C's: customer wants and needs, cost, convenience, and communication.

4 P's of marketing

Also known as the "marketing mix," the 4 P's of marketing represent the core aspects of a product or service that make up the basis of an executable campaign. They are product, price, place, and promotion.

5 P's of marketing

The 4 P's of marketing (product, price, place, and promotion) with the addition of "people," a category that refers to staff members involved in the process of selling goods or services to customers.

A/B testing

Also referred to as split testing, A/B testing is a method in which a marketer presents two versions of a creative, copy segment, or other message to an audience. These two versions are nearly identical with only one aspect changed. The difference in responses determines which variant—A or B—produces better results and should be used going forward.

Ad fatigue

The phenomenon of audience overexposure to an ad to the extent that they tune out completely and stop paying attention to the message. This is detrimental to an ad campaign and negatively impacts ROI.

Affective override

The point at which emotion overtakes the process of rational decision making. In this state consumers are more receptive to emotional messaging and are more likely to make a purchase or take action.

Affiliate links

Promotional links that attribute sales to a marketing affiliate. Affiliates are generally paid regularly, based on attributed sales.

Alt text

A text description that accompanies an image online. Alt text is normally not visible but is detected by screen readers that help visually impaired web users browse the internet. Also known as "alt tags" or "alt descriptions," alt text accompanying images demonstrates to search engines that a site is accessible to the largest possible number of internet users and is looked upon favorably by ranking algorithms.

Audience

All members of a market segment, either in or outside of a digital space, that a message is tailored to reach.

Audience temperature
The level of awareness and interest members of an audience have regarding their own pain points, solutions to those pain points, and the solutions offered by certain products or services. Members of an audience with low awareness are considered "cold"; high-awareness audience members are "warm" or "hot."

Average order value (AOV)
The total value of all orders within a given period divided by the number of customers.

Awareness marketing
Efforts intended to increase brand awareness and recognition by reaching members of a target market who may not know enough about a product or service to consider purchasing it.

B2B
Business-to-business, or brand-to-brand, refers to businesses that market and sell their products or services to other businesses.

B2C
Business/brand-to-consumer refers to a business that markets and sells its products or services to individuals for personal use.

Behavioral segmentation
The act of dividing consumers into groups based on behavior patterns exhibited as they interact with a brand and its products/services.

Behavioral targeting
The practice of placing ads based on the internet browsing history of prospective customers.

Benefit
The customer value that a feature adds to a product or service.

Bounce rate
The percentage of visitors to a page who leave without navigating to another page on the same site. Generally, visitors that bounce do not convert.

Brand
The sum of perceptions, opinions, and feelings that are associated with a company, product, or person. A brand is everything the public thinks it knows about your offering, both real and perceived.

Brand positioning
The strategic approach a brand takes in the marketplace to set itself apart from other offerings.

Brand positioning matrix
A visual representation of brand positions within an industry. The plotting criteria, such as expensive vs. budget or premium vs. cheap, varies from industry to industry based on which characteristics are most relevant to customers.

Broad match
A matching option that matches one's ad against the widest range of keyword search queries, resulting in a large number of matches, many of which may not be relevant.

Call to action (CTA)
The immediate action a marketer asks audience members to take in a message. The action could be to make a purchase, join an email list, leave a review, start a free trial—any action that delivers value to both marketer and audience member.

Campaign optimization
The process of assessing and making decisions about a campaign's performance in order to improve its overall quality and success.

Channel

The means through which a marketer reaches potential customers. A channel can be a one-way method of communication, as with television or print media, or a two-way method of communication, as with social media.

Clickbait

Sensationalized copy, particularly a headline, subject line, or linked text, that doesn't deliver on its promise or is otherwise misleading, spammy, or of low value.

Content asset

Each individual piece of content on the internet. Content asset varies greatly in type, size, and value.

Content depth

A ranking factor used by Google and other search engines that evaluates the length and quality of content on a web page. Pages with little content have low content depth and are said to be thin or shallow.

Content management system (CMS)

A web development application that enables someone with no coding experience to create and manage the content on a website.

Content marketing

The marketing practice of creating content that speaks to a particular keyword or customer pain point as a way to increase audience temperature or get members of an audience to take action.

Contextual targeting

The practice of placing an ad that relates to the content of the page on which the ad runs.

Continuity interrupter

A headline, photo, video, or other content that is so surprising or different that it demands the attention of the reader and gets them to stop scrolling.

Conversion

A response to a request someone has made of someone who interacts with their content. A conversion occurs when someone makes a purchase, signs up for a newsletter, enrolls in a special offer, or takes another form of action.

Conversion-based marketing

A catchall term for marketing that is measured by, and has goals based on, producing conversions in a target audience.

Conversion rate

The percentage of visitors to a web page who complete a desired action, such as making a purchase or registering for a newsletter, while they are there.

Copy

As pertaining to marketing, copy is any text designed to persuade the reader to take action.

Cost per acquisition

The cost of acquiring individual paying customers during the course of a campaign.

Cost per action

The cost associated with each individual action taken during a given period.

Cost per impression

The cost associated with showing a message or advertisement to an audience online. Often billed as the cost per thousand impressions.

Customer acquisition cost

The total of all expenses required to convert a prospect into a customer.

Customer avatar

A fictional composite character that reflects the key attributes of an ideal customer and is used to inform the media mix, product features and benefits, and ad targeting.

Customer journey

The combined experiences a customer has with a brand, from first learning about the brand and the problem its products or services solve to making a purchase, and any communication thereafter.

Customer lifetime value
The value of one customer's total purchase amount over the course of their relationship with a brand, minus the cost to initially acquire the customer.

Dark web
Internet content that is hosted on a network separate from the surface web and is only accessible via specialized browsers.

Deep web
Internet content that is not accessible to or indexed by search engines.

Demographic segmentation
The act of dividing a market based on the personal characteristics of potential customers, such as age, gender, education, occupation, and income level.

Demographic targeting
The practice of placing ads on websites and pages where they are most likely to be viewed by visitors of a certain age, race, gender, or other demographic.

Direct to consumer (DTC)
A brand that sells products directly to consumers without the benefit of any third-party wholesalers or retailers.

Downsell
An offer that decreases the value and price of a customer's order in an attempt to close the sale.

Earned media
Posts, reviews, stories, or other buzz about a brand that it does not control or pay for. Earned media often comes with a higher perceived authority than owned or paid media but also comes with the risk of being negative or critical of one's brand.

Email bounces
Email messages that are undeliverable. Full inboxes, overzealous spam prevention, firewalls, server errors, and deleted email accounts can all cause email bounces.

Engagement
Any type of interaction with content, such as likes, comments, or shares. Engagement is an indicator that people are interested in the content and is generally considered positive.

Exact match
A matching option that matches a keyword only with exact search queries and terms.

Feature
An aspect of a product or service that sets it apart from other, similar products or services. Features produce value for customers—this value is known as a benefit.

Firmographic segmentation
A form of B2B market segmentation based on the shared attributes of a group of businesses, such as number of employees, annual revenue, or number of locations.

FOMO
"Fear of missing out," a form of social anxiety stemming from the fear that others have better products or are having more enjoyable experiences.

Form abandonment rate
The percentage of page visitors who start filling out a lead capture, opt-in, or checkout form and fail to complete it.

Geographical segmentation
The act of dividing a market based on where potential customers are physically located.

Hyper-compelling offer
An offer that is perfectly matched to one's target audience and provides overwhelming value.

Impression rate
The number of times an ad or other display message was shown to traffic.

Impression share
The number of top or absolute top impressions received compared to the number of opportunities for top or absolute top impressions.

Impression
A metric representing the number of times content is displayed, regardless of whether it generates any action.

Inbound marketing
The marketing efforts that take place in response to consumers actively seeking out products or services.

Landing page
A single page built with a specific conversion purpose in mind. Generally, ads or other marketing messages are linked to landing pages where traffic is presented with an offer or a request to take action.

Lead magnet
An (often free) valuable content asset that is offered in exchange for the contact information of traffic on a landing page or opt-in form.

Lifecycle marketing
A systematized approach to marketing designed to move members of an audience through a digital marketing funnel.

Lifestyle marketing
A marketing technique that matches a brand with a perceived lifestyle or set of lifestyle traits to encourage members of an audience to associate that brand with a desirable lifestyle.

Mail merge fields
Placeholder fields in emails or other communications that draw personalized attributes from a marketing database to make each message unique to the recipient.

Market research
The process of gathering information about the consumers in a targeted marketing segment. Surveys, questionnaires, polls, and other information-gathering techniques are used to better understand the needs, preferences, and attributes of members of the target market.

Market segmentation
The act of dividing a large market into smaller, more manageable segments based on shared characteristics of those within the market.

Marketable entity
A brand, person, organization or even a concept with the potential to benefit from marketing techniques and practices.

Marketing
A bundle of activities and tasks employed by businesses to make it known that they exist and to convince consumers that the business is likeable and trustworthy enough to buy from.

Marketing automation
The practice of using tools or platforms to automate common marketing tasks such as sending emails, adjusting PPC bids, and compiling and sending reports.

Marketing formula
The unique combination of market, media, and message a brand uses to reach their target audience.

Marketing mix
Also referred to as the "4 P's of marketing," the marketing mix uses four elements to precisely describe the product or service being sold. The four P's in the mix are product, price, place, and promotion.

Match types
Parameters set on keywords to determine how PPC ads are triggered.

Media mix
The combination of earned, owned, and paid media that a brand uses when marketing to audiences. Effective marketers use a blend of all three types to maximize their reach and results.

Microcopy
Small copy segments such as those that make up or support calls to action.

Mobile-first indexing
The decision from Google's search engine to index the mobile version of a site or web page first and prioritize that version of the site over a desktop version.

Native advertising
Advertising that uses formatting, color palettes, and other design elements to help it blend into surrounding content to prevent ad fatigue.

New media
Any content or media that is delivered digitally.

Off-page SEO
SEO efforts such as generating backlinks and improving a site's technical structure.

Offer
Any presentation of value to an audience that requires the reader or recipient to take action. Offers are most often associated with a purchase but can include opting in, trying a sample, or any other marketing objective.

Old media
Usually referring to technologies that preceded the personal computer / internet age, such as telephone, television, radio, newspapers, billboards, etc.

On-page SEO
The process of optimizing web pages for specific key phrases.

Out-of-home advertising
Any marketing tactic encountered outside of one's home, such as messages on billboards, buildings, city buses, etc.

Outbound marketing
The marketing efforts a company directs toward its target audience, even though the audience did not request the conversation.

Owned media
Any content one creates and places on a channel that they own, such as a website, blog, or social site. Owned media offers the highest degree of control over the content of the messages being shared.

Paid media
Marketing paid for by a company to promote and direct traffic to its own brand or product. The most common form of paid media is advertising.

Paid search placement
Programmatic advertising that appears in search results pages.

Pain points
Problems and challenges faced by people. Products and services are designed to speak to and alleviate pain points.

Pareto principle
Also called the 80/20 rule, this principle states that 80 percent of one's revenue will come from 20 percent of their customers. As applied to email marketing, it states that at least 80 percent of copy should be of pure value to customers, and no more than 20 percent should be designed to get customers to buy.

Pay per click
A programmatic advertising billing model in which advertisers are charged every time one of their ads is clicked on.

Pay per impression
A programmatic advertising billing model in which advertisers are charged every time one of their ads is shown to an individual.

Penetration pricing
A strategy in which products are priced lower than the market price in order to gain attention, capture market share, and "penetrate" a market. This strategy is often used by brands with new products that are attempting to break into a new market.

Phrase match
A matching option that matches one's ad against keywords that include a phrase they designate.

Platform
A tool that links marketers and consumers within a channel.

Product lifecycle
A series of stages reflecting how consumers respond to a product or service in the marketplace.

Programmatic advertising
A method of buying and optimizing digital campaigns automatically instead of having to interact and negotiate with humans, increasing efficiency and transparency for both advertisers and publishers.

Prominence metrics
Metrics that provide an estimation of the visibility of an ad on search results pages.

Promotional mix
A set of marketing approaches that includes advertising, public relations, personal selling, and sales promotion. The mix is used in different ways and combinations to optimize promotional efforts.

Psychographic segmentation
The act of dividing a market into groups based on the values, emotions, and interests of consumers.

Pull marketing
Tactics that "pull" customers along a pathway toward the purchase of a product or service. Like inbound marketing, it targets customers who are actively seeking a product or service.

Push marketing
Outbound marketing efforts that "push" a message out to an audience, whether the audience is actively seeking the message or not. A radio ad is an example of push marketing.

Quality score
A metric used by search engines, in conjunction with the bid, to determine how prominently a given ad will be displayed online. Influential factors include the landing page quality and load time.

Reach
The total number of people who see one's content, regardless of where it is displayed.

Reachable size
The portion of a target market that a marketer can reach in a cost-effective manner.

Responsive design
Web design that scales content to render correctly on a variety of screen sizes, such as those of phones, tablets, and computer monitors.

Retargeting
A method of advertising that targets traffic that has visited a site.

Sales cycle
A map of the specific steps a buyer goes through when making a purchase.

Sales funnel
A sales-oriented representation of the journey customers will take before making a purchase.

Sales page
A stand-alone page designed for the express purpose of generating a sale. The page should contain information about the product and its benefits and a call to action, at a minimum.

Scaling down

The act of decreasing an ad budget, normally because the ad is not producing the desired number of sales.

Scaling up

The act of increasing an ad budget to optimize the number of people who will see an ad that is doing well and producing results.

Search engine optimization (SEO)

The practice of optimizing a website and the pages on it to produce content that search engines see as relevant and reward with higher placements on search results pages.

Search index

The record of pages a search engine has collected and draws from when a user initiates a search.

Search intent

The goal of a search engine user that can be extrapolated from the key phrase they have entered.

Sender reputation

A score assigned to email senders by internet service providers to separate compliant senders from email spammers.

SERP (search engine results pages)

The pages shown to search engine users in response to their search query. Search engine results pages contain both paid and organic results.

SERVE

An acronym representing five categories of digital marketing efforts. The categories are increasing Sales, facilitating an Exchange of communication between marketer and customer, Reducing marketing costs, increasing Value conveyed to customers, and Extending the reach of the brand in digital space and beyond.

Service marketing mix

A marketing mix normally employed by businesses built around delivering a core service. The mix includes the 4 P's of marketing (product, price, place, and promotion), plus "people," "process," and "physical evidence."

Serviceable available market (SAM)

The part of a total addressable market (TAM) that resides within a market that one's product or service is designed for or able to reach.

Shiny object syndrome

The state of being seduced by new products and tools, causing one to vary from their marketing plan instead of staying on track.

SMART goal setting framework

A set of defined qualities designed to help one determine business goals. SMART stands for Specific, Measurable, Actionable, Relevant, and Time-bound.

Social content

Any content created specifically to be used on social networks.

Social media campaign

A planned, coordinated series of actions on social platforms, performed with the intent of achieving a specific goal or goals.

Social media marketing

Marketing intended for social platforms, including tasks such as posting text, images, and videos intended to keep followers informed and engaged.

Social proof

Compelling marketing messaging that revolves around the experiences, endorsements, or number of other customers.

Spam

Any type of messaging or advertising that is low in quality, unwanted, untargeted, and does not offer value to the viewer or recipient.

Squeeze page

A type of landing page designed to get visitors to provide their contact information in exchange for something of value, normally a lead magnet.

Subscriber churn

The ongoing gains and losses of subscribers to an email list.

Surface web

The part of the internet that is indexed by search engines.

Swipe file

A collection of copy, creatives, or other marketing material that is gathered over time. The contents of a swipe file are collected to act as inspiration for a marketer in their own campaigns.

Target market

The portion of a serviceable available market (SAM) at which marketing efforts and resources are aimed. Members of one's target market are most likely to buy the product or service they offer.

Technical SEO

The process of optimizing a website to make it easier for search engines to access, crawl, interpret, and index.

Tiering

A form of B2B market segmentation that groups customers based on their potential value. Tiering often applies to customer lifetime value.

Total addressable market (TAM)

The total number of potential customers for a particular product or service. If one sells generic vehicle floor mats, for instance, everyone who owns a vehicle is part of their TAM.

Traffic

The flow of web users who can be reached with marketing efforts.

Upsell

An offer that increases the value and price of a customer's order.

Value Ladder

A series of offers that increase in value as customers move from being prospects to being buyers and brand advocates.

Value pricing

A strategy that seeks to set pricing according to customers' perceived value of a product. Because customer perception can be manipulated, this pricing strategy may not represent the true value of a product.

Value proposition

The ways in which a business distinguishes itself from its competition and convinces customers to choose it over other options.

Viral marketing

A strategy that depends on websites or other users to pass a marketing message to other sites or users, creating the potential for rapid and exponential spread.

Web crawlers

Indexing bots that crawl the web and report back to search engines in order to build and maintain the search index that engines use to return information in response to search queries.

Web hosting company

A hosting service provider that owns and rents out space on their servers for businesses or individuals to store their website files.

YMYL (your money or your life)
Content that focuses on what is
most important to members of an
audience and is meant to inspire
and excite.

References

CHAPTER 1

Choi, David. 2016. "The first television commercial ever aired 75 years ago today." *Business Insider*. July 1. https://www.businessinsider.com/first-television-commercial-ever-2016-6.

Ad Age. 2003. "Television." September 15. https://adage.com/article/adage-encyclopedia/television/98901.

Internet Live Stats. 2013. Google Search Statistics. November 4. https://www.internetlivestats.com/google-search-statistics/.n.d. Maryville University. https://online.maryville.edu/blog/how-does-digital-media-affect-the-marketing-mix/.

n.d. Maryville University. https://online.maryville.edu/blog/how-does-digital-media-affect-the-marketing-mix/.

CHAPTER 5

Robinson, Richard. 2015. "Vision - Creating a World Without ALS." ALSA.org. Accessed February 14, 2022. http://web.alsa.org/site/DocServer/Vision_Winter_2015.pdf?docID=122341&_ga=2.43202924.855738741.1567482896-1424647728.1558037434.

CHAPTER 6

Motley, Calvin. 2020. "Taylor Swift's Earned an Easy $26 Million for This Endorsement." *Showbiz CheatSheet*. October 8. https://www.cheatsheet.com/entertainment/taylor-swifts-earned-an-easy-26-million-for-this-endorsement.html/.

CHAPTER 7

Godskind, Ken. 2009. "5, 10, 15 seconds? How Long Will You Wait For a Web Page to Load?" *SmartBear*. October 14. https://smartbear.com/blog/5-10-15-seconds-how-long-will-you-wait-for-a-web-p/.

CHAPTER 8

Google AdSense Help. n.d. About the ad auction. Accessed February 14, 2022. https://support.google.com/adsense/answer/160525?hl=en.

CHAPTER 9

Vodafone. 2017. "25 years since the world's first text message." December 4. https://www.vodafone.com/news/technology/25-anniversary-text-message.

Smith, Alexander. 2017. "Pepsi Pulls Controversial Kendall Jenner Ad After Outcry" *NBC News*. April 5. https://www.nbcnews.com/news/nbcblk/pepsi-ad-kendall-jenner-echoes-black-lives-matter-sparks-anger-n742811.

CHAPTER 10

Campaign Monitor. 2019. "24 Email Marketing Stats You Need to Know." July. https://www.campaignmonitor.com/resources/infographics/24-email-marketing-stats-need-know/.

CHAPTER 11

Clifford, Catherine. 2018. "The brilliant business lesson behind the emails Jeff Bezos sends to his Amazon executives with a single '?'." *CNBC* May 7. https://www.cnbc.com/2018/05/07/why-jeff-bezos-still-reads-the-emails-amazon-customers-send-him.html.

CHAPTER 12

Baymard Institute. 2020. "46 Cart Abandonment Rate Statistics." December 20. https://baymard.com/lists/cart-abandonment-rate.

Soulo, Tim. 2017. "How long does it take to rank in Google? (A study by Ahrefs)" *Ahrefs*. February 7. https://ahrefs.com/blog/how-long-does-it-take-to-rank/.

Index

4 C's of marketing, 29
4 P's of marketing, 27
5 P's of marketing, 29
80/20 rule, 219

A

Abandoned-cart messages, 221
Abandoned-cart sequences, 260–261
"About us" pages, on website, 107
Absolute top impression rate, 186
Absolute top impression share, 187
A/B testing, 212, 270
Abundance mindset, 98
Ad(s)
    display, 173, 173*f*
    help-wanted, 274
    in-stream, 174
    outstream, 174–175
    recruitment, 274
    search, 169
    SERP text, 168–169, 169*f*, 175, 176f
    Shopping, 175
    video, 174–175
Ad blockers, 172*f*, 172–173, 175
AdBlock Plus, 173
Ad creatives, 269
Ad fatigue, 44, 269
Ad groups, 170
Advertising
    awareness, 79–80
    behavioral targeting of, 174
    contextual targeting of, 173
    costs of, 48
    demographic targeting of, 173
    digital forms of, 22
    digital marketing funnels and, 253
    display, 171–174
    human resources recruitment, 274
    keywords for, 176–181
    metrics for, 181–187
    native, 45–46, 168
    as offer, 79
    out-of-home, 24–25
    as paid media, 44, 165, 267
    paid search, 168–171
    pay-per-click, 166
    pay-per-impression, 166–167
    profit-motive nature of, 45
    programmatic, 165–168, 178, 263, 269

SERP text ads, 168, 169*f*
social media. *See* Social media advertising
    traditional, 22, 165
    video, 174–175
Advertising campaign, 263
Affective overdrive, 20
Affiliate links, 144–145
Ahrefs, 266
Alexa, 203
Allbirds, 175
ALS Ice Bucket Challenge, 94–95, 158
Alt text, 146
AMA. *See* American Marketing Association
Amazon, 120, 166, 251–252
American Dental Association, 119
American Marketing Association, 14
Anniversaries, 221–222
AOL Instant Messenger, 219–220
AOV. *See* Average order value
Apple, 173
Artists, 4–5
Ask Jeeves, 136
Attributes, in customer avatar, 59–60
Audience
    contact information from, 235, 241
    definition of, 42
    social media marketing, 198–199
Audience temperature, 154–156, 155*f*
Avatar. *See* Customer avatars
Average cart value, 40–41
Average order value, 40–41
Average time on page metric, 126–127
Awareness advertising, 79–80
Awareness marketing, 24–25, 232, 234

B

B2B
    customer journey in, 71
    market segmentation in, 69–70
    social media platforms for, 198
B2C
    customer journey in, 71–72, 72*f*
    market segmentation in, 69
BBB. *See* Better Business Bureau
Behavior, in customer avatar, 59–60
Behavioral segmentation, of market, 66–67
Behavioral targeting, 174
Behavior-based automation
    abandoned cart sequences, 260–261

lead-nurturing sequences, 260
list hygiene, 262
re-engagement sequences, 261–262
user activity as basis of, 257
welcome sequences, 257–260
Benefit
definition of, 18
feature versus, 17–19, 18f
Better Business Bureau, 121
Biden, Joe, 196
Bing, 136, 177
Birthdays, 221–222
Blendtec, 158
Blind auctions, 166–167
Blogs, 48, 282–283
Books, 153
Borden, Neil, 26
Bots, 138–139, 142–143, 148
Bottom-of-the-funnel marketing, 236–237
Bounce-back coupons, 252
Bounce rate, 126, 225
Brand
credibility of, 30
customer relevancy of, 30
definition of, 19
differentiation of, 30
direct-to-consumer, 29
lack of control of, in earned media, 46
marketing for defining of, 19
value of, 57, 243, 249
Brand awareness
examples of, 24
positive, 55
social media campaign to increase, 193
Brand image, 45
Branding, 15
Brand perception, 55
Brand positioning
definition of, 30
matrix for, 30–31, 31f
Branson, Richard, 15
Broad match keywords, 178–179
Budget
digital marketing funnel, 238–239
marketing, 99–100
paid search advertising, 170
Buffett, Warren, 47
Business students, 5
Business-to-business. See B2B
Business-to-consumer. See B2C
Buyer persona. See Customer avatars

C
CAC. See Customer acquisition cost
California Consumer Privacy Act, 128
California legislation, 128–129
California Privacy Rights Act, 128–129

Call to action
button/form, 109f, 114–115
copy with, 113
definition of, 23
in email copy, 215f, 216, 221, 224
as offer, 79
Campaign
advertising, 263
objectives of, 269f
optimizing of, 263–265
paid search. See Paid search campaign
social media, 192–195
Campaign Monitor, 209
CAN-SPAM Act, 216–217
Canva, 146, 202
Carousel ads, 201–202
CCPA. See California Consumer Privacy Act
CD players, 58
CDs, 58–59, 155
Celebrity proof, 119, 119f
Certification, proof through, 121, 122f
Challenges, 94–95, 158
Channels
controllable, 47
definition of, 41–42
Chat, 203–204
Chatbots, 203
Checkout, 242
Clickbait, 112
ClickFunnels, 127
Click-through rate, 183–184, 224
Closing the sale, 242, 250–251
Clothing brands, 68
CLV. See Customer lifetime value
CMO Survey, 100
CMS platforms. See Content management software platforms
Cold audience, 155–156
Collect leads phase, of lifecycle marketing, 239–240
Communication, 20
Competition, in paid media, 44
Competitors, 97
Compliance
California legislation, 128–129
European Union, 129–130
overview of, 127–128
Constant Contact, 210
Consumer expectations, 278
Contact page on website, 106
Container Gardening, 60
Content
audience temperature and, 154–156, 155f
content management software platforms for, 140–141, 146
content marketing versus, 153
conversing, 161
convincing, 159–160, 160f
customer avatar and, 248, 265
defining of, 151–153

depth of, 143–144
educational, 158
encouraging action by, 148
entertaining, 157–158
high-value, 151
for human readers, 148
images as, 151–152
importance of, 150–151
inspirational, 158–159
inventory of, 154
key performance indicators for, 162
length of, 145
for machine readers, 137–147
multimedia-rich, 146
physical, 152–153
readability of, 148
reading level of, 148
return on investment for, 161–162
search intent as focus of, 148
social, 156–161. *See also* Social content
social media and, 268
strategic role of, 153–154
thin, 144–145
troubleshooting of, 265–267
video as, 152
written, 151
Content assets
definition of, 151
inventory of, 154
low-quality, 154
objective of, 153
return on investment for, 161–162
specialization of, 154
Content management software platforms, 140–141, 146
Content marketing
content versus, 153
definition of, 25, 151
paid search and, 170
Content Marketing Institute, 282
Contextual targeting, 173
Continuity interrupters, 112
"Conversational agents," 203
Conversing content, 161
Conversion(s)
cost per acquisition and, 185–186
definition of, 43
as social media metric, 207
Conversion-based marketing, 25–26
Conversion rate, 125–126, 185–186, 207, 224
Convert phase, of lifecycle marketing, 239*f*, 241–242
Convincing content, 159–160, 160*f*
Copy
email, 214–215, 215f
landing page, 109*f*, 113–114
Copyblogger, 283
Copywriters, 113
Copywriting Success Blueprint, 114

Cost(s)
competitor's effect on, 97
customer acquisition, 39
customer avatars and, 247
as obstacle, 97–98
reducing of, 94
Cost per acquisition, 185–186
Cost per action, 185
Cost per click, 166–167, 181–182
Cost per impression, 166–167
Countdown timers, 124, 125*f*
Coupons, 220–221, 244–245, 252
CPA. *See* Cost per acquisition
CPC. *See* Cost per click
CPI. *See* Cost per impression
CPRA. *See* California Privacy Rights Act
Create phase, of lifecycle marketing, 239*f*, 243–245
Credibility
of brand, 30
of owned media, 48
of paid media, 45
CRM. *See* Customer relationship management
CTA button/form, 109*f*, 114–115, 216. *See also* Call to action
CTR. *See* Click-through rate
Customer(s)
anticipating the needs of, 271–272
attributes of, 59–60, 64
behavioral segmentation of, 66–67
behavior of, 59–60
capturing of, 248
clarifying of, 17
converting of, 222–223, 237, 253
delivering product to, 243, 250–251
demographic information of, 57
email subscribers converted to, 222–223, 237
endorsements from, 244
engagement with, 249
expectations of, 278
goals of, 57–58
impressing of, 243–244, 251–252
loyalty of, 54, 66–67
marketing to reach, 17
millennials as, 278–279
multiplying of, 244, 252–253
pain points of, 58–59, 110, 154, 155
satisfaction of, 193
tiering of, 70, 71*f*
value ladder for, 75–77, 76*f*, 82*f*
values of, 57–58
Customer acquisition cost, 39
Customer avatars
attributes in, 59–60
behavior in, 59–60
case study example of, 245–246, 246*f*
content matched with, 248, 265
copy based on, 113
costs as driving factor for, 247

definition of, 56, 180
demographic information in, 57, 180
in digital marketing strategy, 247
example of, 61–62
goals in, 57–58
keywords and, 180–181
media diet in, 60
for multiple market segments, 62
pain points in, 58–59
questions used to create, 56–57
resources for building, 61–62
targeting of, 248
values in, 57–58
Customer journey, 71–72, 72f, 157
Customer lifetime value
average order value and, 40–41
budgeting based on, 100
calculating of, 38–40
cost per acquisition and, 186
definition of, 38
digital marketing funnel and, 238
impressing of customers to create, 244
overview of, 37–38
product design and, 38
tracking of, 39
Customer relationship management, 220, 283
Customer relationships, 91
Customer service, 271–272

D

Damage control, 203–204
Dark web, 137–138
Data
firmographic, 69–70
psychographic, 68–69
quantitative, 69
Data collection
description of, 93–94
social media advertising, 200–201
Deep web, 137
Delivering of product, 243, 250–251
Deloitte's CMO Survey, 100
Demographic information, 57
Demographics
in customer avatar, 57
market segmentation based on, 64–65
Demographic segmentation, 64–65
Demographic targeting, 173
Digiday, 283
Digital billboards, 171
Digital marketers
description of, 3–4
market demand for, 5
role of, 270
SEO by, 135
Digital marketing. See also Marketing
advantages of, 33–34

audience for, 4–5, 42
automating of, 98
business objectives for, 90–91
channels in, 41–42
conversions in, 43
customer service and, 271–272
engagement in, 43
goal of, 25
impressions in, 43
key concepts in, 41–43
for local businesses, 3
misconceptions about, 1–2
objectives of, 89–91, 95
outsourcing of, 5
platforms in, 41–42
process design and, 273
product design and, 272–273
reach in, 43
reasons for, 2–3
results of, 3
role of, 270–274
strategic pricing and, 273
traditional marketing versus, 33–34
traffic in, 42
Digital marketing campaign
objectives of, 269f
optimizing of, 263–265
troubleshooting poor performance in, 265–270
Digital marketing funnel
action phase of, 232f, 233, 235, 238f
advertising to direct customers to, 253
awareness phase of, 232, 232f, 238f
bottom of, 236–239
budgeting for, 238–239
building of, 245–253
case study of, 245–253
consideration phase of, 232, 232f, 234, 238f
cooperation in, 251
engagement and advocacy phase of, 232f, 233, 236, 238f
lifecycle marketing for. See Lifecycle marketing
marketing strategy and, 238
middle of, 234–236
offer portion of, 249–250
onboarding emails to guide customers to, 222
overview of, 231–232
phases of, 232–239
sales cycle, 236–237, 242
schematic diagram of, 232f, 238f
top of, 233–234
welcome email sequences in, 259–260
Digital Marketing Strategic Planning worksheet, 14
Digital Marketing Tool Kit, 105
Digital music players, 59
Diminishing inventory, 124
Direct messaging, 219
Direct response marketing, 23–24
Direct-to-consumer brands, 29

Discount pricing, 28
Display ads, 173, 173*f*
Display advertising, 171–174
Downsell/downselling, 78–79
DTC brands, 29
DuckDuckGo, 136
Duct Tape Marketing, 283

E

Earned media
    asking for, from customers, 244
    definition of, 46, 131, 237
    description of, 43*f*–44*f*, 46–47, 47*f*, 49, 50*f*
    journalists and, 132–133
    positive, 237
    press releases as, 133
    risks associated with, 131
    traffic attracted through, 131–133
    user proof as, 120
e-commerce, 220, 242, 251
Educational content, 158
Email
    abandoned-cart messages in, 221
    address collection, 240
    anatomy of, 212–217
    bounce rate for, 225
    call to action in, 215*f*, 216, 221, 224
    CAN-SPAM Act compliance of, 216–217
    click-through rate for, 224
    compliance information, 216
    components of, 212–217
    conversion rate for, 224
    copy of, 214–215, 215*f*
    coupons in, 220–221
    "from" label of, 213
    headlines, 215*f*, 215–216
    intimacy of, 219
    life events in, 221–222
    metrics for, 223–228
    on mobile devices, 222
    narrative in, 221
    offer with, 241–242
    onboarding, 222
    open rate for, 224
    opt-out option in, 217
    personalization of, 219–222
    reach of, 209
    return on investment of, 209
    sender reputation of, 227–228
    signatures in, 221
    spam complaints for, 227
    statistics regarding, 209
    subject line of, 213–214, 215*f*, 217–218
    unsubscribe rate for, 225–226
    value of, 241
    video in, 215
Email bounces, 225

Email list
    description of, 209–210
    growth rate of, 226–227
    hygiene of, 262
    metrics for, 223–228
    subscribers, 210–212
    unsubscribing from, 218, 225–226
Email sequences
    abandoned cart sequences, 260–261
    description of, 222–223, 249
    lead-nurturing, 260
    re-engagement, 223, 261–262
    sales sequences, 260
    welcome, 222, 258–260, 259*f*
Email service providers
    automation services of, 258
    bounce rates, 225
    description of, 210
    list hygiene tools from, 262
    tech-enabled personalization methods, 220–222
Email subscribers
    80/20 rule for, 219
    A/B test for, 212
    churn of, 217
    contact with, 218
    converting of, 217–219
    customer conversion of, 222–223, 237
    growth rate metric for, 226–227
    lead magnet for generating, 210–212
    life events of, 221–222
Emotion
    affective overdrive and, 20
    purchasing and, 16–17, 19, 59
Endorsements, 119
Engagement
    customer, 249
    definition of, 43
    social media, 205
Entertaining content, 157–158
Entrepreneurs
    description of, 4–5
    offers and, 81–83
    tunnel vision by, 16
European Union, 129–130
Exact match keywords, 178, 180
Expert proof, 118*f*, 118–119

F

Facebook
    advertising on, 196, 197*f*, 198, 267–268
    Chat, 202–203
    description of, 2, 42, 166–167, 174, 189, 190, 202
    Messenger, 202–203
Failure, as "jumping-off point," 95
FAQs page, 106
Fat-head keywords, 149, 150*f*
FCC. *See* Federal Communications Commission

Fear of missing out, 85, 120, 214
Feature
    benefit versus, 17–19, 18f
    definition of, 18
Federal Communications Commission, 45–46
Federal Trade Commission, 216
"Feeding the funnel," 232
Firmographic segmentation, 69–70
Fiverr, 146
Follower count, 205–206
FOMO, 85, 120, 214
Ford, Henry, 58
Form abandonment rate, 127
Franklin, Benjamin, 25
"Free," 85–86
Freelancers, 5
Friendster, 189
"From" label, of email, 213
Fundraisers, 192–193
Funnel. *See* Digital marketing funnel

G

Gates, Bill, 150–151
GDPR. *See* General Data Protection Regulation
General Data Protection Regulation, 129–130
General Motors, 90
Gen Z, 278–279
Geographical segmentation, 65
GetResponse, 210
GIFs, 152
Gmail, 262
Goal(s)
    of customer avatar, 57–58
    of customers, 57–58
    of marketing, 13–14
    for offer, 80
    SMART, 91–92, 194
    social media campaign, 193–194
Goal setting
    in action, 95–96
    reasons for, 92–93
Golf Digest, 60
Google
    Ads, 168, 172
    AdSense, 172
    advertising on, 166–167
    algorithms used by, 135–136
    alternatives to, 136–137
    Analytics, 206, 267
    Campaign URL Builder, 225
    display advertising on, 171–172
    Keyword Planner, 176
    mobile-first indexing by, 142–143
    programmatic advertising, 166
    Quality Score, 184
    Search Console, 266–267
    search engine of, 2, 25, 135–136

    SEO for website placement on, 134
    Shopping, 175, 176f
    Tag Manager, 267
    website indexing by, 138–139
Graphics, on landing pages, 109f, 115–116
Graphics interchange format. *See* GIFs
Growth rate, of email list, 226–227

H

Hard bounce, 225
Hashtags, 192–193
Headlines
    email copy, 215f, 215–216
    landing page, 109f, 111–113
helpareporter.com, 132
Help a Reporter Out, 132
Help-wanted ads, 274
High-value content, 151
Home Fresh, 38–40, 91–92
Home & Gardens, 60
Hootsuite, 205, 282
Hot audience, 155–156
"How-to" queries, 233
HubSpot, 205
HubSpot Academy, 283
Hulu, 174
Human resources recruitment, 274
Hyper-compelling offer, 83–87, 242, 249

I

Image(s)
    alt text with, 146
    as content, 151–152
    in email copy, 215
    on landing pages, 109f, 115–116, 151–152
    on-page SEO and, 146
Image ads, 201
Impressing of customers, 243–244, 251–252
Impression rate, 186–187
Impressions, 43
Impression share, 186–187
Inbound marketing
content marketing as, 25
description of, 22f, 22–23
tactics of, 22f
Influencers
description of, 4–5
endorsements from, 119
personal selling by, 29
Inspirational content, 158–159
Instagram, 29, 190, 197f, 202, 268
In-stream ads, 174
Inventory, diminishing, 124
iPhone, 27

J

Jantsch, John, 283

Jarvis, Richard, 202
Jenner, Kendall, 204
Journalists, 132–133

K

Keap, 210
Kettering, Charles, 90
Key performance indicators, 162
Keyword Planner, 176
Keywords
    ads matched with, 170–171
    advertising, 176–181
    assessment of, 266–267
    broad match, 178–179
    customer avatars and, 180–181
    description of, 135, 143
    exact match, 178, 180
    fat-head, 149, 150f
    long-tail, 149, 150f
    match type, 177–180
    owning of, 150
    phrase match, 178–180
    selecting of, 176–181
    stuffing of, 149
    troubleshooting of, 266–267
Kleenex, 24–25

L

Lack of familiarity, 98–99
Lack of money, 97–98
Lack of time, 98
Landing pages
    average time on page metric for, 126–127
    bounce rate for, 126
    conversion rate for, 125–126
    copy on, 109f, 113–114
    countdown timers on, 124, 125f
    CTA button/form, 109f, 114–115
    definition of, 108
    diminishing inventory on, 124
    effectiveness of, metrics for measuring, 125–127
    features of, 109f
    form abandonment rate for, 127
    graphics on, 109f, 115–116
    headlines on, 109f, 111–113
    images on, 109f, 115–116, 151–152
    marketing psychology practices applied to, 117–124
    metrics for measuring effectiveness of, 125–127
    opt-in form, 109f, 111, 211f
    opt-in pages, 109f, 110–111, 117, 263
    pop-ins, 123f, 124, 125f
    role of, 108–109
    sales pages, 111–116
    scarcity on, 122–123
    social proof on. *See* Social proof
    urgency on, 122–123
    video on, 109f, 115–116, 146, 152
    video sales pages, 116, 116f
    webinar registration, 117, 117f
Lead magnet, 110, 210–212, 211f, 235, 240
Lead-nurturing sequences, 260
Leadpages, 127
Legislation, 128–129
Lifecycle marketing
    attract phase of, 246–248
    capture phase of, 248
    close/deliver phase of, 250–251
    collect leads phase of, 239f, 239–240
    convert phase of, 239f, 241–242
    create phase of, 239f, 243–245
    definition of, 239
    digital marketing funnel and, 239–245
    engage phase of, 249
    impress stage of, 251–252
    multiply phase of, 251–252
    offer phase of, 249–250
    schematic diagram of, 253f
    target phase of, 245–246
Life cycle of product, 27–28, 28f
Life events, 221–222
Lifestyle marketing, 68
Lifetime value. *See* Customer lifetime value
LinkedIn, 196, 197f, 198
Links
    affiliate, 144–145
    off-page SEO, 146–147
    SERPs affected by, 147
List hygiene, 262
Live chat, 203
Local businesses, 3
Location-based segmentation, 65
Logo, 19
Long-tail keywords, 149, 150f
Low-quality content assets, 154
Loyalty of customers, 54, 66–67
Lush, 221

M

Machine readers, SEO for, 137–147
Mailchimp, 210
Mail merge fields, 220
Market
defining of, 53–55
    definition of, 20
    media and message with, 20–21, 21f
    serviceable available, 53–55, 55f
    total addressable, 53–55, 55f
    untapped, 247
Marketable entity, 15
Marketers
    customers and, 17
    sales as goal of, 93
    target audience and, communication between, 93
Marketing. *See also* Digital marketing

4 C's of, 29
4 P's, 27
5 P's, 29
awareness, 24–25, 232, 234
books as tool for, 153
bottom-of-the-funnel, 236–237
brand defined through, 19
budget for, 99–100
content. *See* Content marketing
conversion-based, 25–26
definition of, 14–16
direct response, 23–24
emotional space and, 19–20
FOMO-focused, 85
goals for, 13–14
importance of, 16–20
inbound. *See* Inbound marketing
industry statistics on, 100
lifecycle. *See* Lifecycle marketing
lifestyle, 68
methods of, 15
middle-of-the-funnel, 234–236
objectives of, 17–20, 28, 89–91, 95. *See also* Objectives
outbound. *See* Outbound marketing
personal aspect of, 14
processes involved in, 14
pull, 22
push, 22
sales revenue for, 100
sales versus, 13
social media, 191–195
spending on, 99–100
top-of-the-funnel, 233–234
traditional, 13–14, 33–34
viral, 94–95
Marketing automation
    behavior-based. *See* Behavior-based automation
    benefits of, 257
    definition of, 257
    importance of, 98
    lead-nurturing sequences, 260
    in lifecycle marketing, 241
    sales sequences, 260
Marketing formula, 20, 26, 32*f*
Marketing mix
    alternative interpretations of, 29–30
    definition of, 26
    example of, 32–33
    service, 29
Marketing obstacles
    competitors as, 97
    lack of familiarity as, 98–99
    lack of money as, 97–98
    lack of time as, 98
    obsolescence as, 97
Marketing plan
    budget in, 99–100

definition of, 96
    description of, 28
    importance of, 95–96
    as road map, 96
Marketing professionals, 5
Marketing psychology, 117
Marketing strategy
    brand positioning in, 32
    building of, 31–32
    closing phase of, 242, 250–251
    description of, 21
    digital marketing funnel and, 238
    product design and, 16
    strategic goals and, 26
Marketing students, 5
Market research, 17
Market segmentation
    B2B, 69–70
    B2C, 69
    by behavior, 66–67
    definition of, 63
    by demographics, 64–65
    firmographic, 69–70
    importance of, 63
    by location, 65
    by psychographics, 67–69
Market segments
    business fit with, 64
    definition of, 20
    distinction among, 63–64
    identification of, 63–64
    reachable size of, 64
Match type, 177–180
MAUs. *See* Monthly active users
McKinsey & Company, 271
Media
    definition of, 20
    for direct response marketing, 23
    earned. *See* Earned media
    market and message with, 20–21, 21*f*
    new, 33
    old, 33–34
    owned. *See* Owned media
    paid. *See* Paid media
Media diet, 60
Media mix
    components of, 43*f*–44*f*, 43–49
    definition of, 43
    earned media, 43*f*–44*f*, 46–47, 47*f*, 49, 50*f*
    owned media, 43*f*, 45, 48–49, 49*f*–50*f*
    paid media, 43*f*–45*f*, 43–46, 48–49, 50*f*
    social media and, 194–195
Meetup, 189
Memes, 152
Message
    definition of, 20
    market and media with, 20–21, 21*f*

Messaging, 202–203
Messenger, 202–203, 237
Metrics
    for content, 161–162
    conversions, 207
    customer service, 272
    email marketing, 223–228
    follower count, 205–206
    for landing pages, 125–127
    online advertising, 181–187
    reach, 206
    return on investment, 132, 161–162, 175, 206–207
    social media, 195, 204–207
Microcopy, 115
Microsoft, 136, 150
Middle-of-the-funnel marketing, 234–236
Millennials, 278–279
Mobile devices
    email design for, 222
    mobile-first indexing for, 142–143
Mobile-first indexing, 142–143
Money-back guarantees, 250
Monthly active users, 196, 197f
Moz, 134, 282
MP3 players, 58–59, 155
Multimedia-rich content, 146
Myspace, 189

N

Native advertising, 45–46, 168
Native design, 168
Negative social media, 203–204
Neil Patel's blog, 283
Netiquette, 86
New Balance, 175, 176f
New media, 33
New York Times, 202

O

Objectives, marketing
    changing of, 95
    defining of, 89–91
    reasons for focusing on, 92–93
    SMART goals, 91–92
Obsolescence, 97
Offer
    A/B test for, 212
    anatomy of, 80–81
    audience for, 80
    call to action as, 79
    crafting of, 79–83
    customer ascension from, 80–81
    definition of, 79
    in digital marketing funnel, 249–250
    downsell, 78–79
    email with, 241–242
    "free" with, 85–86

goal for, 80
    hyper-compelling, 83–87, 242, 249
    product of, 80
    scarcity with, 85
    understanding of, 81–83
    upsell, 77–78, 250
    urgency of, 83–84, 123
Off-page SEO, 139, 146–147
Old media, 33–34
On-page SEO
    content depth, 143–144
    content length, 145
    definition of, 139, 143
    multimedia-rich content, 146
Open rate, for emails, 224
Opt-in form, 109f, 111, 211f
Opt-in pages, 109f, 110–111, 117, 263
Opt-out option, in email, 217
Order fulfillment, 243
Organic reach, 268
Organic results, 135–136, 157, 169f, 176f
Organic search marketing, 165, 265–267
"Our story" pages, on website, 107
Outbound marketing
    awareness marketing as, 24–25
    description of, 21–22
    direct response marketing as, 23–24
    tactics for, 22f
Outlook, 262
Out-of-home advertising, 24–25
Outsourcing, 5
Outstream ads, 174–175
Owned media
    description of, 43f, 45, 48–49, 49f–50f
    in middle-of-the-funnel marketing, 236
    in social media campaign, 195

P

Paid media
    advertising as, 44, 165, 267
    description of, 43f–45f, 43–46, 48–49, 50f, 108
    in middle-of-the-funnel marketing, 236
Paid messaging, 45
Paid search, 168–171
Paid search campaign
    description of, 170–171
    keyword selection for, 178
    quality score for, 184–185
Pain points, 58–59, 110, 154, 155
Papworth, Neil, 202
Pareto principle, 219
Patel, Neil, 283
Pay-per-click advertising
    click-through rate, 183–184
    cost per acquisition, 185–186
    cost per click, 166–167, 181–182
    description of, 166, 181

metrics for, 181
   quality score, 184
Pay-per-impression advertising, 166–167
Penetration pricing, 28
Pepsi, 203
Perception, of brand, 19
Personalization of email, 219–222
Personal selling, 29
Photo libraries, 146
Phrase match keywords, 178–180
Physical content, 152–153
Pinterest, 166, 190, 197*f*
Place, 29
Platforms
   definition of, 41–42
   social media. *See* Social media platforms
PlayStation, 192
Podcasts, 161–162
Point-of-sale systems, 242
Poor Richard's Almanac, 25
Pop-ins, 123*f*, 124, 125*f*
POS systems. *See* Point-of-sale systems
Post-purchase coupons, 67
PPC advertising. *See* Pay-per-click advertising
Press releases, 133, 158
Price
   customer journey and, 72
   definition of, 28
Pricing, strategic, 273
Privacy, 277–278
Process design, 273
Product
   branding of, 19
   customer journey and, 72
   definition of, 27
   maturity of, 28
   placement of, 29
   price for, 28
   product life cycle of, 27–28, 28*f*
   promotion of, 29
Product design
   customer lifetime value and, 38
   description of, 272–273
   marketing strategy and, 16
Product launch, 92
Product life cycle, 27–28, 28*f*
Profits, 90–91
ProfNet, 132
profnet.com, 132
Programmatic advertising, 165–168, 178, 263, 269
Prominence metrics, 187
Promotion, 29
Promotional messages, 133
Promotional mix, 29
Proof in wisdom of the crowd, 120, 121*f*
Proof through certification, 121, 122*f*
Psychographic segmentation, 67–69

Pull marketing, 22
Purchasing, emotion and, 16–17, 19, 59
Push marketing, 22

Q
Q-Tip, 24
Quality guarantees, 250
Quality score, 184
Quantitative data, 69
Quora, 166
Qwoted, 132
qwoted.com, 132

R
Rand, Paul, 272
Reach
   definition of, 43, 48
   organic, 268
   social media, 206
Reachable size, 64
Reach metrics, 206
realtor.com, 150
Reddit, 190
Re-engagement email sequence, 223, 261–262
Remarketing, 171, 237
Responsive design, 142–143
Retargeting, 171, 184, 192
Return on investment
   description of, 132, 161–162
   email, 209
   outstream video ads, 175
   social media, 206–207
ROI. *See* Return on investment
Rule of Seven, 264

S
SaaS companies, 237
Sales
   digital marketing objectives for, 90
   as marketer goal, 93
   marketing versus, 13
   revenue from, for marketing, 100
Sales and marketing department, 15
Sales conversion, 43
Sales cycle, 236–237, 242
Sales funnel. *See* Digital marketing funnel
Sales letter, 24
Sales pages, 111–116
Sales psychology, 117
Sales sequences, 260
SAM. *See* Serviceable available market
Scarcity
   in email copy, 215
   on landing pages, 122–123
   with offer, 85
Scarcity mindset, 98
Search ads, 169, 201

Search Console, 266–267
Search engine(s). *See also* specific search engine
    content depth evaluations by, 144–145
    how they work, 135–136
    organic results from, 135–136, 169*f*, 176*f*
    paid results, 135–136
    spiders used by, 138–139
    web crawlers used by, 138–139
Search Engine Journal, 282
Search engine optimization
    definition of, 134
    for human readers, 148
    for machine readers, 137–147
    off-page, 139, 146–147
    on-page. *See* On-page SEO
    paid search and, 170
    SERPs, 135
    site speed importance for, 140–142
    technical. *See* Technical SEO
    troubleshooting of, 266
Search engine result pages. *See* SERPs
Search index, 135
Search intent, 135–136, 148, 233–234
Segmentation of market. *See* Market segmentation
Self-marketing, 15
Selling
    downselling, 78–79
    upselling, 77–78, 250
    value ladder in, 75–77, 76*f*, 82*f*
Semrush, 205
Sender reputation, 227–228
SEO. *See* Search engine optimization
Sequences, email, 222–223
SERPs
    description of, 135, 140–142, 147
    text ads, 168–169, 169*f*, 175, 176*f*
SERVEs
    in action, 95–96
    description of, 92–94
Serviceable available market, 53–55, 55*f*, 247
Service launch, 92
Service marketing mix, 29
Shiny object syndrome, 96
Shipping, 243, 278
Shopping carts, 221, 260–261
Siri, 203
Site. *See* Website
Site speed, 140–142
Six Degrees, 189
SMART goals, 91–92, 194
SMS, 202–203, 237
Snapchat, 197
Social content
    conversing, 161
    convincing, 159–160, 160*f*
    definition of, 156
    educational, 158

    entertaining, 157–158
    inspirational, 158–159
    types of, 156–161, 157*f*
Social media
    audience engagement using, 231
    content and, 268
    damage control from, 203–204
    definition of, 189
    evolving nature of, 189–191
    follower count for, 205–206
    growth of, 189
    lead magnets on, 210–212
    media mix changes on, 194–195
    Messenger, 202–203
    metrics for, 204–207
    negative, 203–204
    organic reach on, 268
    programmatic advertising on, 269
    SMS, 202–203
    troubleshooting of, 267–269
Social media advertising
    audience targeting and building, 198–199
    carousel ads, 201–202
    creatives, 201–202
    data collection, 200–201
    image ads, 201
    messaging, 201–202
    platform(s) for, 196–198
    prevalence of, 196
    spending on, 196
    story ads, 202
    testing of, 200–201
    video ads, 201
Social media campaign, 192–195
Social media engagement, 205
Social media marketing, 191–195
Social media platforms. *See also* specific platform
    dashboards on, 205
    market share of, 190–191, 191*f*
    selection of, for advertising, 196–198, 197*f*
Social media reach, 206
Social proof
    celebrity proof, 119, 119*f*
    definition of, 118
    description of, 109*f*, 222
    expert proof, 118*f*, 118–119
    proof in wisdom of the crowd, 120, 121*f*
    proof through certification, 121, 122*f*
    user proof, 120
    uses of, 121–122
Soft bounce, 225
Spam, 214, 227
Spiders, 138–139
Split testing, 270
Squarespace, 140
Squeeze pages, 109*f*, 110–111, 117
Startup business, 100

Statista, 190, 209
Stock photo libraries, 146
Story ads, 202
Strategic pricing, 273
Students, 5
Subject line, of email, 213–214, 215*f*, 217–218
Subscribers, email
    80/20 rule for, 219
    A/B test for, 212
    churn of, 217
    contact with, 218
    converting of, 217–219
    customer conversion of, 222–223, 237
    growth rate metric for, 226–227
    lead magnet for generating, 210–212
    life events of, 221–222
Subscription model, 40
Surface web, 137–138
Swift, Taylor, 119*f*
Swipe files, 113

T
Tag Manager, 267
TAM. *See* Total addressable market
Target audience
    conversion of, 43
    marketer and, communication between, 93
    message for, 20
    social media marketing, 199
Target market
    brand positioning for, 30
    definition of, 30, 53–54
    market segmentation for, 69
    members of, 54, 60
    penetration pricing for, 28
Technical SEO
    definition of, 139
    mobile-first indexing, 142–143
    site page structure, 139–140, 143
    site speed, 140–143
Television, 2
Text messaging, 202–203
Tiering, 70, 71*f*
TikTok, 190, 197
Timers, countdown, 124, 125*f*
Top impression rate, 186
Top impression share, 186
Top-of-the-funnel marketing, 233–234
Total addressable market, 53–55, 55*f*
Traditional marketing, 13–14, 33–34
Traffic
    capturing of, 131–163, 248
    compliance considerations for, 127–130
    definition of, 42
    directing of, 165–187
    earned media for attracting, 131–133
Trulia, 150

Trump, Donald, 196
Tumblr, 190
Twitter, 46, 132, 166, 190–191, 197*f*
Twitter Ads, 191
twitter.com, 132
Two-way messaging, 15–16

U
UL. *See* Underwriters Laboratories
Unbounce, 127
Underwriters Laboratories, 121
Unsubscribe rate, 225–226
Unsubscribing from email list, 218, 225–226
Untapped markets, 247
Upsell/upselling, 77–78, 250
Upwork, 146
Urgency
    in email copy, 215
    on landing pages, 122–123
    of offer, 83–84, 123
URL inspection tool, 266
USDA Organic seal, 121
User proof, 120
UTM codes, 207, 224–225

V
Value, delivering of, 243
Value-added upsell, 77
Value ladder
    description of, 75–77, 76*f*, 82*f*, 231, 237, 244
    lead magnets and, 110
    objectives and, 94
Value pricing, 28
Value proposition, 94
Values, of customers, 57–58
Values-based messaging, 68
Video(s)
    as content, 152
    in email, 215
    as entertaining content, 157–158
    on landing pages, 109*f*, 115–116, 146
Video ads, 174–175, 201
Video advertising, 174–175
Video sales pages, 116, 116*f*
Vimeo, 215
Viral marketing, 94–95
Virgin Atlantic, 15
Virgin Group, 15
Virgin Mobile, 15

W
Web crawlers, 138–139
Web hosting company, 142
Webinar registration landing pages, 117, 117*f*
Website
    "about us" pages on, 107
    affiliate links on, 144–145

attention span of user, 140–141
checkout, 242
company information on, 106–107
contact page on, 106
content of. *See* Content
as dedicated sales environment, 107
display advertising on, 172
FAQs page on, 106
functions of, 106–108, 108*f*
indexing of, by Google, 138–139
as informational resource, 106–107
landing pages of. *See* Landing pages
mobile-first optimization of, 142–143
"our story" pages on, 107
as owned media asset, 107
page structure of, 139–140
as point of contact, 106
responsive design of, 142–143
speed of, 140–142
as tool, 105–108
value of, 105–106
Welcome email sequence, 222, 258–260, 259*f*
Wire services, 133
Wisdom of the crowd, proof in, 120, 121*f*
Wix, 140
WordPress, 140
World Wide Web, 15
Written content, 151

Y
Yahoo!, 177, 262
YMYL topics, 159
YouTube, 167, 174, 215

Z
Zero-based budget, 100
Zillow, 150

Notes

WHAT DID YOU THINK?

We rely on reviews and reader feedback to help our authors reach more people, improve our books, and grow our business. We would really appreciate it if you took the time to help us out by providing feedback on your recent purchase.

It's really easy, it only takes a second, and it's a tremendous help!

—— NOT SURE WHAT TO SHARE? ——

Here are some ideas to get your review started...

- *What did you learn?*
- *Have you been able to put anything you learned into action?*
- *Would you recommend the book to other readers?*
- *Is the author clear and easy to understand?*

TWO WAYS TO LEAVE AN AMAZON REVIEW

Use the camera app on your mobile phone to scan the QR code or visit the link below to record your testimonial and get your free book.

or

www.quickstartguides.review/digital

SCAN ME   VISIT URL

GET YOUR NEXT
QuickStart Guide®
FOR FREE

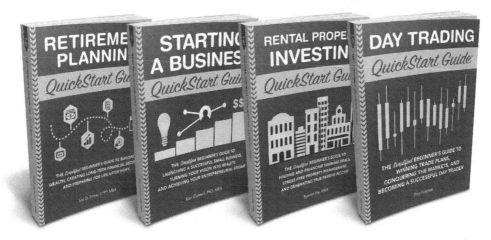

Leave us a quick video testimonial on our website and we will give you a **FREE *QuickStart Guide*** of your choice!

RECORD TESTIMONIAL

SUBMIT TO OUR WEBSITE

GET A FREE BOOK

TWO WAYS TO LEAVE A VIDEO TESTIMONIAL

Use the camera app on your mobile phone to scan the QR code or visit the link below to record your testimonial and get your free book.

SCAN ME

or

www.clydebankmedia.com/free-qsg

VISIT URL

SAVE 10% ON YOUR NEXT
QuickStart Guide®

USE CODE: QSG10

CLYDEBANK MEDIA

QuickStart Guides®

PROUDLY SUPPORT ONE TREE PLANTED

One Tree Planted is a 501(c)(3) nonprofit organization focused on global reforestation, with millions of trees planted every year. ClydeBank Media is proud to support One Tree Planted as a reforestation partner.

Every dollar donated plants one tree and every tree makes a difference!

Learn more at www.clydebankmedia.com/charitable-giving or make a contribution at onetreeplanted.org

Made in the USA
Columbia, SC
09 January 2023

75862638R00183